# My Xbox®

## Xbox 360®, Kinect™, and Xbox LIVE®

Bill Loguidice
Christina T. Loguidice

**que®**

800 East 96th Street
Indianapolis, Indiana 46240 USA

# My Xbox®

## Copyright © 2012 by Que Publishing

All rights reserved. No part of this book shall be reproduced, stored in a retrieval system, or transmitted by any means, electronic, mechanical, photocopying, recording, or otherwise, without written permission from the publisher. No patent liability is assumed with respect to the use of the information contained herein. Although every precaution has been taken in the preparation of this book, the publisher and author assume no responsibility for errors or omissions. Nor is any liability assumed for damages resulting from the use of the information contained herein.

ISBN-13: 978-0-7897-4896-6
ISBN-10: 0-7897-4896-7

Library of Congress Cataloging-in-Publication Data is on file

Printed in the United States of America

First Printing: February 2012

## Trademarks

All terms mentioned in this book that are known to be trademarks or service marks have been appropriately capitalized. Que Publishing cannot attest to the accuracy of this information. Use of a term in this book should not be regarded as affecting the validity of any trademark or service mark.

## Warning and Disclaimer

Every effort has been made to make this book as complete and as accurate as possible, but no warranty or fitness is implied. The information provided is on an "as is" basis. The authors and the publisher shall have neither liability nor responsibility to any person or entity with respect to any loss or damages arising from the information contained in this book.

## Bulk Sales

Que Publishing offers excellent discounts on this book when ordered in quantity for bulk purchases or special sales. For more information, please contact

**U.S. Corporate and Government Sales**

**1-800-382-3419**

**corpsales@pearsontechgroup.com**

For sales outside of the U.S., please contact

**International Sales**

**international@pearson.com**

**ASSOCIATE PUBLISHER**
Greg Wiegand

**ACQUISITIONS EDITOR**
Loretta Yates

**DEVELOPMENT EDITOR**
Todd Brakke

**MANAGING EDITOR**
Kristy Hart

**SENIOR PROJECT EDITOR**
Lori Lyons

**COPY EDITOR**
Apostrophe Editing Services

**INDEXER**
Erika Millen

**PROOFREADER**
Kathy Ruiz

**TECHNICAL EDITOR**
Tim Barrett

**PUBLISHING COORDINATOR**
Cindy Teeters

**BOOK DESIGNER**
Anne Jones

**COMPOSITOR**
Bronkella Publishing

# Contents at a Glance

# Table of Contents

# About the Authors

**Bill Loguidice** is a top business, technology, staffing, and creative professional, a noted videogame historian and subject matter expert, and a critically acclaimed author. Bill is also the cofounder and managing director for the online publication, *Armchair Arcade*, one of *PC Magazine*'s Top 100 Websites.

As a leading videogame and computer historian and collector, Bill personally owns and maintains more than 400 different systems from the 1970s to the present day, including a large volume of associated software, accessories, and literature. It is from these great resources and his sincere passion for the topic that Bill is often called upon to provide subject matter expertise to both public and private media interests.

Bill has coauthored numerous books, including *Vintage Games: An Insider Look at the History of Grand Theft Auto, Super Mario and the Most Influential Games of All Time*; *Wii Fitness For Dummies*; and *Motorola ATRIX For Dummies*. He is also a writer and producer on the feature film documentary from Lux Digital Pictures, *Gameplay: The Story of the Videogame Revolution*.

Website: www.armchairarcade.com

**Christina Torster Loguidice** is a scientific, technical, and medical editor and writer. Over her publishing career, she has overseen numerous peer-reviewed medical journals and healthcare technology magazines, including *Surgical Rounds, Cardiology Review, Resident & Staff Physician, Oncology Net Guide*, and *OncNurse*. Christina is currently the editorial director of *Annals of Long-Term Care: Clinical Care and Aging*, which is a monthly peer-reviewed clinical journal that reaches healthcare professionals caring for individuals residing in long-term care facilities. She reports from several medical conventions annually.

Christina has always had a keen interest in technology and fitness and nutrition, and is the coauthor of *Wii Fitness For Dummies*. She enjoys working out in her home gym with her husband and using the virtual gyms afforded by various gaming platforms. Christina also holds an AFTA personal trainer certification.

## Dedication

*To our beautiful girls, Amelie and Olivia. Always know that we you love you both more than anything!*

## Acknowledgments

Thanks as always to all our family (Ulla, Wolfgang, Jody, Bill, Brigitta, Alicia, and Rob) for their support, both direct and indirect. It's appreciated more than we can ever express. Thanks to our literary agent, Matt Wagner, for continuing to be a trusted partner. Last, but certainly not least, thanks to everyone at Pearson Education and Que for their extraordinary professionalism and assistance with this project, including Loretta Yates, Todd Brakke, Kristy Hart, Lori Lyons, Tim Barrett, Cindy Teeters, and Anne Jones.

# We Want to Hear from You!

As the reader of this book, *you* are our most important critic and commentator. We value your opinion and want to know what we're doing right, what we could do better, what areas you'd like to see us publish in, and any other words of wisdom you're willing to pass our way.

As an associate publisher for Que Publishing, I welcome your comments. You can email or write me directly to let me know what you did or didn't like about this book[md]as well as what we can do to make our books better.

*Please note that I cannot help you with technical problems related to the topic of this book. We do have a User Service group, however, where I will forward specific technical questions related to the book.*

When you write, please be sure to include this book's title and author as well as your name, email address, and phone number. I will carefully review your comments and share them with the author and editors who worked on the book.

Email:   feedback@quepublishing.com

Mail:    Greg Wiegand
         Associate Publisher
         Que Publishing
         800 East 96th Street
         Indianapolis, IN 46240 USA

# Reader Services

Visit our website and register this book at quepublishing.com/register for convenient access to any updates, downloads, or errata that might be available for this book.

Learn to set up, position, configure, and control your new home entertainment centerpiece.

In this chapter, you learn about the components that come with your Xbox 360 console and how to set it up.

# Getting Started

Before you can enjoy your Xbox 360 console and its rich multimedia capabilities, you need to free it from its packaging and set it up. Although this task isn't difficult, it may feel overwhelming if you don't have much experience hooking up electronics. Having a good understanding of all the features and goodies that come with your system can make this task considerably easier. In this chapter, you learn about all the physical components of your Xbox 360 console and how to hook everything up so that you'll be on your way to playing games and having fun in no time.

## Unboxing Your Xbox 360

Taking your Xbox 360 out of the box can be a surprisingly exhilarating experience, and unlike assembling furniture, no tools are required to put it together, except for your hands. However, before you start trying to hook it up, it's wise to familiarize yourself with your model and all its parts so that you can plan accordingly. For instance, you ultimately want to place your Xbox in a location where there is enough clearance around the unit to ensure none of its ventilation openings are blocked. If a wireless Internet connection is not available, you want to place your console close enough to make a wired connection to an available router or other network connection. If you also purchased Kinect, you need to make sure that you have a proper place for it as well (see "Setting Up Your Kinect" in Chapter 10, "Getting to Know Kinect," for more on this). Finally, if you place your Xbox in a spot where the cables going to the TV are not easily accessible, you may want to purchase a better AV cable in advance so that you do not have to hook it all up again.

## Understanding the Xbox 360 Models

Following the launch of the first Xbox 360 console in November 2005, numerous models have been released. This book outlines the two current Xbox 360 S models: Xbox 360 4GB and Xbox 360 250GB, both of which you can purchase alone or bundled with Kinect, a video sensor that enables a "controller-free gaming and entertainment experience."

The Xbox 360 4GB and the Xbox 360 250GB have many similarities. They each include five standard USB 2.0 ports and one custom port for the Kinect sensor (outlined in Chapter 10 and Chapter 11, "Using Kinect") and have built-in Wi-Fi and optical digital audio. They are also sleeker, smaller, and run quieter and cooler than their predecessors. So, what distinguishes one model from the next? It essentially boils down to storage space, price, and whether it includes a wired headset.

- **Xbox 360 4GB**—This model features 4GB of internal flash storage. Although this may be enough storage space if you use the system for basic gaming, you may quickly run out of space if you use it to store downloadable videos and games, for instance; however, stand-alone hard drives and other removable storage options are available, which are discussed later in this chapter. Xbox 360 4GB is considered to be the entry-level model, generally retailing for $100 less than the 250GB bundles.

- **Xbox 360 250GB**—This model comes with a wired headset and a 250GB hard drive. It retails for approximately $100 more than the equivalent 4GB bundles.

>>> Go Further

## LOOKING FOR A DEAL ON AN OLDER XBOX 360 CONSOLE?

Be an informed buyer when shopping for an older model Xbox 360. These models, which were typically white, went by various designations, including "Pro", "Premium", "Elite," and "Arcade". While being slightly larger in size, more prone to failure, and outside of warranty coverage might be something you can live with if the price is right, it's what you're doing without that might make the purchase of a discontinued model a poor value proposition. All Xbox 360s prior to the S have only three USB ports, have no dedicated Kinect sensor input (although they can still be used when powered by a wall socket), and lack both built-in wi-fi and S/PDIF optical audio connectors. On top of these negatives, retailers like Amazon often run specials on new Xbox 360 systems, with savings of $50 or greater not uncommon.

## Breaking Down the Components

Before you hook up your system, it might be helpful to familiarize yourself with the various ports and plugs on the Xbox console and the other components that come with the system, including the composite AV cable, optional headset, power supply, and wireless controller.

## Xbox 360 Console

Your Xbox 360 includes numerous buttons, ports, and other components. Now review the external anatomy of your Xbox 360 console to get a better handle on its parts.

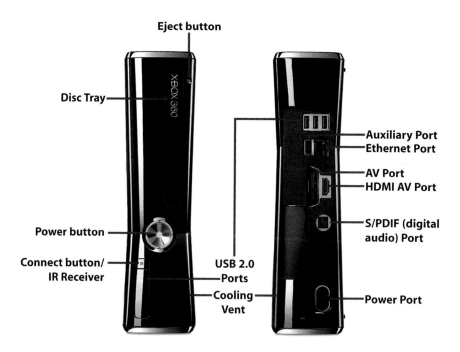

- **Auxiliary Port**—This is the dedicated Kinect port, handling both data and power for this motion control camera device.

- **AV Port**—AV stands for *audio video*. AV cables attach to this port and to your TV, establishing a connection between your console and TV.

- **Connect button/IR Receiver**—Press this button when you want to connect additional wireless controllers to your console.

- **Cooling Vent**—Enables heat to escape from your console. This vent should never be blocked.

- **Disc Tray**—This is where you load and unload a CD or DVD disc after pressing the Eject button or selecting the Eject option from a menu. (No model of Xbox supports Blu-ray discs.)

- **Eject button**—Touch this button when you want to open the Disc Tray.

- **Ethernet Port**—This is a network port, enabling a wired connection.

- **Hard Drive**—If installed, this is typically the main drive where you can store all your data.

- **HDMI AV Port**—HDMI stands for *high-definition multimedia interface*. This port enables you to use a standard HDMI cable, which must be purchased separately, to provide the highest quality video and audio output to compatible displays.

- **Power button**—Touch this button to turn your console on or off.

- **Power Port**—This is the port where you can insert the power cord from the AC adapter.

- **S/PDIF (digital audio) Port**—S/PDIF stands for *Sony-Phillips Digital Interface*. This sound port enables you to connect your console to an external audio system via a TOSLINK connector, providing high-quality digital output.

- **USB 2.0 Ports**—USB stands for *universal serial bus*. These ports enable you to attach peripheral devices to your console, such as a wired controller or a Flash Drive for additional storage capacity. Your console has five of these ports: two in front and three in back.

## Composite AV Cable

Your Xbox 360 console comes with a Composite AV cable. This cable connects your Xbox console to your TV, providing audio and video output. Because this cable establishes a standard-definition (SD) connection, it should be used only on older TVs, unless you don't mind low-quality visuals and sound. See "Connecting to Your TV" in this chapter for more on this cable and which cables and connections to use to fully tap the potential of your Xbox 360 console.

**The standard definition cable that comes in the box should be the first item you replace if your TV has connections for something other than composite input.**

## Wired Headset

The optional Wired Headset, which plugs into your controller, enables you to chat with your friends on Xbox LIVE. It comes bundled only in with the Xbox 360 250GB console. If you find the Wired Headset annoying, wireless options are available, and you can use wired and wireless headsets together on the same console.

### Don't Want to Use a Headset to Chat?

The Kinect sensor features a built-in microphone, and you can use it to chat with friends sans headset when you connect to Xbox LIVE.

## Power Supply

The power supply, which provides electrical energy to your Xbox 360 console, comes in two parts, including a brick-like AC adapter and a two-prong power cord that goes from the AC adapter to a standard wall outlet.

## Wireless Controller

Your Xbox 360 wireless controller features 2.4GHz wireless technology, enabling you to play up to 30 feet away from your console. Although your console comes with one controller, it can support up to four controllers at any given time.

# Setting Up Your Xbox 360

Now that you have a good handle on all your Xbox 360's parts, it's time to hook it up so that you can start enjoying your new system. This process won't take long, provided you've already secured a proper place for your console and do not need to move heavy furniture or lots of knickknacks out of the way.

## Positioning Your Xbox

You can position your Xbox 360 so that it lies horizontally or stands vertically. Although positioning your console is easier than baking a premade pie, you still need to follow a few rules.

- Assess the intended spot for your console carefully; it should be placed on a flat, level, stable, hard surface that is free of dust and debris, enabling for plenty of ventilation, and is not too close to any heat sources, such as a radiator, heat register, or even things like cable boxes and sound systems.

- Place the console so that it is entirely on the intended surface; no part of your console should be dangling precariously in the air.

- Check that all ventilation openings on the console are unobstructed.

## Connecting to Your TV

Connecting your Xbox 360 to your TV or monitor is the most important part of the setup process because this connection can have a direct impact on how you experience the sound and visuals of games and movies that you play through your console. Although you are given a composite AV cable to establish this connection, your console supports cable types that offer superior output. To ensure your TV hook-up is optimized, you should carefully consider all options before proceeding.

- **Composite AV cable**—This cable, which is included with your Xbox 360, provides a standard-definition picture and analog stereo audio output. It does not support high-definition resolutions, and its video signal is poor compared with the other outlined cable types; thus, it is *not* recommended for high-definition TVs/monitors. Even standard-definition displays may benefit from use of either an S-Video or component AV cable.

- **S-Video AV cable**—S-Video stands for *separate video*. Though audio is the same, the picture quality produced by this cable is a step up from a composite AV cable, but there are better options yet, especially for high-definition TVs/monitors.

**The S-Video AV cable is a step up from the Composite AV cable, but does not support HD video output.**

- **Component HD AV cable**—Based on the "HD" in its name, some may assume that this cable is just for high-definition TVs/monitors, but it also works with standard-definition TVs/monitors with this input. Though audio is the same, the quality of this cable's video signal is superior to both composite and S-Video AV cables, but there are yet better options for high-definition TVs/monitors.

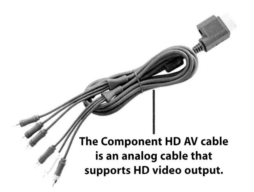

**The Component HD AV cable
is an analog cable that
supports HD video output.**

- **VGA HD AV cable**—VGA stands for *video graphics array*. This cable, which cannot be used on standard-definition TVs, displays high-definition graphics up to 1080p on high-definition TVs/monitors using the VGA input.

**The VGA HD AV cable supports a wide range of resolutions and
is a good choice when connecting to older computer monitors.**

- **HDMI cables**—HDMI stands for *high-definition multimedia interface*. If you have a high-definition TV/monitor, this is the Cadillac of cables, as it provides high-definition video output and superior audio output via Dolby Digital 5.1 Surround Sound, all through just one cable. Several HDMI cables can work with your Xbox 360, including version 1.3 and version 1.4. The former is the most common type and can be used on any high-definition TV/monitor; however, if your display supports 3D, you should opt for version 1.4, preferably 1.4a, which has defined mandatory 3D formats for broadcast, game, and movie content.

**An HDMI cable delivers HD video and digital surround sound over a single cable.**

- **Optical Audio cable**—This optional digital audio cable plugs into the S/PDIF port on the console and because it carries no video signal is used with one of the other listed cables. The optical audio cable is designed to help you extract the best sound possible from the system, supporting the same Dolby Digital 5.1 Surround Sound as HDMI. To make use of this cable, you need a home theater receiver or TV/monitor that has digital audio inputs. This is most commonly used with one of the non-HDMI cables, unless you need a separate audio cable to connect to a sound system.

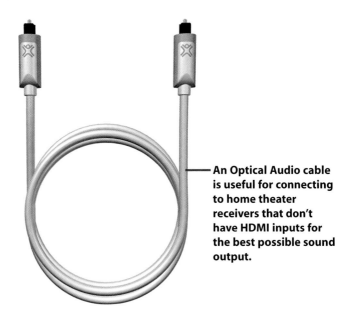

**An Optical Audio cable is useful for connecting to home theater receivers that don't have HDMI inputs for the best possible sound output.**

The following table provides an overview of the resolutions and audio output provided by each of the cable types and the configuration of their connectors.

| Cable | Supported Resolution | Supported Audio | Connector |
|---|---|---|---|
| Composite AV Cable | 480i | Analog Stereo | Composite Video (yellow), Left Audio (white), Right Audio (red) |
| S-Video AV Cable | 480i | Analog Stereo | S-Video (DIN), Composite Video (yellow), Left Audio (white), Right Audio (red) |
| Component HD AV Cable | 480i, 480p, 720p, 1080i, 1080p | Analog Stereo | Y Component (green), PB Component (blue), PR Component (red), Composite Video (yellow), Left Audio (white), Right Audio (red) |
| VGA HD AV Cable | 640x480, 848x480, 1024x768, 720p, 1280x768, 1280x1024, 1360x768, 1440x900, 1680x1050, 1080p | Analog Stereo | VGA (DE-15), Left Audio (white), Right Audio (red) |

| Cable | Supported Resolution | Supported Audio | Connector |
|---|---|---|---|
| HDMI Cable (version 1.3) | 480p, 720p, 1080i, 1080p | Stereo LCPM, Dolby Digital 5.1, Dolby Digital with WMA pro | HDMI |
| HDMI Cable (version 1.4) | 480p, 720p, 1080i, 1080p; includes support for 3D on 3D TVs for select content | Stereo LCPM, Dolby Digital 5.1, Dolby Digital with WMA pro> | HDMI |
| Optical Audio Cable | N/A | Stereo LCPM, Dolby Digital 5.1, Dolby Digital with WMA pro | TOSLINK |

### Connecting a Composite AV Cable

**1.** Plug the AV connector on the composite cable into the AV port on your console.

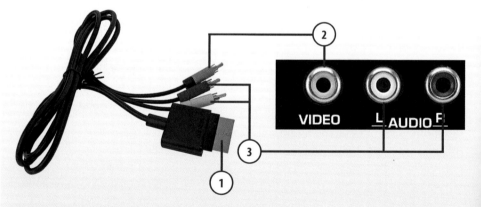

**2.** Plug the yellow connector on the composite cable into the yellow video input on your TV/monitor.

**3.** Plug the red and white audio connectors on the composite cable into the corresponding red and white audio inputs on your TV/monitor.

4.  Select the video input for your TV/monitor that matches the connection type used.

## Have Only One Audio Input on Your TV?

Your TV is monaural, also called a mono TV, meaning it has only one speaker and therefore only one audio jack. Connect the white connector to the single audio input.

## Connecting an S-Video AV Cable

1.  Plug the AV connector on the S-Video cable into the AV port on your console.

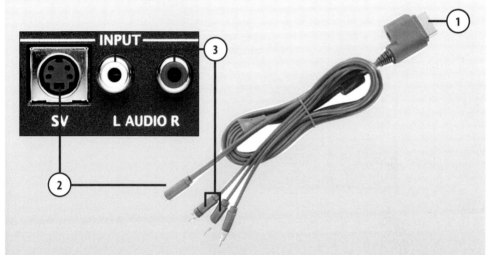

2.  Plug the S-Video connector on the cable into the S-Video input on your TV. The yellow composite video connector should remain unconnected.

3.  Plug the red and white audio connectors on the cable into their corresponding red and white audio inputs on your TV, amplified speaker system, or receiver.

## Connecting a Component HD AV Cable

1. Set the switch on the AV connector for your TV/monitor to "HDTV" if your TV supports a screen resolution of 480p or higher, or to "TV" if it does not.

2. Plug the connectors on the component HD AV cable into the corresponding color input jacks on the TV/monitor; if present, the yellow composite video connector should remain disconnected.

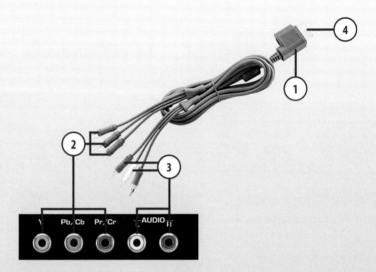

3. Plug the red and white audio connectors on the component HD AV cable into the corresponding audio ports on your TV/monitor or sound system.

4. Plug the AV connector on the component HD AV cable into the AV port on your console.

## It's Not All Good

If your AV connector is set to HDTV and you find that your console does not display on your TV, you may need to set the switch to TV during initial setup. When your console starts up, it then displays in standard definition. You can then go to the Display Settings and select to display in HD. The console then prompts you to flip the switch on your cable to HDTV. When you restart your console, it is now in HD mode.

## Connecting a VGA HD AV Cable

1.  Plug the AV connector on the VGA HD AV cable into the AV port on your console.

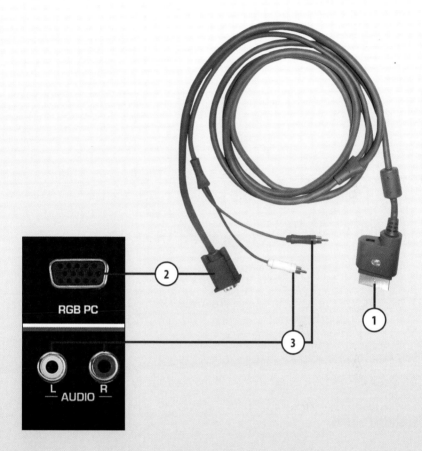

2.  Plug the VGA connector on the VGA HD AV cable into the VGA port on your TV/monitor.

3.  Plug the red and white audio connectors on the VGA HD AV cable into the corresponding audio ports on your TV/monitor or sound system.

## Connecting an HDMI Cable

1. Plug one end of the HDMI cable into the HDMI port on your console.

2. Plug the other end of the HDMI cable into the HDMI port on your high-definition TV/monitor.

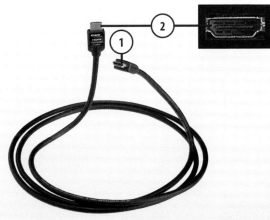

## Connecting an Optical Audio Cable

1. After plugging in one of the video  as described in the previous sections, plug one end of the optical audio cable into the S/PDIF port on your console.

2. Plug the other end of the optical audio cable into the S/PDIF, optical audio, or TOSLINK port on your home theater receiver or TV/monitor.

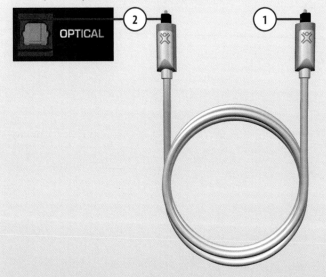

3. Ensure that your home theater receiver or TV/monitor is set to the correct optical audio input.

Go Further

## TV GAME MODE

If you notice a delay between your button presses and what is displayed on screen, you may want to enable Game Mode on your TV. This optional setting, which is available on many of today's HDTVs, is designed to speed up image processing. Minimizing display lag is particularly important when using the Kinect sensor. Refer to the manual that came with your TV to see if Game Mode is an option.

### Connecting the Power Cord

1. Insert the power supply cord into the Xbox 360 console.

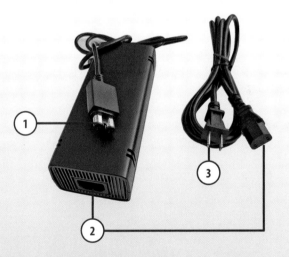

2. Connect the AC power cord and the power supply, ensuring a secure connection between the two.

3. Plug the AC power cord into a wall outlet.

## Setting Up Your Controller

Getting your controller hooked up couldn't be easier, considering it comes wirelessly connected to your console directly out-of-the-box; however, you need to insert the batteries. The controller accepts disposable AA batteries, also known as *LR6 batteries*; these are included. Low yield rechargeable batteries are not recommended because they can drain quickly.

### Inserting Batteries

1.  Separate the battery pack from the controller by pressing the tab at the top of the AA battery pack and pulling it away from the controller.

2.  Insert two AA batteries into the bottom of the battery pack, ensuring the positive (+) and negative (–) ends are inserted as marked on the battery pack.

3.  Slide the AA battery pack back into the controller and push it into the controller until it snaps back into place.

## Don't Want to Worry About Running Out of Batteries?

You can avoid running out of batteries and simultaneously help the environment by purchasing an Xbox 360 Play and Charge Kit, which comes with a
rechargeable battery pack that enables approximately 30 hours of play per
charge, and a cord that can plug into any USB port on your console or computer, enabling you to use your controller as a wired controller while the battery
pack charges.

## Connecting Additional Controllers

Unless you are perfectly content playing solo offline, you will want to add
additional controllers to your console, or have the ability to connect your
friends' controllers to your console; up to four controllers can be used. Follow
these steps to achieve either objective.

1.  Turn your console on by pressing the power button.

2.  Press and hold the Xbox Guide button in the middle of the controller until it turns on,
    as demonstrated by the Guide button lighting up.

3.  Press the Connect button on the console and wait for the console lights to spin.

4. Press and hold the Connect button on the back of the controller until the controller lights spin; after the lights on both the controller and console have spun and flashed once, your controller is connected.

## Using Your Controller

Although every game and application (for example, Netflix) has its own set of controls, which are outlined in the game instructions or in the application's menu, some components and buttons have fairly consistent usage patterns.

### Understanding Digital and Analog

You'll hear a lot about "digital" and "analog" when it comes to your controller. Digital uses discrete values, and analog uses a continuous range of values. The digital D-pad and buttons register as on or off. For instance, with the D-pad, if you move an in-game character left, it simply moves left. The analog sticks and triggers enable a finer degree of control. For instance, with the analog stick, you can control how quickly an in-game character moves left.

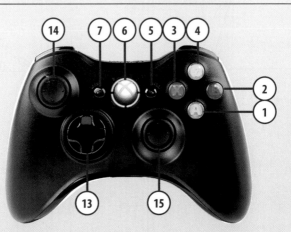

1. **A button**—A green button generally used to accept selections.

2. **B button**—A red button generally used to go back to previous screens or to exit a screen.

3. **X button**—A blue button often used to backspace text, or cancel or end a selection.

4. **Y button**—A yellow button that often brings up a menu.

5. **Start button**—A button that turns on your controller and can be used to pause and unpause your game, movie, music, or other media.

6. **Xbox Guide button**—A button that powers your console on and off (if held for longer than 3 seconds). When your console is on, lightly pressing this button gives you immediate access to the Xbox Guide, which provides a menu of navigation and console setting options. This button is divided into four lighted quadrants, each of which is assigned a number. The quadrant that is lit corresponds with your controller's position or player number.

7. **Back button**—A button that is sometimes used to pull up in-game menus, and similar to the B button, can take you to the previous screen when browsing menus.

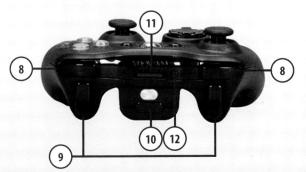

8. **Left and right bumpers**—Buttons that act as quick scroll buttons in menu screens, with the right bumper scrolling right and the left bumper scrolling left. These are often abbreviated as LB and RB.

9. **Left and right triggers**—Analog buttons that act as up and down quick scroll buttons in menu screens, with the left trigger scrolling down and the right trigger scrolling up.

10. **Battery pack**—Stores the batteries that give your wireless controller the power to function.

11. **Charge port**—Only used if you purchase an Xbox 360 Play and Charge kit, which enables you to use your controller while you recharge your rechargeable battery pack by turning your controller into a wired controller.

12. **Connect button**—A button used to pair the controller to the console if not previously linked.

13. **Directional pad (D-pad)**—A digital control that provides eight-directional input, enabling you to go up, down, left, right, up and left, up and right, down and left, and down and right. Some games do not enable use of the D-pad for movement but map certain in-game functions to it.

14. **Left stick**—The primary analog stick, functions much like a D-pad, but due to its analog nature (detecting minute movements) is not as precise when navigating menus. It also functions as a button when you press down on it, often bringing up secondary functions or in-game menus.

15. **Right stick**—The second analog stick, often used to look around and adjust the camera angle in games that provide this functionality. It is also sometimes used for moving around in games, though use of the left stick for this function is much more common. The right stick also functions as a button. For instance, in games that enable you to adjust the camera angle, pressing the button may return the camera vantage point to the center.

## Powering On for the First Time

Now that you have your Xbox 360 hooked up and your controller ready to go, you can turn on your console. However, before you can start play-ing with your new toy, you need to go through a quick console setup. The Xbox 360 does a good job of prompting you. If unsure of some-thing, follow these steps.

1.  Turn on your console by touching the Power button on your con-sole.

2.  Press the Xbox Guide button on your controller.

3.  Press the A button on your con-troller.

4.  Highlight your language using the controller's D-pad or the left stick, and then press the A button to select.

5. Now you see the Welcome screen, which also mentions the Kinect Sensor if you already have one hooked up. Press A on your controller to continue, or if the Welcome screen is in a language that you can't read, press B on your controller to go back to step 4.

6. At the Console Settings screen, press A to continue.

7. At the Locale screen, highlight the country where you will be using your console, and press A to continue.

8. You now see the Display Settings screen. Your Xbox 360 does its best to automatically detect the correct resolution; however, it is best to select Yes to change your display settings to optimize them. Otherwise, select No and skip to step 10.

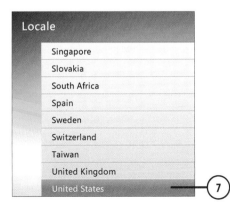

**9.** At the Settings screen , the number of options available varies, depending on your TV and cable hookup. Refer to "Connecting to Your TV" earlier in this chapter to determine optimal settings for your display and cable type. Choose the best setting shown; don't worry about choosing incorrectly. The system tests your selection and returns you to the Settings screen within 10 seconds if it is not compatible. After you make a compatible selection, you can press A to continue.

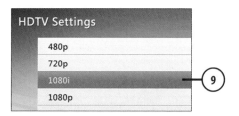

**10.** Now you see the Auto-Off information screen. Press A on your controller to continue.

**11.** At the Content Controls screen, you can turn Content Controls On or Off. If you choose Off, proceed to step 13. If you opt to turn it on, you have the default restrictions displayed for games, movies, and TV. After initial setup is complete, you can further customize these settings. Refer to "Adjusting Content Controls" in Chapter 4, "Getting to Know Your Xbox."

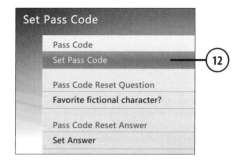

**12.** At the Set Pass Code screen, follow the prompts to set  your pass code, establish your pass code reset question, and set your passcode reset answer. Refer to "Choosing Family Settings" in Chapter 4 for additional details. When you finish configuring these settings, select Done and press A.

13. Now you are done with the console setup and will be brought back to the Console Settings screen. Press A to continue or B to go back if you want to change anything.

14. At the Connect to the Internet screen, press A to continue.

15. At the Internet Connection screen, you can connect to Xbox LIVE. Select Connect Later, or refer to Chapter 2, "Networking Your Xbox," for instructions on how to connect.

16. At the Gamer Profile screen, press A to continue.

17. Enter your profile name, and press the Start button on your controller when done.

18. Select an avatar that best represents you, or you can refer to Chapter 3, "Personalizing Your Xbox Experience," if you want to fully customize an avatar now.

19. At the Save Profile screen, highlight Done and press A to continue. If you want to Join Xbox LIVE or to Customize Profile, you can do so before proceeding. Turn to Chapters 2 and 3, respectively, for detailed instructions.

20. After you finish reading the information on the Network and Xbox LIVE screen, press A to continue. If you've already connected your Kinect Sensor, proceed to the next step. Otherwise, you're now ready to begin your Xbox odyssey!

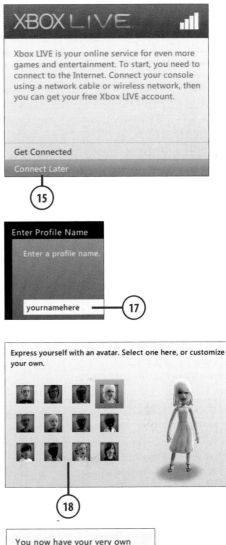

21. At the Kinect Sensor screen, press A to continue.

22. Now you see the Sensor Placement screen. Read the recommendations, make any needed adjustments based on these recommendations, and select the Sensor Placed item by pressing A to continue.

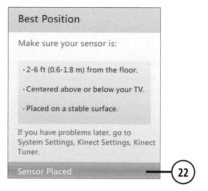

**Best Position**

Make sure your sensor is:

· 2-6 ft (0.6-1.8 m) from the floor.

· Centered above or below your TV.

· Placed on a stable surface.

If you have problems later, go to System Settings, Kinect Settings, Kinect Tuner.

Sensor Placed ————————(22)

23. At the Background Noise screen, press A to test. After a short test, you are told if your background noise level is OK. If it is not OK, follow the recommended steps and retest. Otherwise, press A to continue.

24. Now you are at the Speaker Volume screen. Press A to Play the test. After a short test, you are told if your speaker volume is OK. If it is not OK, follow the recommended steps and retest. Otherwise, press A to continue.

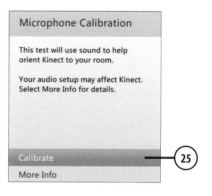

**Microphone Calibration**

This test will use sound to help orient Kinect to your room.

Your audio setup may affect Kinect. Select More Info for details.

Calibrate ————————(25)

More Info

25. At the Microphone Calibration screen, press A to Calibrate. After the calibration sounds finish playing, press A to continue .

26. At the Chat Microphone screen, select On for chat and press A to continue if you want to use Kinect's built-in microphone for games and Xbox LIVE parties. Otherwise, select Off for chat and press A to continue.

27. You are now asked to move in front of the Kinect Sensor and wave to interact with Kinect.

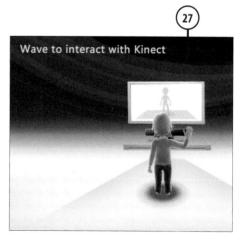

(27)

**Wave to interact with Kinect**

**28.** At the Select an Option screen, use your left or right hand to hover over Continue until the circle around the hand icon is completely rendered.

**29.** At the Congratulations screen, just like in the previous step, use your hand to select Done. You are now at the main menu, ready for fun .

## Playing Discs

Your Xbox 360 can play game discs licensed by Microsoft specifically for this platform; region 1 DVDs, which are sold in the United States, Canada, Bermuda, and U.S. territories; and any CD music/audio discs.

### Spare Your Discs!
Never move your Xbox 360 with a disc in the disc tray because there is a risk of the disc getting scratched by the console's DVD drive, rendering the disc unusable.

## Inserting and Removing Discs

1. Touch the Eject button lightly to open the disc tray.

2. Remove the disc or place the disc with the label facing out into the grooves of the disc tray, ensuring it is secure.

3. Touch the Eject button again or lightly push on the outside of the disc tray to close it.

### Warning

You can eject a disc at any time, but you may lose unsaved data.

## Manually Ejecting Discs

Although your Xbox is a well-built piece of electronic equipment, you may at some point find yourself with an Eject button that does not function properly. This can be especially disconcerting if your favorite game is stuck in there, but do not fret. It is possible to reclaim your disc; all you need for this feat is a straightened paper clip.

1. Disconnect your console from the power cord and any other cables.

2. Locate the yellow sticker underneath the ventilation vents, which will be on the top of the console if positioned vertically as shown to the right. Insert the straight end of a paper clip into the eject hole, which is located just above the yellow sticker.

3. After the disc tray pops out, pull the tray out the rest of the way with your fingers.

## Setting Up Your Headset

A headset enables you to chat with friends and family on Xbox LIVE. You can also use a headset to transmit voice commands in games that support this functionality. If you purchased the Xbox 360 250GB console, you received a wired Xbox 360 Headset with your unit. However, if you opted for the 4GB version, you need to purchase a headset separately, provided you need one. Fortunately, numerous wired and wireless headsets are available for your Xbox 360, including many by third-party manufacturers, and they range in price from a few dollars to $100 or more. You can check online retailers such as Amazon.com to find the one that best suits your needs.

### Connecting Your Headset to the Controller

These instructions pertain only to the Xbox 360 Headset by Microsoft, which is the wired headset that comes with the Xbox 360 250GB console and can be purchased separately for about $20.

1. Turn the volume knob on your headset all the way down.

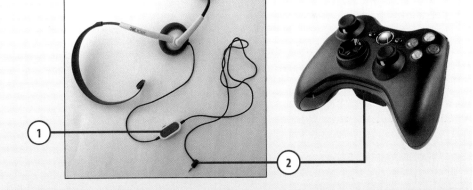

2. Plug the 2.5-mm headset connector into the controller expansion port, which is located on the front of your controller.

3. Place the headset over the top of your head and adjust the microphone so that it is located approximately 1 inch away from your mouth, with the microphone opening pointed toward your mouth; this can prevent your breathing from being transmitted.

4. Turn your volume up to a level that suits you and go ahead and start your game or chat session.

## Using Your Headset

The headset is simple to use. There are only two functions on the headset's control that you need to be aware of. In addition to these functions, the headset's control can be clipped to your shirt for easy access.

- **Mute button**—Sliding this button on the headset control turns off voice transmission.

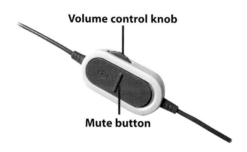

**Volume control knob**

**Mute button**

- **Volume control knob**—Rotating this knob enables you to adjust the listening volume of your headset.

## It's Not All Good

As with all things electronic, sometimes problems do arise. Here's some of the common problems that you may encounter with the headset and how to troubleshoot them. First, always makes sure the headset is properly plugged into your controller, that the volume is at an appropriate level, and that the mute button isn't enabled.

After that, if other players still can't hear you, make sure you haven't muted your voice in the Xbox Guide, by going to the Guide's Settings menu, selecting Voice, and clearing the Mute checkbox if it's enabled. You might also check your game manual to ensure a particular game doesn't require you to press a button to enable voice communication.

If this doesn't solve the problem, or if you can't hear anyone you're on chat with despite having the volume up and ensuring a proper connection with your controller, it's entirely possible there's something wrong with your headset. The cables on these headsets tend to get jostled around a lot and they can eventually fail, requiring you to purchase a new one.

# Setting Up Storage

If you purchased the Xbox 360 250GB model, your console comes equipped with a hard drive; however, you can also purchase a hard drive to bump up the storage capacity of the 4GB model. In addition, both models accept a USB flash drive and other removable storage, giving you plenty of options for saving games and other media. There is also an option for saving your profile and saved games online, referred to as Cloud Storage, which is discussed in Chapter 2.

## Removing and Attaching Your Hard Drive

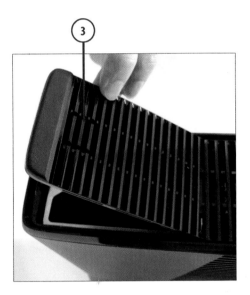

1. Turn off your console and unplug all cables.

2. If your console is in the vertical position, place it horizontally; make sure there is no disc in the disc tray before proceeding with this step.

3. Locate the hard drive cover release, and push the slats on the release in the direction of the disc tray to remove the hard drive cover.

4. Pull the hard drive tab to remove the hard drive from the console.

5. To insert a hard drive, simply slide it back into place, and snap the hard drive cover closed.

## Using a USB Flash Drive or Other Storage Device with Your Console

Your Xbox 360 has five USB 2.0 ports; although, the two front ports are the most easily accessible, making them ideal for removable storage. You can use these ports to connect a 1GB or greater capacity USB flash drive or other device containing a hard drive, such as a portable music player, to your Xbox 360. However, only USB flash drives formatted with the Windows FAT32 file system work on the console; Macintosh or Linux formats are not compatible. If you purchase a USB flash drive that is not preconfigured for the Xbox, you need to format your USB flash drive for use as an Xbox storage device before you can use it to save a game or other media. If you prefer not to have to go through the additional configuration steps, you can purchase a preconfigured Xbox 360 USB flash drive by SanDisk, which start at about $20.00.

## Connecting a USB Flash Drive

1. Locate the USB 2.0 ports on the front of your console; they are located behind the small slot to the left of your console's Power button.

2. Plug your USB 2.0 Flash Drive or other USB storage device into one of the ports.

## Configuring a Flash Drive

If you need to configure your Xbox 360 flash drive, follow these steps:

1.  Go to System on the Settings channel and press A.

2.  Highlight Storage and press A.

3.  Highlight the USB Storage Device and press A.

4.  Decide whether you want to format the entire USB flash drive for your Xbox 360, which erases anything contained on that drive, or just part of it.

5.  To format the entire USB flash drive, select Configure Now and confirm that you want to erase all data on the drive. To format only part of the USB flash drive, select Customize, adjust the Reserved Storage slider to indicate how much space you want to allocate for Xbox storage (512MB is always reserved for system use), and select Configure. Your Xbox 360 tests the drive. If it passes, it will now list as a memory unit under the Storage Devices menu, which also indicates how much space is available on your device.

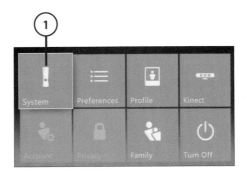

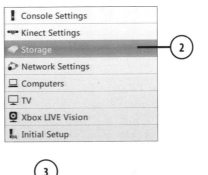

## Transferring Content Between Consoles

If you have another Xbox 360, you may want to transfer the content on its hard drive to your new console. To accomplish this task, you can use one or two USB flash drives, allowing anywhere from 8GB to 32GB of data to be transferred. This method works best if you have only a small amount of data to transfer, such as gamer tags, profiles, and a saved game or two. If you have a large amount of data to transfer, you will be better served using an Xbox 360 hard drive transfer cable to move everything over to your new console. Regardless of which method you use, you need to make sure that you have the latest dashboard software installed on the old system.

## It's Not All Good

After you transfer content over, it will no longer be available on the old hard drive; thus, there is always the risk of losing data. Although it may be tempting to buy a cheap transfer cable from a third-party vendor, there is no protection if the cable is defective and your hard drive is wiped clean of your valuable data.

### Transfer Using a USB Flash Drive

This method works only if both the old and new Xbox 360 consoles are operational. It may also be time-consuming, requiring this process to be repeated several times to transfer all data over, depending on how much data you transfer and the capacity of your USB flash drive.

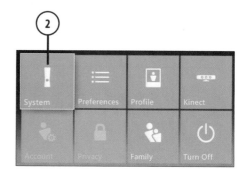

1. Plug your configured USB flash drive into your old Xbox 360.

2. Turn on your old console and go to the System menu under the Settings channel.

3. Select Storage.

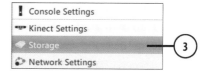

**4.** Choose your hard drive and press Y for Device Options.

**5.** Select Transfer Content.

**6.** Select the Memory Unit.

**7.** By default, all content is selected to transfer. Remove the check-mark from any content you don't wish to transfer, or press X to clear the checkmarks from all the content in a given category. Select Start to continue.

**8.** Once finished, power off your console and remove the USB flash drive.

**9.** Plug the USB flash drive into your new Xbox 360 and power it on. Repeat the same steps as above, except instead of transferring from a hard drive to a USB flash drive, you are transferring from the USB flash drive to a hard drive.

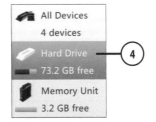

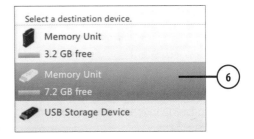

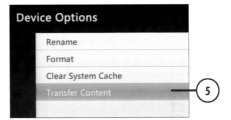

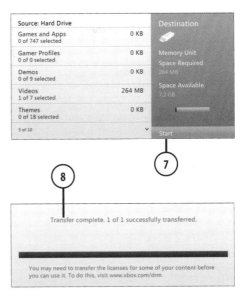

## Transfer Using a Hard Drive Transfer Cable

An Xbox 360 Data Transfer Cable, which is sold separately, is required for this step. A hard drive transfer can take several hours to complete, depending on how much content you have stored, so you may want to plan accordingly.

1. Remove the hard drive from your old Xbox 360 console. If this console is another Xbox 360 S unit, go to the "Removing and Attaching Your Hard Drive" section under "Setting Up Storage" earlier in this chapter to see how to do this. If you have an original Xbox 360 console, follow these directions:

   a. Turn off your original Xbox 360 console.

   b. Locate your console's hard drive, which is at the top if the console is placed vertically or on the left if the console is placed horizontally.

   c. Press the Release button on the hard drive.

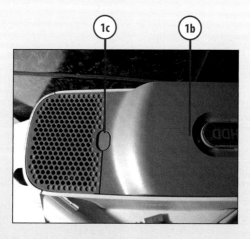

   d. Lift the hard drive away from the console.

2. Attach the transfer cable to your old hard drive.

3. Attach the other end of the transfer cable into a USB port on your new console.

4. Turn on your new console.

5. When a transfer content screen appears asking "Do you want to transfer content now?" select "Yes; transfer to console." Note: If this screen does not appear, you need to update your dashboard. How to do this is described in the next section.

6. Select Start to begin the content transfer. When complete, you can sign in to Xbox LIVE to access all your old content.

## Updating Your Dashboard

Xbox 360 software is periodically updated to provide you with new features and to keep your peripherals, such as your Kinect sensor, optimized. You can use four methods to get your Xbox 360 update: installing from Xbox LIVE, copying to a USB flash drive, burning to a CD or DVD, and installing from a game disc. (This option is available only if your game disc includes a newer version of the console software than what is currently on your system.) To install the console software from a game disc, just follow the prompts when you start the game. To install using the other methods, follow the directions outlined in this section.

## Updating via Xbox LIVE

This is the easiest way to update your
Xbox 360 console software, but it
requires an Internet connection. If
you do not have an Internet connection, but would like to establish one,
see "Connecting to Your Home
Network" in Chapter 2.

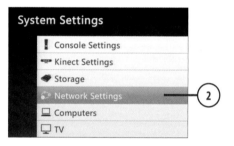

1. Go to the Settings channel and
   select System.

2. Highlight Network Settings and
   press A to continue.

3. Select the Wired Network or the
   name of your wireless network, if
   prompted. If necessary, enter the
   wireless network's password.

4. Select Test Xbox LIVE Connection.

5. If prompted to update the console software, select Yes, Continue.

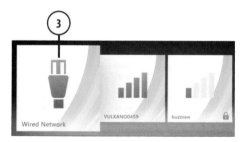

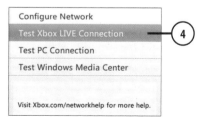

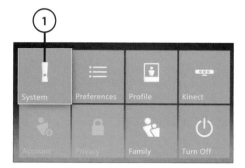

## RECEIVED A CONNECTION ERROR OR EXPERIENCED AN UPDATE PROBLEM?

*>> Go Further*

If you receive an Xbox LIVE connection error (for example, Connection Not Available, IP Address Not Found, Inability to Connect to Wireless Network), visit the Xbox LIVE Connect Solution at http://support.xbox.com/en-us/pages/xbox-live/troubleshoot/connection-issues/cant-connect-to-xbox-live-wizard.aspx, which can help you troubleshoot the problem by asking you a series of questions and then providing detailed instructions on how to overcome it. If the console software does not download successfully, visit http://support.xbox.com/en-us/pages/xbox-360/how-to/update-xbox-360/system-updates.aspx#Troubleshooting, to access troubleshooting strategies. Alternatively, you can try downloading your update via a USB flash drive or CD/DVD, as outlined in this chapter.

## Updating Using a USB Flash Drive

This method requires access to a computer and a USB flash drive formatted with what is known as the Windows FAT32 file system. If you have a Macintosh or Linux, don't fret because the FAT32 file system is compatible with either operating system.

1. Plug your USB flash drive into a USB port on your computer.

2. Download the console update .zip file at www.xbox.com/system-update-usb.

3. Click Save to save the file on your computer.

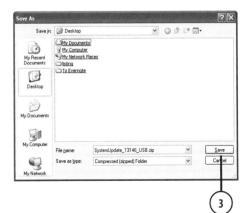

4. Right-click the file from where you saved it (here I've saved it to my Windows desktop) and click Extract All… to unzip the file.

5. Copy the file's contents to the root directory of your USB flash drive.

6. Unplug the USB flash drive from your computer.

7. Plug the flash drive into a USB port on your Xbox 360.

8. Restart your Xbox 360; the installation program starts automatically.

9. Select Yes when prompted to update the console software.

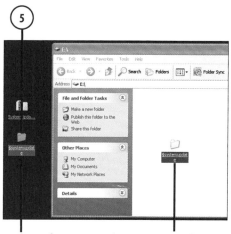

**Copy the extracted folder…**     **…to the USB flash drive**

## Updating Using a CD or DVD

This method requires you to have access to a computer that enables you to burn CDs or DVDs.

1. Follow steps 2–4 under "Updating Using a USB Flash Drive."

2. Insert a blank, writeable CD or DVD into your computer.

3. Copy the extracted contents of the .zip file to the root directory on your CD or DVD, and choose to write (burn) the files to the disc.

4. When the burn is complete, remove the CD or DVD from your computer, and insert it into Xbox 360's disc tray.

5. Restart your Xbox 360; the installation program starts automatically.

6. Select Yes when prompted to update the console software.

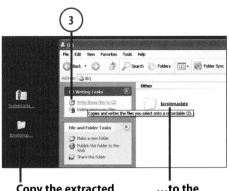

**Copy the extracted folder...**          **...to the writeable disc**

# Understanding Your Warranty

As long as your device's case has not been opened or tampered with, the warranty period on your Xbox 360 and the Kinect sensor, discussed in Chapters 10 and 11, is 1 year. During this time, you can return the console and sensor to Microsoft for servicing free of charge, provided troubleshooting does not resolve your problem. To send your Xbox 360 or Kinect sensor to Microsoft for servicing, visit www.xbox.com/en-US (U.S. residents only). Alternatively, you can call (800) 4MY-XBOX.

If your console or sensor is no longer under warranty, you can still send them to Microsoft for servicing should any problems arise. At this time, if you submit your request online, servicing costs approximately $100, whereas if you submit via phone, it can cost around $120. Turnaround time on repairs varies by state, but generally ranges between 12 and 19 days.

## Register Your Xbox 360

Registering your Xbox 360 makes it easier to keep on top of your warranty and gives you access to rewards, offers, and other information. To register your console, go to www.xbox.com/registermyxbox. The process takes approximately 3 minutes.

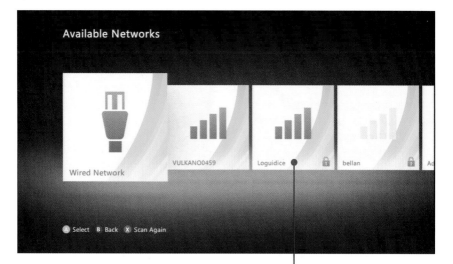

Learn to connect your Xbox 360 via both wired and wireless network connections, and learn the benefits of the various Xbox LIVE memberships.

In this chapter, you learn how to connect your console to the Internet, access Xbox LIVE, and make purchases through your console.

- → Establishing a Wireless Connection
- → Setting Up a Wired Connection
- → Joining Xbox LIVE
- → Understanding Xbox LIVE Memberships
- → Understanding Microsoft Points

# Networking Your Xbox

To maximize your enjoyment of the Xbox 360, you need to hook it up to the Internet. You can achieve this via a wireless or wired connection. When your Xbox is networked, you can join Xbox LIVE, which enables you to connect with friends, download and play games, and have instant access to a substantial media library.

## Connecting to Your Home Network

Unlike its predecessors, the Xbox 360 4GB and 250GB have built-in wireless networking, enabling you to connect your console to your home network without needing to purchase a separate wireless networking adapter. If you prefer to establish a wired connection, which generally provides the fastest and most reliable connection, this is still an option, but you need to purchase an Ethernet cable.

If your home is not yet equipped with broadband Internet access, you should consider setting up a high-speed connection to tap the full potential of your console. After you decide whether to set up a wireless or wired connection, see "Establishing a Wireless Connection" or "Establishing a Wired Connection," respectively, to determine what you need to start. After you purchase the necessary items, refer to your network hardware's instruction manual for guidance on setup. Although the process is generally straightforward, each manufacturer and system can have specific configuration and setup requirements, making coverage of such intricacies well beyond the scope of this book.

If you already have high-speed Internet access via DSL or a cable modem, networking your Xbox 360 takes just a few minutes as you'll see in the following sections.

## Establishing a Wireless Connection

Xbox 360 supports 802.11b/g/n wireless networks. To establish a wireless network connection, you need three things: (1) a high-speed Internet connection (that is, cable modem or DSL service; satellite, 3G or 4G mobile connections, and dial-up services are either not recommended or supported); (2) a router, bridge, or wireless access point (WAP) compatible with Xbox LIVE (that is, any router, bridge, or WAP marked as "Compatible with Windows 7," "Works with Windows Vista," or "Certified for Windows Vista"); and (3) a minimum of 128MB of storage space on your console (if you plan to join Xbox LIVE).

Follow these steps to connect your Xbox 360 to your wireless network. You will not be able to continue past step 2 if you have an Ethernet cable connected, so if you wish to switch from wired to wireless, disconnect the cable first.

### Finding Network Hardware Compatible with Xbox LIVE
If you need to purchase network hardware to wirelessly connect to Xbox LIVE or want to upgrade your current hardware, you can find a list of compatible hardware at http://support.xbox.com/en-us/xbox-live/get-started/connecting/network-hardware-compatible-xbox-live.

1. Go to the Settings channel and select System from the menu.

2. Scroll to Network Settings and press A to select it.

3. Scroll to the wireless network you want to use and press A to select it. If your wireless network is password protected, proceed to the next step; otherwise, go to step 5.

4. At the Network security screen, enter your wireless network password and select Done.

5. When successfully connected, the Network settings screen appears and shows Network, Internet, and Xbox LIVE as Connected. Keep in mind that your console is not yet connected to Xbox LIVE, but the capability to access Xbox LIVE is now there should you want to join.

## Update Console Software

After step 5, you may receive a prompt to update your console software. If this occurs, select Yes and follow the onscreen prompts. For additional information on updating your console software, turn to "Updating Your Dashboard" in Chapter 1, "Getting Started."

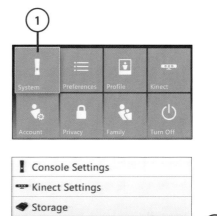

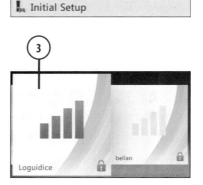

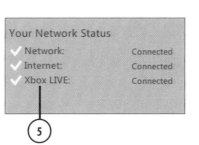

*Go Further*

## LOOKING FOR A WIRELESS PERFORMANCE BOOST?

If you find your wireless connection to be sluggish, you can consider investing in a Powerline AV Network Kit. These easy-to-use devices enable you to create a high-speed network connection anywhere in your home via an adaptor that plugs directly into any electrical wall outlet. No need to run wires! Many brands are available. Visit online sites such as Amazon.com to read reviews and find the one that best suits your needs.

## Establishing a Wired Connection

To establish a wired connection, you need four things: (1) a high-speed Internet connection (that is, cable modem or DSL service; satellite, 3G or 4G mobile connections, and dial-up services are either not recommended or supported); (2) a router and modem compatible with Xbox LIVE (that is, any routers or modems marked as "Compatible with Windows 7," "Works with Windows Vista," or "Certified for Windows Vista"); (3) an Ethernet cable, which must be purchased separately; and (4) a minimum of 128MB of storage space on your console (if you plan to join Xbox LIVE).

Follow these steps to get your Xbox 360 wired to your home network.

### The Long and Short of Ethernet Cables

Ethernet cables enable high-speed wired Internet connections. Be sure the Ethernet cable that you purchase is a CAT-5, CAT-5e, or Cat-6 and the appropriate length. The cable needs to reach from the back of your console to your network port or router. Many lengths are available, so you should have no trouble finding one that meets your needs. Amazon.com tends to have the best deal on cables, and it can be useful to read customer reviews before purchase.

## Making the Hardware Connections

Before you can connect your Xbox 360 to your wired home network, you have to connect your console to your network port or router (or modem) via the Ethernet cable. Because both ends of the cable are the same, this is a breeze.

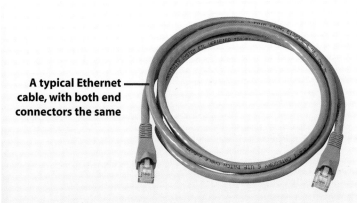

**A typical Ethernet cable, with both end connectors the same**

1. Plug one end of the Ethernet cable into a network port or port on your router. If your Xbox is the sole device on your home network, you can plug it directly into the modem.

2. Plug the other end of the Ethernet cable into the back of your Xbox 360.

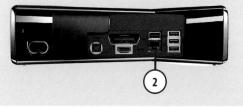

## Testing Your Connection

After the hardware connections are established, you have to test your connection.

1. Go to System under the Settings channel and press A to select it.

2. Scroll to Network Settings and press A to select it.

3. On the Available Networks screen, select Wired Network.

4. On the Network Settings screen, select Test Xbox LIVE Connection.

5. When successfully connected, the Network settings screen appears and shows Network, Internet, and Xbox LIVE as Connected. Keep in mind that your console is not yet connected to Xbox LIVE, but the capability to access Xbox LIVE is now there should you want to join.

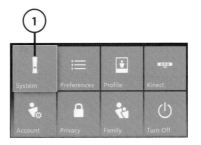

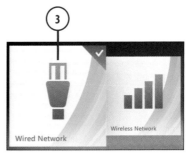

# Examining Xbox LIVE

Xbox LIVE is a service offered by Microsoft Corporation that enables online multiplayer gaming and access to various digital media. It was first made available in 2002 and has evolved considerably since then, with new features added regularly, including extension of the service to other platforms, such as Windows Phone and Windows 8. It is available as a free service and as a subscription-based service. Joining Xbox LIVE is crucial to getting the most out of your console.

## Understanding Xbox LIVE Memberships

The Xbox LIVE free service is known as Xbox LIVE Free (it was previously known as Xbox LIVE Silver), whereas the paid service is known as Xbox LIVE Gold. The latter offers access to considerably more services, as demonstrated in the following table, which compares select features. There is also a Family Pack option, which provides four Xbox LIVE Gold memberships so an entire household can enjoy the extra benefits at a reduced cost. In addition, the Family Pack enables you to gift point allowances to family members, view reports about your family's Xbox LIVE activities, and receive occasional discounts on family-friendly games.

Although an Xbox LIVE Gold membership makes more features and services accessible to you on your Xbox 360, many of these have additional requirements (for example, a Netflix subscription to access Netflix content). In addition, much of the digital content on the Xbox LIVE Marketplace is not free. For example, the only downloadable games generally free are ad-supported games. Making purchases from the Xbox LIVE Marketplace requires purchasing Microsoft Points. See "Understanding Microsoft Points" later in this chapter.

**COMPARISON OF SELECT FEATURES AND SERVICES OFFERED BY XBOX LIVE FREE VERSUS XBOX LIVE GOLD***

| Feature | Xbox LIVE Free | Xbox LIVE Gold | Additional Requirements |
|---|---|---|---|
| Avatar creation and customization | Yes | Yes | None |
| Downloadable content | Yes | Yes | None |
| Family Settings | Yes | Yes | None |
| Free demos and game previews | Yes | Yes | None |
| Game Room | Yes | Yes | None |

## COMPARISON OF SELECT FEATURES AND SERVICES OFFERED BY XBOX LIVE FREE VERSUS XBOX LIVE GOLD* *CONTINUED*

| Feature | Xbox LIVE Free | Xbox LIVE Gold | Additional Requirements |
|---|---|---|---|
| MSN access | Yes | Yes | None |
| Roaming profiles | Yes | Yes | None |
| Text with friends | Yes | Yes | None |
| Kinect Fun Labs | Yes | Yes | Kinect |
| Voice chat | Yes | Yes | Headset or Kinect |
| Xbox LIVE arcade access | Yes | Yes | None |
| Zune video | Yes | Yes | Microsoft Points |
| Avatar Kinect | No | Yes | Kinect |
| Cloud Storage | No | Yes | None |
| ESPN access | No | Yes | ESPN3-affiliated ISP |
| Facebook access | No | Yes | Facebook account |
| Halo Waypoint | No | Yes | None |
| Hulu Plus access | No | Yes | Hulu Plus account |
| iHeartRadio access | No | Yes | None |
| IPTV access | No | Yes | IPTV account |
| Last.fm access | No | Yes | Last.fm account |
| Netflix access | No | Yes | Netflix account |
| Online Multiplayer Gaming | No | Yes | None |
| Party chat | No | Yes | Headset or Kinect |
| Skype access | No | Yes | Headset or Kinect and Skype account |
| Twitter access | No | Yes | Twitter account |
| Video Kinect | No | Yes | Kinect |
| YouTube access | No | Yes | YouTube account |
| Zune music | No | Yes | Zune Pass |

*Microsoft is continually updating and adding services, so more services will be available than are outlined here.*

## Save on Xbox LIVE Gold Membership

You can purchase an Xbox LIVE Gold membership directly through your Xbox, but you can likely save some money if you shop around. Check other retailers before you buy, such as game stores and online retailers. At Amazon.com, for instance, you can opt to purchase a card that contains a code that gives you access to Xbox LIVE for a certain amount of time, or you can opt to receive the code via email after you make your payment. If using a third-party retailer, be sure to use one that is reputable, especially if you opt to receive your code electronically.

# Joining Xbox LIVE

When you know which Xbox LIVE membership you want, you can set up your Xbox LIVE account. Follow these steps to get your Xbox LIVE membership.

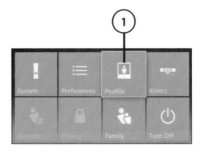

1. Go to Profile under the Settings channel, and press A to select it.

2. Select Join Xbox LIVE.

3. At the Exit Session screen, select Yes.

4. At the Welcome to Xbox LIVE screen, press A to continue.

5. At the first Join Xbox LIVE screen, enter your first name, scroll to Done, and press A to proceed.

6. Enter your email address, scroll to Done, and press A to proceed.

7. Enter your password, scroll to Done, and press A to proceed.

8. Enter your password again to confirm it, scroll to Done, and press A to proceed.

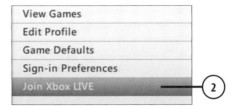

9. At the Secret Question screen, select the question you would like to answer should you need to have your password re-sent to you in the future. After you enter your answer, scroll to Done, and press A to proceed.

10. At the Account Protection screen, select and enter either an SMS number or alternate email address. If you do not want to have an alternate way to verify your identity, press X to skip.

11. Enter your date of birth, and press A to continue.

12. Press A to proceed after you confirm your information. If you need to change anything, select any line to edit and press A to continue.

13. At Your current privacy settings screen, press A to continue.

14. At the Terms and preferences screen, select Accept and press A to continue.

15. After your Xbox LIVE Free account is created, the Congratulations! screen appears, which includes a preassigned Gamertag that can be changed once for free. Press A to continue.

16. At the Xbox LIVE Gold screen, press A to Continue.

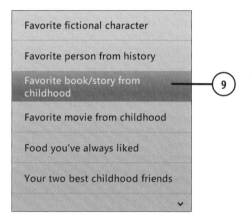

Favorite fictional character

Favorite person from history

Favorite book/story from childhood

Favorite movie from childhood

Food you've always liked

Your two best childhood friends

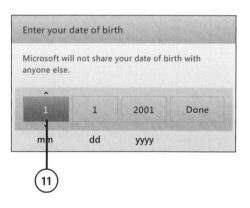

Enter your date of birth

Microsoft will not share your date of birth with anyone else.

| 1 | 1 | 2001 | Done |
| mm | dd | yyyy | |

XBOX LIVE.

Your free account is now active.

Your gamertag: **UtmostSuperset0**

You can change it once for free. After signup, open your profile and select Edit Profile, Gamertag.

Continue

**17.** At the Xbox LIVE Gold Memberships screen, select the membership option you would like, and press A to continue. Select Upgrade Later if you are happy with Xbox LIVE Free membership.

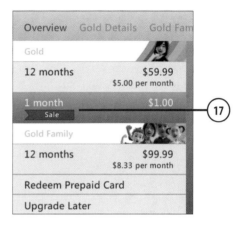

### Upgrade Later

Even if you want to upgrade to Xbox LIVE Gold, you may want to select Upgrade Later. Microsoft has various offers, so sometimes selecting Upgrade Later automatically gives you a free trial to Xbox LIVE Gold. If no such offer is available, you can always go back and upgrade your membership.

## Changing Your Preassigned Gamertag

A Gamertag is your username on Xbox LIVE and other platforms, including Windows Phone and Games for Windows LIVE. Because it identifies your profile on Xbox LIVE and is the method people use to locate you on Xbox LIVE, you may want to customize it.

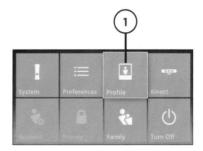

**1.** Go to Profile under the Settings channel, and press A to select it.

**2.** Scroll down to Edit Profile and press A.

**3.** Press A to select Gamertag.

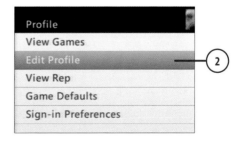

4. At the Change Gamertag screen, select Enter a New Gamertag to pick your own. You can also choose Get Suggestions if you want to see some available options to select or edit.

5. At the Change Gamertag screen, enter a new Gamertag, scroll to Done, and press A to continue.

6. After you input an available Gamertag, a second Change Gamertag screen appears. If you are happy with your moniker, select Yes, use this gamertag. Confirm the change.

### Name Changes

Choose your Gamertag carefully because you can edit it only once for free. Future name changes cost you 800 points.

# Paying for Xbox LIVE Gold Membership with a Credit Card

If you decide to pay for Xbox LIVE Gold membership, follow these steps:

1. Follow steps 1 through 16 under "Joining Xbox LIVE."

2. At the Xbox LIVE Gold Memberships screen, select one of the paid options, and press A to continue.

3. At the first Billing Info screen, enter your first name, scroll to Done, and press A to continue.

4. Enter your last name, phone number, and email address on their respective screens, scrolling to Done, and pressing A to continue after each.

## Registering a Payment Type for the First Time

You can purchase Xbox LIVE Gold membership directly through your console, but if your credit card information is not already in the system, this can be time-consuming. To speed up purchasing your Gold membership and avoid having to go through countless screens, log into your Xbox LIVE account through your computer at www.xbox.com and select My Account, which appears on the top right of the screen or directly under your avatar when you select Social from the top navigation bar. Choose Manage Payment Options and input your information. You can also add PayPal as a payment option. For more on this, see "Paying for Purchases with PayPal" later in this chapter.

5. At the Select Payment Option screen, select Credit Card and press A to continue.

6. At the first Credit Card Info screen, select your credit card type, and press A to continue.

7. Enter your name as it appears on your credit card, scroll to Done, and press A to continue.

8. Enter your credit card number and its verification code, scrolling to Done, and pressing A to continue after you enter them.

9. Enter your credit card's expiration date, scroll to Done, and press A to continue.

10. At the Credit Card Confirmation screen, press A to continue after you verify your information. If anything needs to be corrected, press B to go back to previous screens.

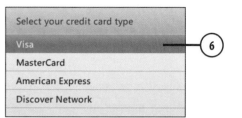

Select your credit card type

Visa — 6

MasterCard

American Express

Discover Network

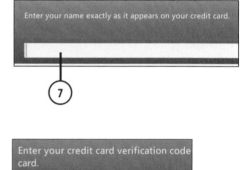

Enter your name exactly as it appears on your credit card.

7

Enter your credit card verification code
card.

8

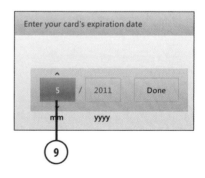

Enter your card's expiration date

5 / 2011 Done

mm yyyy

9

11. At each of the Billing Address screens, enter the requested information: address, city, state, and zip code, scrolling to Done, and pressing A to continue for each screen.

12. Press A after confirming your information. If anything needs to be corrected, press B to go back.

13. At the Xbox LIVE Gold Memberships screen, select Confirm Purchase. If you decide you don't want the Xbox LIVE Gold membership, select Cancel.

## Avoid Automatic Renewals

When you purchase Xbox LIVE Gold membership through your Xbox, it automatically renews until you cancel it. If you receive a promotional deal, it is only good for the initial trial. Upon renewal, you will be charged whatever the going price is for the option that you initially selected. If you want to avoid automatic renewals, purchase a card or code for Xbox LIVE Gold membership from other retailers instead of paying for it through your console with a credit card.

## Redeeming a Prepaid Card

1. Follow steps 1 through 16 under "Joining Xbox LIVE."

2. At the Xbox LIVE Gold Membership screen, select Redeem Prepaid Card.

3. At the Redeem Code screen, enter the 25-character code from your prepaid card (do not include spaces or hyphens; hyphens appear automatically), scroll to Done, and press A to continue.

4. At the Confirm screen, make sure Redeem Now is selected, and press A to continue.

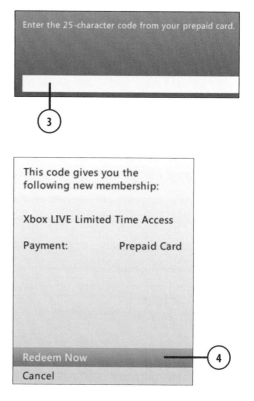

Enter the 25-character code from your prepaid card.

③

This code gives you the following new membership:

Xbox LIVE Limited Time Access

Payment:          Prepaid Card

Redeem Now                              ④

Cancel

# Understanding Microsoft Points

Microsoft Points are the currency that you use to purchases digital content from the Xbox LIVE Marketplace. This digital content includes games, game add-ons, accessories for your avatar, and videos. You can buy Points directly through your Xbox 360 or from other retailers. As of this writing, if you purchase these Points directly through your Xbox 360, you can buy as few as 400 Points ($4.99) or as many as 6,000 Points ($74.99). Third-party retailers generally sell prepaid cards that contain 1,600 or 4,000 Microsoft Points. Some retailers allow you to opt to receive the code to redeem your Microsoft Points immediately upon purchase via email, rather than having to wait for the card with the code to arrive in the mail; however, some delays in accessing codes have still been reported with this option.

Points that are purchased do not expire, but if you are awarded Points through promotions, these can have expiration dates. However, when you use your Points to make a purchase, Xbox LIVE automatically uses those with the nearest expiration date.

## It's Not All Good

**Buyer Beware**

If you opt to receive your Microsoft Points code electronically from a third-party retailer, be sure to buy only from a reputable company. There have been reports of individuals receiving bogus codes from some online retailers.

## Adding Microsoft Points to Your Account

Follow these steps to add Microsoft Points to your account.

1. Select Account from the Settings channel.

2. Go to the Account Management blade, select Add Microsoft Points, and press A to continue.

3. At the Add Microsoft Points screen, select the number of points that you want to add and press A to continue.

4. At the Points Purchase screen, select Confirm Purchase. If you do not yet have a credit card or PayPal tied to your account, Xbox LIVE prompts you for your billing information.

## It's Not All Good

There have been two major criticisms regarding the need to purchase Microsoft Points to buy digital content from the Xbox LIVE Marketplace or the Games for Windows – LIVE Marketplace. First, Microsoft Points must be purchased in blocks, so you almost always have to buy more points than you immediately need. Second, using Points insulates you from the true costs of the products you are purchasing because Points simply do not feel like currency to most people; however, approximately 80 Points is equivalent to $1.00.

There are several Xbox LIVE Points Converters on the Web. You can find a particularly good one at http://thewrongadvices.com/2007/03/05/xbox-live-points-converter. This calculator enables you to covert points to dollars and vice versa between six different currencies.

## Redeeming Codes

Follow these steps to redeem your Microsoft Points via a code.

1. Go to the Settings channel and select Account.

2. At the Account Management screen, select Redeem Code.

3. At the Redeem Code screen, enter the 25-character code from your prepaid card, scroll to Done, and press A to select.

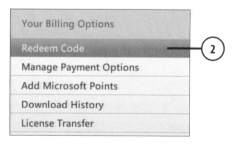

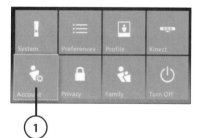

4. At the Confirm screen, make sure Redeem Now is selected, and press A to continue.

**Add Microsoft Points**

From the Account Management screen, you can also opt to Add Microsoft Points. The same steps apply as outlined in "Adding Microsoft Points to Your Account."

---

This code gives you the following new membership:

Xbox LIVE Limited Time Access

Payment:              Prepaid Card

Redeem Now       ④

Cancel

## Paying for Purchases with PayPal

PayPal is a free service that enables you to securely make payments and transfer money over the Internet. When you sign up for a PayPal account, you link your checking or savings account, or debit or credit card, to PayPal. You can also add money to your PayPal account via MoneyPak, which works like a cash top-up card.

When you have a PayPal account, which can be set up at www.paypal.com, you can link your Xbox LIVE account to your PayPal account, giving you another means to make purchases through your console. To link your PayPal account to your Xbox LIVE account, go to www.xbox.com/paypal and follow the instructions. You can also add your PayPal account directly on your Xbox by following these steps.

1. Go to the Settings channel and select Account.

2. At the Account Management screen, select Manage Payment Options.

3. From the Manage Payment Options screen, select Add PayPal.

4. Enter your email address and password, then select Next.

5. Select Accept to authorize PayPal as a payment method. You now see that your PayPal account is ready to use.

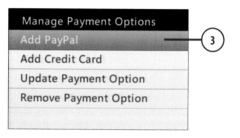

## Accessing Xbox LIVE Anywhere

LIVE Anywhere is a concept by Microsoft to bring Xbox LIVE features and services to a variety of platforms, promoting cross-platform communication while allowing users to maintain a unified identity through one Gamertag. Currently, besides the Xbox 360, the other two platforms actively using the LIVE concept are Games for Windows – LIVE and Windows Phone.

Because Games for Windows – LIVE and Xbox LIVE connect to the same service, you need only one account to access the features offered by each one, such as multiplayer gaming, voice chat, text chat, and achievements. You can also use the same pool of Microsoft Points to make purchases on the Games for Windows – LIVE Marketplace, which even includes some online multiplayer titles that enable PC gamers to play against Xbox 360 gamers.

Through Windows Phone, you can connect and play games with your friends, regardless of your geographic location. The phone uses your Xbox LIVE avatar and gamer profile to keep track of your scores and wins. It also enables you to see which of your friends are online and what they are up to on their consoles, PCs, or Windows Phones.

**If you're a Windows Phone owner, you have access to all of your Xbox LIVE information on the go.**

## Connecting to Your Xbox on the Web

Xbox LIVE members can access their account information on the Web at any time by logging into Xbox LIVE at www.xbox.com. When logged in, you can keep track of your friends, monitor your achievements, edit your avatar, queue games to download to your Xbox 360, send and receive messages, redeem Microsoft Points, and more.

**Accessing your Xbox LIVE information from the Web is just as feature rich as accesing it from your console.**

# Understanding Updates

The Xbox 360 console software is periodically updated, providing you with new features and services. Having your console connected to Xbox LIVE ensures you always have the latest console software, as you are automatically prompted to update your software when an update becomes available. Turn to Chapter 1 for more information on updating your dashboard.

1. When an Update Required screen pops up, scroll up to Yes, and press A to select it.

2. When the Update in Progress screen disappears, your console may restart, and you are good to go.

Customize your    Shop for more
avatar.              items.

BillLog

Change My
Features

Change My
Style

Marketplace

Save and Exit

Awards

Gamer Picture

Choose New
Avatar

A Select

Earn avatar        Snap a Gamer
awards.            Picture.

In this chapter, you learn how to add a personal touch to your Xbox 360 experience by creating your own profile, building an avatar, and accessorizing your system with just the right add-ons.

→ Creating a Profile
→ Building an Avatar
→ Exploring the Dashboard
→ Signing In to Your System
→ Managing Profiles

# Personalizing Your Xbox Experience

Power is good. Control over that power is even better. Your Xbox 360 gives you the control you need to make using it a unique experience. Not only can you create your own user profile complete with gamer picture, you can also build an avatar in your—or anyone else's—likeness. As part of this control, you'll also learn about all the options available from the Xbox 360 Dashboard and the ways in which you can accessorize your system with just the right enhancements and add-ons.

# Establishing User Profiles

Your profile, which establishes your presence on Xbox, includes several components, such as profile name or Gamertag (profile name if you have an Xbox
LIVE account), Gamerscore, and Gamer picture. Turn to "Digging into Your
Profile" in Chapter 4 to learn more about the various components and how to
flesh out your profile. Although you can have as many profiles as your hard
drive or other storage device can hold, any profile you want Xbox LIVE access
for needs to be signed up for an Xbox LIVE Free or Xbox LIVE Gold account.
See "Joining Xbox LIVE" in Chapter 2 for more on this. Profiles not tied to Xbox
LIVE remain offline and have no dependence on or interactivity with the
Xbox Live service.

Why have offline accounts? Perhaps not everyone in your household uses the
Xbox 360 enough to warrant signing up for Xbox LIVE, or maybe you only
want your friends to know about your achievements in *Call of Duty: Modern
Warfare 3* and not that you are also a *High School Musical 3: Senior Year
DANCE!* game junkie.

## It's Not All Good

**Beware of Account Headaches**

If you establish an offline account, you can convert the account to an Xbox
LIVE account at a later date, but you likely won't be able to retain your cur-
rent profile name, unless you have selected something highly unusual that
has not already been taken by someone on Xbox LIVE. As described in
"Joining Xbox LIVE" in Chapter 2, you are given a randomly generated
Gamertag, but you can customize it once for free.

You should also keep in mind when creating profiles that there is no way to
merge an offline account with an Xbox LIVE account down the road, so
achievements earned on one account can't be transferred to another once
you decide it is OK to let your friends know about your little *High School
Musical 3: Senior Year DANCE!* addiction. While several potential workarounds
are described on the Web, we have yet to find one that actually works.

# Creating a Profile

The first step in the personalization process is to create a profile. If you followed the steps in "Powering On for the First Time" from Chapter 1, "Getting Started," or "Joining Xbox LIVE" from Chapter 2, "Networking Your Xbox," you have a basic profile to modify and can skip straight to "Building an Avatar." Otherwise, if you want to create another or new profile, begin with the first step.

1. From the Social channel, highlight Sign In or Out, and press A on your controller to select it.

2. Select Create Profile.

3. If you have only one memory device attached to your console, proceed to step 4. If you have more than one memory device attached to your console, an image similar to the one shown to the right appears. Select the storage location of your choice.

---

### Which Storage Location?

If you plan to use your Profile on another console without Internet access, you can put it on removable storage that you can take with you, such as a USB Flash Drive (refer to Chapter 1). To learn how to move, delete, or recover your Xbox LIVE Gamertag, refer to the "Moving, Deleting, and Recovering a Gamertag" section found later in this chapter.

---

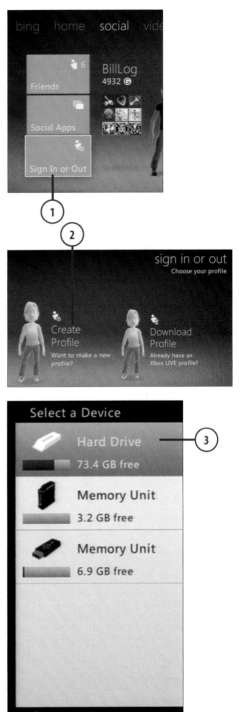

4. Enter a profile name of up to 15 characters. When satisfied with your profile name, select Done or press Start on your controller.

5. At the choose avatar screen, move the D-pad or Left Stick on your controller left or right until you settle on an avatar picture that you think would make a good starting point. Press the A button when you're happy with your selection.

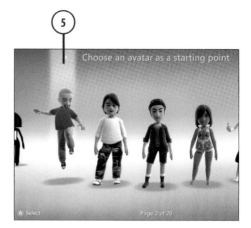

6. If you like the avatar you've selected, scroll to the Save and Exit icon. If not, select "Choose New Avatar." If you want to change your selected avatar's physical appearance, choose "Change My Features."

## Tweaking Your Avatar

To change your avatar's clothes, select "Change My Style," or select "Marketplace" to purchase new garb and other items from the Avatar Marketplace. You can also take a picture of your avatar by selecting "Gamer Picture." All of these avatar customization options are discussed in detail in "Building an Avatar" later in this chapter.

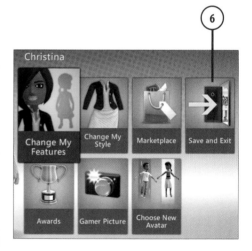

## Signing In

Now that you have one or more pro-files, you need to know how to sign in to the Gamertag of your choice.

1. Go to the Social channel, high-light Sign In or Out, and press A on your controller to select it.

2. Highlight the profile you want to sign in and press A to select.

3. You're now successfully signed in and can navigate the Xbox 360 Dashboard as your selected pro-file.

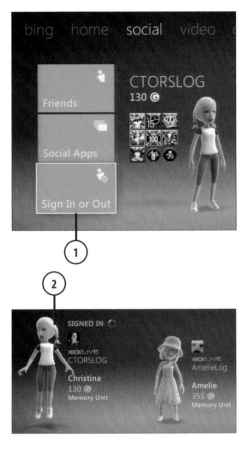

# Building an Avatar

Building your avatar, or digital representation, is one of the most enjoyable aspects of profile setup. You get to play around with your digital representa-tion's appearance without any repercussions, unlike real life. You can shape and mold your avatar as much as you want. If you don't like a selected tattoo or hair style, for instance, you simply change it with a button press. Use your avatar to express yourself, and don't worry about letting your alter ego come out.

## Selecting a Base to Work From

Before you can customize your avatar, you need to select one to work with. Follow these steps to get started:

1.  If you're already signed in with the profile you'd like to build your avatar for, proceed to step 2. Otherwise, follow steps 1–3 from "Signing In" above.

2.  Highlight and select your avatar under the Social channel.

3.  Select Customize Avatar.

4.  You see all the customization options to the right of your avatar; these are individually described in the following sections, starting with Change My Features.

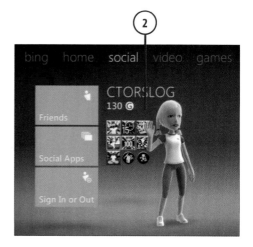

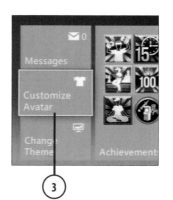

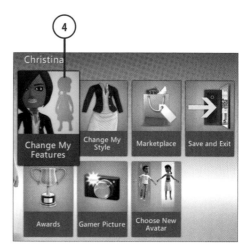

## EDITING YOUR AVATAR ON THE WEB

If you signed up for Xbox LIVE (refer to Chapter 2), you can also edit your avatar online at http://live.xbox.com/en-US/AvatarEditor?xr=shellnav. Because this is designed primarily for Games for Windows – LIVE or Windows Phone users without access to a real Xbox 360, you have access to most of the same editing and configuration options. This is also great for when you're away from your console and want to further perfect your digital representative. As if you needed another way to while away the hours on the Web!

## Change My Features

To change your avatar's facial features, body size, and coloring, simply follow these steps. If you're not already at the Customize Avatar screen, follow steps 1 through 4 from the previous page.

1. At the Customize Avatar screen, select Change My Features.

2. At the My Features screen, use the Left Stick or D-pad to move between the eight categories. There are minor variations in naming and options, depending upon whether you chose a female or male as a starting point. Select a category to edit by pressing A on your controller. Choose from among the following categories:

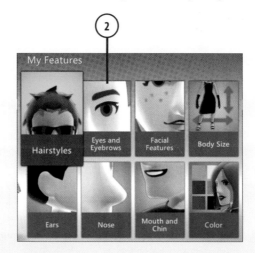

- **Hairstyles**—Move left for hairstyles generally styled to the left and move right for hairstyles generally styled to the right.

- **Eyes and Eyebrows**—Select between editing Eyes or Eyebrows. After selecting the type of Eyes or Eyebrows that you want, choose the color.

- **Facial Features**—If you have a female avatar, you go straight to editing Facial Features. If you have a male avatar, select between editing Facial Hair or Facial Features.

- **Body Size**—Move the Left Stick or D-pad left or right to make your avatar thinner or heavier. Move the Left Stick or D-pad up or down to make your avatar taller or shorter.

- **Ears**—Select one of the nine ear types. Normal ear types, such as round, are most easily visible when no hair is blocking them and are best seen when viewing your avatar from the side. Fantasy ear types, such as Elven and Fantasy, are more obvious regardless of hairstyle or view.

- **Nose**—There are 18 nose types to choose from. Be sure to give your avatar a whirl to see how it looks from the side.

- **Mouth and Chin**—Select between editing Chin or Mouth. There are many mouth options to choose from, including fantasy types, such as Bunny and Vampire.

- **Color**—There are eight categories for color. Some of the categories, such as Facial Hair Color, appear as grayed out if your avatar has no facial hair.

## Navigation Guide

Each of these categories uses the same controls for navigation. Use the Left Stick or D-pad to move between the various options when you are in one of the aforementioned eight customization options. Once you find a feature that you want (like a particular hairstyle under the "Hairstyles" category), highlight it and press A to select it. You can use the Left and Right Triggers to rotate your avatar for a better look. If you change your mind at any time, press B to go back to the screen you want.

## Duck!

If you are in a zoomed-in view of your avatar's upper body, you can bonk your avatar on the head by pushing up on the Right Stick and then pulling it down quickly.

**3.** Press B to return to the Customize Avatar screen.

**4.** Select another category, or choose Save and Exit to save your changes and return to the Xbox 360 Dashboard.

## Want to Have More Fun with Your Avatar?

Pressing the Right Stick causes your avatar to burp. Pressing the Right Bumper makes your avatar smile. Pressing the Left Bumper makes your avatar express a random emotion. Useful tip? No. Fun? Yes!

## Change My Style

If you want to change your avatar's clothing, makeup, and accessories, follow these steps. If you're not already at the Customize Avatar screen, follow steps 1 through 4 from the "Selecting a Base to Work From" section.

**1.** At the Customize Avatar screen, select Change My Style.

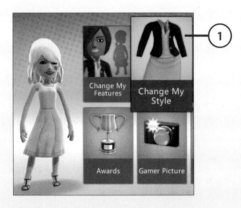

**2.** At the My Style screen, use the Left Stick or D-pad to move between the eight categories. Select a category to edit by pressing A on your controller.

- **Tops, Headwear, Bottoms, and Shoes**—These categories are gender-specific and have different options for male and female avatars.

- **Accessories**—Select between editing Glasses, Wristwear, Gloves, Rings, or Earrings. These categories are gender-specific and have different options for male and female avatars, though some options may be considered a bit unusual by some (such as hot pink sweatbands for a male avatar).

- **Props**—Props are animated objects that your avatar interacts with. You can only get props inside some games or by purchasing them at the Avatar Marketplace. If you're on a console with an active Internet connection and using a profile with an Xbox LIVE account, you can visit the Avatar Marketplace by pressing Y on your controller. If you have already acquired props for your avatar, you can move the Left Stick or D-pad to rotate between the items.

- **Dress Up**—This category features various preconfigured clothing ensembles or costumes. For male avatars, some outfits come with matching shoes. For female avatars, only the dress is included, though some outfits, such as the Cheerleader Dress, would have benefitted from including preconfigured shoes.

## Navigation Guide
Navigating between each of the above categories requires the same controls. Use the Left Stick or D-pad to move between the various items. Use the Left and Right Triggers to rotate your avatar for a better look. If you change your mind at any time, press B to go back. Press A to make your selection and return to the My Style screen. Press Y to go to the Avatar Marketplace.

- **My Outfits**—Put together a killer look? This is the place to save your present outfit for posterity and later access. Press A to save your outfit, and if applicable choose a device to save it to. Enter a name for your outfit, and select done or press the Start Button to confirm. You are now back at the My Outfits screen, where you can use the Left Stick or D-pad to select between your various saved outfits. Press the X button to delete an outfit. When you're happy with your selection, press A to return to the My Style screen.

3. Press B to return to the Customize Avatar screen.

4. Select another category, or choose Save and Exit to save your changes and return to the Xbox 360 Dashboard.

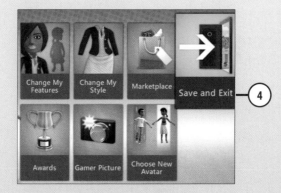

## Marketplace

Not satisfied with the free clothing, accessories, and props? If your console is connected to the Internet and your present profile has an Xbox LIVE account (refer to Chapter 2), you can visit the Avatar Marketplace to buy specialty items for your avatar. Profiles not tied to Xbox LIVE are restricted to the standard options. You can access the Avatar Marketplace from within the Change My Style category by pressing Y on your controller. Otherwise, follow these steps to go directly to the Marketplace to purchase the latest fashions from an online inventory. If you're not already at the Customize Avatar screen, follow steps 1 through 4 from the "Selecting a Base to Work From" section to get there.

1.  At the Customize Avatar screen, select Marketplace. The Marketplace rectangle has a sparkle in its upper-right corner if there is new content since your last visit.

2.  At the Avatar Marketplace screen, use the Left Stick or D-pad to move between the upper marketplace highlights or lower category tiers of Most Popular, Lifestyle Collections, Game Styles, and All. Select a highlighted option by pressing A on your controller.

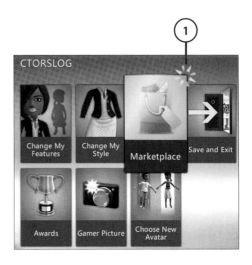

3. Use the Left Stick or D-pad to move between the various purchasable items. Use the Left and Right Triggers to rotate your avatar for a better look. If you change your mind at any time, press B to go back. Press A to purchase an item using Microsoft Points (refer to Chapter 2). Press X to go to the My Style screen, and follow along from step 3 under "Change My Style."

4. Press B to return to the Customize Avatar screen.

5. Select another category, or choose Save and Exit to save your changes and return to the Xbox 360 Dashboard.

## Accessing Purchased Content

Only the profile that purchases an item can use it. If you move your profile to a different console, you need to download purchased items again, but you don't need to pay for them again. Refer to the section, "Transferring Content Licenses to a New Console" in Chapter 5 for more information on transferring avatar items and other purchased content from the Xbox LIVE Marketplace to a new console.

## Accessing Awards

After performing certain functions or playing through certain games, you can earn awards that take the form of new items for your avatar to wear or use. Some awards may not yet be accessible, but if you select one of these potential awards, a brief description appears letting you know how to earn it. Follow these steps to access information on potential awards and use already earned awards. If you're not at the Customize Avatar screen, follow steps 1 through 4 from the "Selecting a Base to Work From" section to get there.

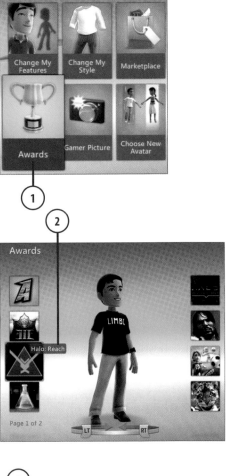

1. At the Customize Avatar screen, select Awards.

2. At the Awards screen, use the Left Stick or D-pad to move between the various games and applications you've played that have available or potential awards. Press A on your controller to make a selection or B to go Back.

3. At the game-specific awards screen, select an award. If you find an earned clothing item or prop, you can use the Left and Right Triggers to rotate your avatar for a better look. If you change your mind at any time, press B to go back.

4. Press B to return to the Customize Avatar screen.

5. Select another category, or choose Save and Exit to save your changes and return to the Xbox 360 Dashboard.

## Gamer Picture

Proud of your avatar? Have an Xbox LIVE profile? Why not take a picture?
Follow these steps to do just that. If you're not already at the Customize
Avatar screen, follow steps 1 through 4 from the "Selecting a Base to Work
From" section to get there.

1. At the Customize Avatar screen, select Gamer Picture.

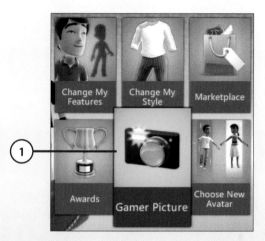

2. At the Basic Mode Gamer Picture screen, use the Left Stick or D-pad to move between
the various avatar pose options. Use the Left and Right Triggers to rotate your avatar
for a better look. To create your own custom pose, press X on your controller for
Advanced Mode.

---

### Change Your Mind?

If you change your mind at any time, press B to go back. You can also skip creating a custom pose by selecting among the existing options, pressing A, and
proceeding to step 5.

---

**3.** At the Advanced Mode Gamer Picture screen, use the controls as shown on the screen to manipulate the image of your avatar. Press Y to use a prop. Press the Left Bumper to change your avatar's expression. The expression only remains for a few seconds after you release the Left Bumper. If you like an expression, hold the Left Bumper down until you've taken your avatar's photo by pressing the Right Bumper.

## Posing

Your avatar's photo is displayed in the Preview window. If you like the pose in the Preview window, press A on your controller to get to the Gamer Picture screen where you can select a backdrop. If you prefer to return to Basic Mode instead, press X.

4. At the Choose Backdrop screen, use the Left Stick or D-pad to move between the various backdrop options. Select a highlighted backdrop by pressing A on your controller.

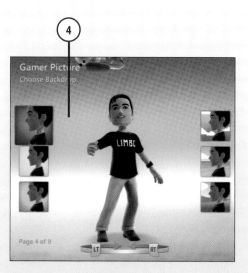

5. Press B to return to the Customize Avatar screen.

6. Select another category or choose Save and Exit to save your changes and return to the Xbox 360 Dashboard.

## Worth a Thousand Words?

The picture that you take of your avatar is the picture that other people see unless you choose a gamer picture. If you already have a gamer picture, the picture of the avatar is added to the list for you to choose from.

## Choosing a New Avatar

If you want to change your avatar's gender or associate a new avatar with your profile, this is the place to do it. Don't worry, you'll still retain any items you've purchased for your avatar from the Xbox LIVE Marketplace; however, after you replace your avatar, you can no longer see the old one, and you lose all your customizations, so proceed with these steps with caution. If you're not at the Customize Avatar screen, follow steps 1 through 4 from the "Selecting a Base to Work From" section to get there.

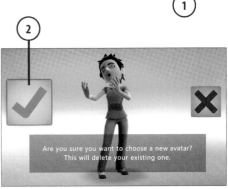

1. At the Customize Avatar screen, select Choose New Avatar.

2. At the Choose New Avatar screen, use the Left Stick or D-pad to move between the green checkmark for choosing a new avatar, which deletes your existing one, and the red x to cancel the action and bring you back to the Customize Avatar screen. Press A to confirm your selection. Press B to go back.

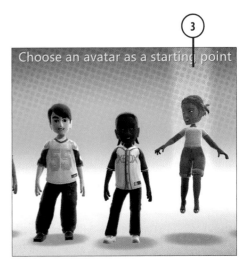

3. If you deleted your existing avatar, select a new avatar as a starting point. Move the D-pad or Left Stick on your controller left or right until you settle on an avatar picture that you think is a good match or would make a good starting point. Press the A button when you're happy with your selection.

4. If you want to customize your newly selected avatar, proceed to step 6 under "Creating a Profile," or if you are happy with it the way it is, select Save and Exit from the Customize Avatar screen.

# Moving, Deleting, and Recovering a Gamertag

The final stage of profile management is to learn how to keep your Gamertag accessible by moving and recovering it. You also learn how to delete your profile in case you ever want to start over from scratch.

## Using a Gamer Profile on Another Console

You can use a USB flash drive to take your profile with you for when you want to play on a different console that does not have Internet access. Follow these steps and you can become portable in no time.

1. Go to the Settings channel and select System by pressing A on your controller.

2. Select Storage.

3. Select the storage device where the profile you want to move is located.

4. Select Gamer Profiles.

5. Select the gamer profile you want to move.

6. Select Move.

7. Select the USB Storage Device to move the profile to.

8. Remove the USB flash drive and take it to the other console. When you return to your console, remember to plug the USB flash drive back in so that you can again sign in to your profile, or simply follow the steps in the next section to recover it.

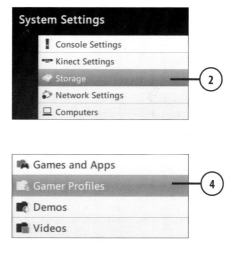

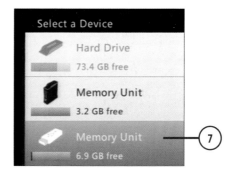

# Recovering Your Gamertag from Xbox LIVE

If you accidentally delete your Xbox LIVE Gamertag or simply want to use it on a different console, follow these steps. You need the email address and password you used to sign in to Xbox LIVE.

1. Press the Xbox Guide Button.

   If you haven't already, make sure to sign out of your account by pressing the X button after bringing up the Xbox Guide.

2. Select Download Profile.

3. Select Download Profile again.

4. At the email address screen, enter the address that you use to sign in to Xbox LIVE profile you want to recover the Gamertag for and then select Done.

5. At the password screen, enter the password that you use to sign in to Xbox LIVE and then select Done.

6. Select the storage device you want to recover the account to.

7. A downloading screen appears
with a status bar. Once the
account is fully recovered, a sign-
in screen appears. By default,
Remember Password is selected;
if this is not your console, remember to uncheck this option. Select
Sign In to finish.

### Xbox LIVE Child Accounts

For Xbox LIVE child accounts, the
associated Xbox LIVE adult
account credentials are required
to complete the recover
Gamertag procedure.

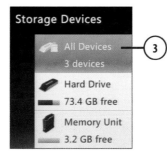

# Deleting a Gamer Profile

If you find that you no longer use a
profile, follow these steps to delete it.

1. Go to the Settings channel, and
select System by pressing A on
your controller.

2. Select Storage.

3. Select All Devices.

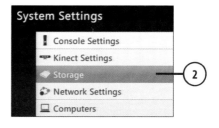

4. Select Gamer Profiles.

5. Select the gamer profile you want to delete.

6. Select Delete.

7. If you want to delete the profile, but leave the saved games and achievements, select Delete Profile Only. If you want to delete the profile and the associated saved games and achievements, select Delete Profile and Items.

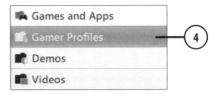

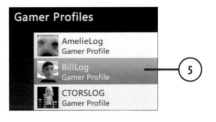

# Navigating the Xbox 360 Dashboard

The Xbox 360 Dashboard divides content, settings, and functions into categories, or channels, each represented by a group of related boxes. All channels and features are visible when logged into Xbox LIVE. For profiles without access to Xbox LIVE, fewer options will be available.

General navigation of the Xbox 360 Dashboard follows:

- **Left Stick** or **D-pad**—Left and right changes your Channel; up, down, left, and right highlights content blocks within a Channel.

- **A Button**—Accepts selections.

- **B Button** or **Back Button**—Back or exit.

- **Left and Right Bumpers**—Quick scroll left and right.

Now take a look at the channels, most of which are covered in greater detail elsewhere in this book.

## Bing Channel

Bing will search for content both on your system and available via the various services, so you can find the exact game, movie, TV show, sporting event, or music you want. See "Searching with Bing" in Chapter 4, "Getting to Know Your Xbox," for more on the Bing channel.

Provides system-
wide search
functionality

## Home Channel

Home is the default dashboard menu, providing quick access to your most recently accessed content, as well as your system's DVD drive. The Home Channel also contains selectable advertisements.

The default dashboard menu, which provides quick access
to your recently accessed content and DVD drive.

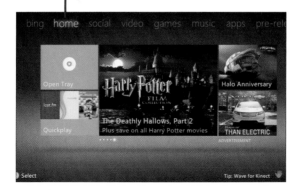

## Social Channel

Social provides access to your Xbox LIVE friends and social media services such as Facebook and Twitter. Refer to Chapters 8 and 9 for detailed information on the Social channel.

**This is your Xbox LIVE friends and social media hub.**

## TV Channel

TV contains television-related apps and offerings from cable operators and providers such as Verizon and Comcast, where you can watch live TV channels if you're a subscriber. The TV channel contains selectable advertisements. Refer to "Watching Other Video Services" in Chapter 6 for more information.

## Video Channel

Video contains downloadable videos, streaming services such as Netflix, live sports, and related content. The Video channel contains selectable advertisements. Refer to Chapter 6 for information on the Video channel.

**This is your hub for video-related content on Xbox LIVE. Some services, such as Netflix, require paid memberships for you to access them.**

## Games Channel

Games contains downloadable games, demos, add-ons, and related content. The Games channel contains selectable advertisements. Refer to Chapter 5 for detailed information on the Games channel.

**This is where you find downloadable games, demos, add-ons, and other content on Xbox LIVE. There are some free titles, but most must be purchased.**

## Music Channel

Music contains streaming music services, music videos, add-ons for music games, and related content. The Music channel contains selectable advertisements. Refer to Chapter 7, "Tuning into the Music Channel," for detailed information on the Music channel.

**This is your portal to the free and paid music services on Xbox LIVE.**

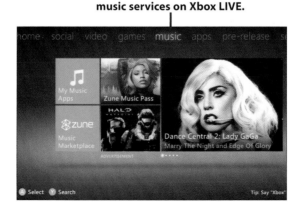

## Apps Channel

Apps provides quick access to all your downloaded applications that are also accessible from the other channels, as well as provides the ability to add new applications. The Apps channel contains selectable advertisements.

**Provides quick access to all your applications and a portal to download more.**

## Settings Channel

Settings provides access to all of your essential system, account, and Kinect settings.

**This channel is your one-stop shop for tweaking key settings and preferences.**

## Xbox Guide

Pressing the Xbox Guide Button on your controller at any time causes the Xbox Guide to pop up on your screen. The Xbox Guide delivers access to condensed (and fast) versions of many of the features found on the Xbox 360 Dashboard. Selecting some menu options ends whatever it is you're doing after providing a warning, whereas selecting other options enables you to return to whatever it is you were doing at the time you summoned the Xbox Guide. You can return to the Xbox dashboard or whatever activity you were doing at any time by pressing Y on your controller or selecting the Xbox Home option. Following is a summary of each of the categories, referred to as blades.

## Profile Blade

The Profile Blade provides quick access to your friends and their activities, messages, and various chat features.

**Pressing the Xbox Guide Button on your controller pulls up this menu, which allows you to perform many tasks more quickly than if you went through the Xbox 360 dashboard.**

## Games Blade

The Games Blade provides quick access to your achievements, awards, and recent activities, including the ability to quick launch the games in your library.

**The Games Blade allows you to access your achievements, awards, recent gaming activities, and all downloaded games, which are stored in your game library.**

## Media Blade

The Media Blade provides quick access to your video, music, and picture libraries, and a connected Windows Media Center PC. There is also a music player so that you can select and play the music that you want in the background of most of your Xbox 360 activities, including games.

**The Media Blade gives you access to non-game-related media. You can also use the built-in music player to select and play music while you perform various activities on your console, including playing games.**

## Marketplace Blade

The Marketplace Blade provides quick access to the various marketplaces and enables you to see your active downloads and redeem codes.

**The Marketplace Blade provides a convenient way to access the Xbox LIVE Marketplace and conduct various activities, such as redeeming a code (for example, if you purchase Microsoft Points from an outside vendor).**

## Settings Blade

The Settings Blade provides quick access to your profile, account, and console settings and preferences. You can also remotely turn off your system from this blade.

**The Settings Blade enables you to quickly access your profile, adjust your preferences, configure family and system settings, as well as manage your account. You can also turn off your console here.**

# Accessorizing Your Xbox

Even though your Xbox 360 comes with everything you need to make it work out-of-the-box, a variety of accessories are available that can make your experience even better. As a bonus, many of these accessories also work with Windows XP or newer PCs, though you need the Wireless Gaming Receiver for Windows, shown here, to make wireless devices compatible.

**The Wireless Gaming Receiver for Windows has a range up to 30 feet, enabling wireless freedom for up to four wireless controllers.**

Now take a look at some of the most useful and fun accessories for your Xbox 360.

# Controllers

For the best in-game control, it's hard to beat the wireless controller that comes with your system. It's a proven, ergonomic design favored by millions of gamers and works out-of-the-box. That doesn't mean there aren't options, though, like the ones described here.

## Wired

There are two main advantages to using a wired controller. One is that you never run out of batteries. Two is that this is the easiest way to use the controller with Windows XP or newer PCs; simply plug it into an available USB port. Naturally, the main disadvantage to a wired controller is that you're tethered to your console, and that wire only goes so far.

Microsoft makes a wired version of the wireless controller that comes with your system, and various third parties, such as PDP who makes the AfterGlow Controller shown here, offer interesting alternatives.

**Some third-party controllers like the one shown here match the look and feel of the official Xbox controller, while others use their own unique designs.**

## Wireless

Just like with the wired controllers, a variety of third parties make alternative gamepads. Microsoft themselves offers two variations on the standard wireless controller that comes with your system. The first is a cosmetic color or artwork variation, like the Halo 3 Spartan Controller.

**Microsoft occasionally releases special editions of its popular controller, like this Xbox 360 Halo 3 Limited Edition Wireless Controller, which features a colorful design by comic book artist Todd McFarlane.**

The other variation is the Wireless Controller with Transforming D-pad and Play & Charge kit, which attempts to address the feeling by some that the D-pad on the standard wireless controller is not suitable for gaming. This controller tries to address that issue with a D-pad that transforms from a plus to a disc, offering additional precision. Other minor tweaks are also present, such as analog sticks with deeper grooves.

**This Xbox 360 Wireless Controller by Microsoft features a D-pad with a raised plus symbol, enabling greater accuracy and control of both directional and sweeping movements.**

## Keyboards

Even though you're only up to Chapter 3, you've probably already become frustrated by how tedious it can be to enter text using the controller. Luckily, there are two simple ways, described next, to eliminate this tedium, which may become too much to bear when you get to Chapter 9 and try to use applications such as Facebook and Twitter.

### Chatpad

Microsoft's Chatpad snaps directly under your existing controller, as shown here. The Chatpad adds little weight and is ideal for those who don't mind typing with their thumbs.

**The Chatpad is a mini keyboard that snaps
directly onto your Xbox controller. It enables
you to enter text much faster than scrolling
through and using the virtual keyboard.**

### USB Keyboards

Remember those USB ports on your console? They're ideal for plugging in standard USB keyboards, such as the one you probably use on your computer. The best part is you don't need to do anything extra to make them work after you plug them in. You can even go wireless as long as the keyboard's wireless USB adapter doesn't require drivers. Microsoft and Logitech are two of the more popular wireless keyboard manufacturers and each has several models that work right out of the box.

## Media Remotes

Even though the standard Xbox 360 controller that comes with your system does a fine job navigating menus, and, of course, playing games, it's not particularly intuitive for controlling music and videos. That's where a media remote comes in handy. Using your system's IR Receiver, a compatible remote control enables you to easily do things such as play, pause, and rewind your media, and duplicate many of the functions found on the standard controller, such as the Xbox Guide Button. Microsoft makes the Universal Media Remote, which can control your Xbox 360, a Windows Media Center PC, and many TVs. The latest Xbox 360 Media Remote from Microsoft, shown below, matches the styling of the Xbox 360 S models and supports the latest media features, including Live TV channels. There are also a wide variety of third-party options and many universal remotes that can be configured to work with the Xbox 360.

**The Xbox 360 Media Remote's top buttons mimic those on the Xbox 360 controller.**

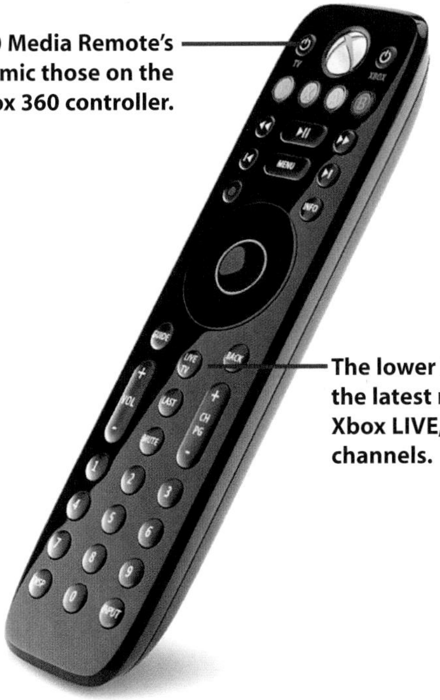

**The lower buttons support the latest media features on Xbox LIVE, such as the Live TV channels.**

## Racing Wheels

Although the left analog stick on the standard wireless controller offers excellent steering control in racing games, nothing quite matches the feel of a steering wheel. Luckily, for the racing game enthusiast, several different types of racing wheels, both wired and wireless, in a variety of price ranges and from a variety of manufacturers, are available. The latest such wheel from Microsoft is the Xbox 360 Speed Wheel, shown here, which features a lightweight, U-shaped, wheel-only design. Instead of foot petals to control gas and brakes, the Speed Wheel uses trigger buttons. A more traditional racing wheel at the lower end of the price range, the Wireless Racing Wheel from Mad Catz, is shown here as well.

**These green bands of light on each handle provide visual cues when necessary.**

**This Wireless Racing Wheel from Mad Catz also includes foot petals.**

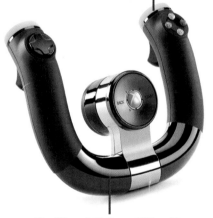

**The Xbox 360 Speed Wheel is compatible with all racing games right out of the box, though functionality is limited in some games.**

# Rhythm Game Controllers

Want to play like a rock star but can't read a note? Want to dance but have two left feet? Rhythm games and their controllers can let anyone—yes, even you—feel like a superstar.

Band games such as *The Beatles: Rock Band* (MTV Games, 2009) and *Guitar Hero World Tour* (Activision, 2008), shown here, work with instrument controllers such as guitars and drums. Karaoke games, such as *Karaoke Revolution* (Konami, 2009) and *Lips* (Microsoft, 2008), work with microphones. Games such as *DanceDanceRevolution Universe 3* (Konami, 2008) work with dance pads, whereas *DJ Hero 2* (Activision, 2010) uses a turntable. Some games, like *Rocksmith* (Ubisoft, 2011), can even teach you how to play a real instrument, which in this case, is the electric guitar. In short, there seems to be no end to the clever ways videogames can make even the most daunting performance challenges fun, educational, and accessible. And speaking of accessible, don't forget Kinect (refer to Chapter 10, "Getting to Know Kinect") and its capability to track your movements sans controller, making it ideal for dance videogames.

**Rhythm game controllers are a lot of fun and can give you a new appreciation for music, though they can be expensive and the items bulky and difficult to store.**

## Big Button Pads

The Big Button Pads, pictured here, presently come bundled with either *Scene It? Light, Camera, Action* (Microsoft, 2007) or *Scene It? Box Office Smash* (Microsoft, 2008), but they also work with other games, such as the downloadable *Uno* (Microsoft, 2006) and *Wits & Wagers* (Microsoft, 2008) games. The Big Button Pads are ideal for party play for trivia- and game-show–style games because they feature a large "buzzer" button on the top.

**Microsoft's Big Button Pads work especially well for trivia games and provide an intuitive buzz-in experience akin to a TV game show.**

## Xbox 360 Arcade Sticks

Fighting and arcade style games are extremely popular on the Xbox 360, but some gamers find playing them with the standard controller unsatisfactory. That's where an arcade stick comes in, which is also often referred to as a fighting stick. Available from a variety of manufacturers, including Hori that makes the Fighting Stick EX2 pictured here, these controllers don't work with every game, but they do offer the hardcore gamer a more authentic arcade experience and more targeted control in the games that do support them.

**If you're not satisfied with the Xbox controller's D-pad, particularly for fighting and classic arcade games, arcade sticks provide a great alternative.**

## Xbox LIVE Vision

You can use Microsoft's Xbox LIVE Vision Camera for video chat, personalized gamer pictures, in-game video chat, and still pictures. It can also provide controller functionality in certain games such as *Pinball FX2* (Microsoft, 2010), where the flippers can be operated. Nevertheless, except for certain legacy games and applications, most of the Xbox LIVE Vision's functionality has been superseded by Kinect (refer to Chapter 10).

**Though mostly superseded by Kinect, Microsoft's Xbox LIVE Vision Camera is still supported and can be found for cheap alone or bundled.**

Search your console
and all of the Xbox
LIVE marketplaces.

Adjust Privacy,
System, and
other settings.

Play game
discs and
DVDs.

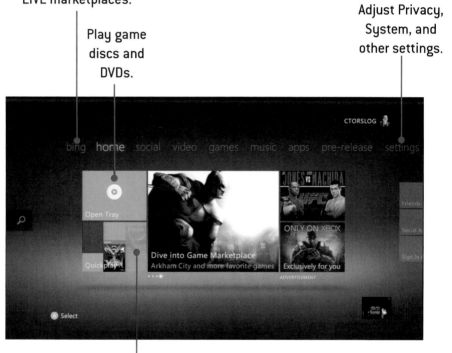

Access your last 11
games or media.

In this chapter, you learn how to use the Home, Apps, and Settings channels to play games, edit profiles, access media libraries, and modify preferences. You also learn how to search for everything with Bing, as well as how to store game saves online.

4

# Getting to Know Your Xbox

The Home, Apps, and Settings channels are three of the most important menu categories with which you should familiarize yourself. These channels are where you start games or videos, edit profiles, access media libraries, and modify all settings. There are also two important features: Bing search and Cloud saves that greatly enhance use of your Xbox.

## Working with Game Discs

Although the "Playing Discs" section in Chapter 1, "Getting Started," explained the high-level details of working with discs, there's actually a bit more you can do than simply inserting and removing discs, which happens from the Open Tray section of the Home channel.

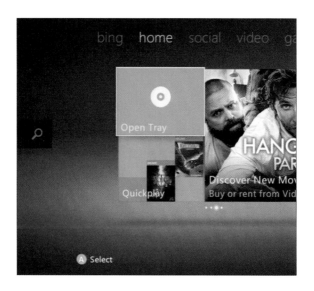

## Playing a Game Disc

To insert a game disc, touch the Eject Button on your console or press A on your controller from the Open Tray section of the Home channel. If your Xbox has a DVD in its tray, press the Y Button instead to open the tray so that you can remove the DVD before inserting your game disc. After you insert the game disc, close the tray. You can do this either by gently pushing the tray back toward the console, touching the Eject button, or pressing A on your controller.

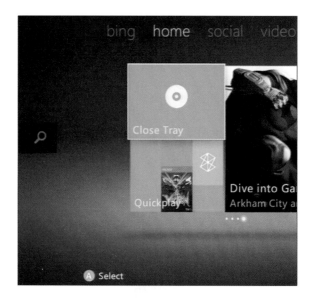

After the disc is read by the console, the default option is for the game to automatically start. You can disable auto-play by selecting Auto-Play within the Console Settings menu under System Settings in the Settings channel. Refer to the "Tweaking System Settings" section later in this chapter for details.

If auto-play is disabled, the console reads the disc and turns the Open Tray option into a Play Game option, like the example shown below. Pressing A starts the game. Pressing X reveals Game Details, which shows related games, an overview with the ability to rate the title, publishing details, downloadable extras to purchase, any achievements you've earned, and an image gallery of in-game screenshots.

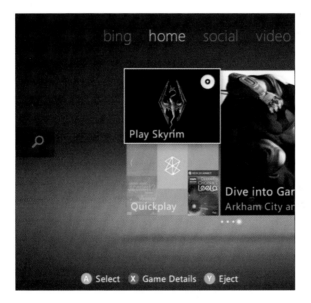

## Installing a Game on Your Hard Drive

If you have a hard drive in your system, you can install your disc games onto it, which can save wear and tear on the disc drive and make certain games load faster. Installing a game on the hard drive requires a minimum of 4GB of free space, and sometimes double that or more. As such, you need to carefully consider what you install. Even after you install the game on your hard drive, the game disc must still be present in the disc drive for validation in order to play the game.

## What About Installing to a Flash Drive?

Although you have the option to install a game to a flash drive with suitable performance and free space, it is not recommended. Because the write speeds of most flash drives are relatively slow, your game's performance may suffer, albeit not nearly as much as running directly off the disc, and there's a maximum 16GB capacity limit, so you'll be limited to installing only one or two games, provided little else is stored on the drive.

To install a game to the hard drive, follow these steps.

1. Insert the game disc per the instructions in the earlier "Playing a Game Disc" section. If your Xbox loads the game (which it does by default), exit it and return to the Home channel.

2. From the Home channel, highlight the game you want to install.

3. Press X on your controller for Game Details, which are only available for Xbox 360 titles.

4. Select Install. If prompted, choose your hard drive as the save destination. A progress indicator appears while your game is installed to your hard drive. Installation of the game takes several minutes.

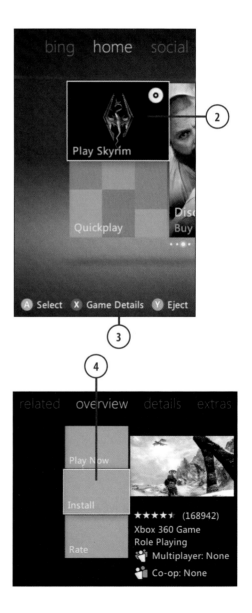

5.  When finished installing, press A
    to continue. You now have the
    option to play the game or delete
    it from the hard drive. Pressing B
    on your controller returns you to
    the Home channel.

    For multidisc games, install each
    disc to your hard drive by follow-
    ing the previous steps.

### Original Xbox Games

Games written for the original
Xbox cannot be installed and
played on the Xbox 360 hard
drive. For more on playing original Xbox games, refer to
"Understanding Backward
Compatibility with the Original
Xbox" in Chapter 5, "Playing on
the Games Channel."

# Deleting a Single Game from Your Hard Drive

To delete a single game from your
hard drive, follow these steps:

1.  Follow steps 1 and 2 from the
    "Installing a Game on Your Hard
    Drive" section.

2.  Select Delete.

3. Confirm the deletion; otherwise, select No or press B on your controller to go back.

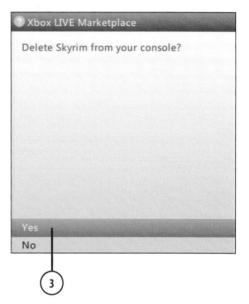

## Copy, Move, or Delete Multiple Games from Your Hard Drive

To copy, move, or delete one or more games from your hard drive, follow these steps:

1. Go to the Settings channel, and select System.

2. Select Storage.

3. Select Hard Drive.

4. Select Games and Apps.

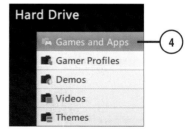

5. Select the game you want to copy, move, or delete, or press Y on your controller for that game's options.

6. Select Copy, Move, or Delete, depending on which action you wish to perform. If you select Copy or Move, proceed to step 7. If you select delete, confirm the deletion.

7. Select the storage device to which you want to copy or move the content.

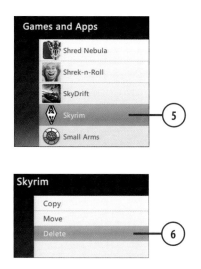

# Digging into Your Profile

After going to the trouble to create a profile in Chapter 3, "Personalizing Your Xbox Experience," you're now ready to reap the rewards and take a look at all the available options that having a profile gives you.

If you aren't signed in, make sure to select Sign In from the Social channel. When you're signed in, highlight your profile, and select it by pressing A on your controller.

**Sign into your profile to interact with all its features.**

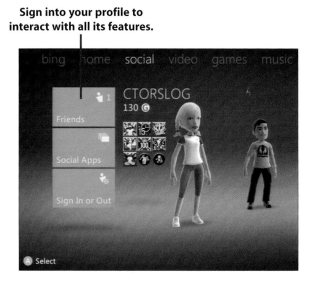

## Main Profile

Your main profile consists of the following options: Messages, Customize Avatar, Change Theme, Achievements, and Change Gamertag, as well as a profile summary. Now take a closer look at the options.

### Messages

Selecting Messages pulls up a Community screen that has four tabs at the top from which you can take specific actions. Some actions include: sending and receiving text and voice messages; inviting someone to chat one-on-one; inviting friends to a party where you can all play games and chat together; invite someone to play a game; or invite someone to become friends. These communication-centric features are why the entire section has the heading of Community. The top four tabs are as follows:

- **Messages**—The first tab you see is the Messages blade. From here, you can create new messages and access and take action on received messages. Refer to "Working with Messages" in Chapter 8, "Getting Social with Friends," for full details on the things you can do with your messages.

- **Friends**—To the immediate left of the Messages blade is the Friends blade, which shows how many of your friends are presently connected and what their status is. You can invite any friends to a party and initiate communications with them. Refer to Chapter 8 for further detail on each of the options.

- **Xbox LIVE Party**—To the immediate left of the Friends blade is the Xbox LIVE Party blade. From here you can invite players to party, invite a party to a game, or conduct a party chat. Refer to Chapter 8 for full party details.

- **Players**—To the immediate right of the Messages blade is the Players blade, which provides a listing of the gamers you've played against online. You can view gamer profiles; send positive or negative reviews of a player's conduct, which affects his or her reputation score; and send friend requests. Refer to Chapter 8 for additional details on interacting with others.

## Customize Avatar

Selecting Customize Avatar brings you to the Customize Avatar screen, which is described in detail in Chapter 3.

## Change Theme

Selecting Change Theme enables you to change your Dashboard's theme. This list includes all preinstalled themes and any themes you download or purchase from the Marketplace.

Select Theme

Xbox 360

Spectrum

Day

Night

AXE Excite Themes

Castle Crashers Dashboard Theme

EA

Family Guy Vol. 4 DVD Theme

Ⓐ Select  Ⓑ Back

## Achievements

The Achievements block shows all games played and their respective Gamerscore and achievements earned, as well as the last time they were accessed. Of all the games you've ever played, it also shows you how many achievements have been earned out of the total possible, and the matching Gamerscore points and possible points.

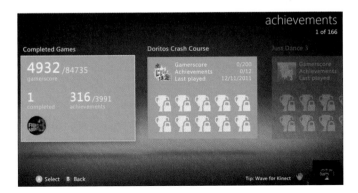

If you're an overachiever, you can select Completed Games to see a listing of all the games you've unlocked all the achievements for and the amount of gamer points earned. Selecting Share Game lets you share your achievements on Facebook.

## Change Gamertag

Selecting Change Gamertag enables you to change your Gamertag to something else for the specified number of Microsoft Points. This area also displays your profile summary.

## Profile Information Under Settings

Outside of your main profile, additional related information exists under the Settings channel. Now take a closer look at these additional options.

### Profile

Selecting Profile enables you to view all the games you've played and their related achievements, edit your high-level profile details, view your reputation, and set game defaults and sign-in preferences. Now review these options for a brief tutorial:

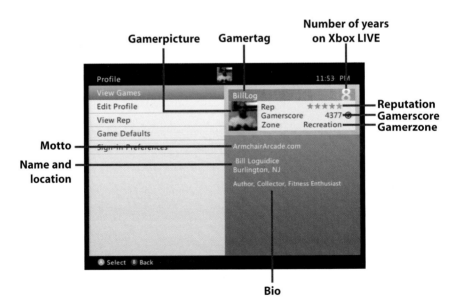

- **View Games**—Selecting View Games enables you to view all the games you've played from most recent to oldest, the Achievements available in each, and what Achievements you've already attained. Getting an Achievement increases your overall Gamerscore. You also see how many gamer points attaining achievements in each game has earned you, which is represented by the number next to the G icon. Selecting a particular game pulls up the Achievements summary screen for that game.

| Achievements | | 4:59 PM |
|---|---|---|
| Air Band 4 of 8 Achievements | | 25 🄶 |
| Build A Buddy 5 of 8 Achievements | | 25 🄶 |
| Madden NFL 11 0 of 24 Achievements | | 0 🄶 |
| NBA 2K11 1 of 50 Achievements | | 15 🄶 |
| NBA JAM: OFE 3 of 12 Achievements | | 15 🄶 |
| Fantastic Pets 5 of 51 Achievements | | 75 🄶 |
| Just Dance Kids 2 2 of 25 Achievements | | 60 🄶 |
| Ⓐ Select   Ⓑ Back   Ⓨ About Gamerscore | | |

## >>> Go Further

# UNDERSTANDING THE GAME ACHIEVEMENTS SCREEN

After selecting a game to view, you see the Achievements summary screen for that game. In the example shown here for *Fight Night Champion* (Electronic Arts, 2011), you see that the first row of Achievements has been unlocked, which accounts for 8 of the 44 possible Achievements attained. The highlighted Achievement is described in the gray bar, with the date it was unlocked and how many gamer points it was worth (25). Achievements that have yet to be attained are represented by the padlocked Trophy icons. Highlighting one of those indicates what you need to do to unlock that Achievement and how many gamer points it's worth. Pressing X lets you share the selected achievement on Facebook. When finished viewing the Achievements, press B to go back.

- **Edit Profile**—Selecting Edit Profile reveals eight options: Gamertag, Gamer Picture, Gamer Zone, Motto, Avatar, Name, Location, and Bio. While most of these terms are straightforward, see the Go Further sidebar for more information.

>>> Go Further

## UNDERSTANDING THE PROFILE COMPONENTS

Your profile consists of several components, some of which are optional for you to include, such as Name, Location, and Bio. What follows is a brief overview of you profile's components so you can optimize your profile to best represent you.

- **Gamertag**—As described in Chapter 2, "Networking Your Xbox," you have only one opportunity to change your Gamertag for free. After that, as of this writing, it costs you 800 Microsoft Points each time you want to change your Gamertag, although Microsoft sometimes has promotions that enable you to take this action for fewer Points.

- **Gamer Picture**—Two types of pictures are tied to your Gamertag: a Gamer Picture, which is viewable by anyone, and a Personal Picture, which is viewable only by people in your friends list. You can use the same image for both, although only the Personal Picture can use one of your own images, as captured with an Xbox LIVE Vision camera or Kinect. You can also opt to Download a Gamer Picture, which takes you to the Marketplace where you can choose between a selection of pictures that are free or cost Microsoft Points.

- **Gamer Zone**—Games that you play online on your Xbox 360 offer a variety of ways to optimally match you up with other players. One of these ways is through your Gamer Zone selection, which includes Recreation, Pro, Family, and Underground. Your choice of Gamer Zone determines which game sessions you are most likely to join. For example, if you choose Underground, which is intended for aggressive, experienced players, you are most likely to play with other Underground players. If there are no suitable game sessions in your preferred zone, you can still play with players from other zones.

- **Motto**—Your Motto is a short phrase of up to 21 characters that encapsulates your beliefs, ideals, or anything else you'd like others to know about you. Standard onscreen keyboard controls apply. Potentially offensive mottos may get reported, so choose wisely.

- **Avatar**—Selecting Avatar brings you to the Customize Avatar screen, which is described in detail in Chapter 3.

- **Name, Location, and Bio**—Unless you specify otherwise, your Name, Location, and Bio are visible to anyone viewing your Profile. To change your online safety settings, refer to the "Privacy Settings" section later in this chapter. Selecting any of the three options brings up the onscreen keyboard where you can enter your text.

- **View Rep**—Your rep is your reputation on Xbox LIVE. Rep is determined by player reviews submitted about you. A high rep means other players like to play with you, and a low rep means many players want to avoid you. By selecting View Rep, you can see a summary of what others think of you and how that feedback breaks down. Similarly, when you leave feedback about others you've played against, their rep is affected. When you avoid a player, you're less likely to be matched with him or her in the future, and if you prefer a player, you're more likely to be matched with him or her in the future.

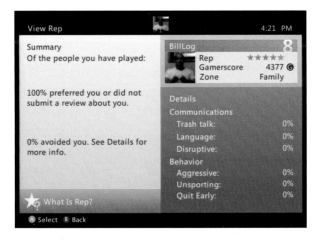

- **Game Defaults**—Selecting Game Defaults enables you to choose default settings for future games so that you don't need to go to the trouble to select common preferences each time. You can set defaults for Action and Racing games and also set General Game Defaults. For instance, one of the options under General Defaults enables you to select a default difficulty level from Easy to Hard. Settings like these can be changed within the options of most games, but choosing your preferences under Game Defaults ahead of time can help to streamline the process.

- **Sign-In Preferences**—Selecting Sign-In Preferences enables you to set whether you want the current profile to automatically sign in, making it the default profile when your system starts up. There is also an option to automatically sign in to Messenger, which enables you to interact with those using Windows Live Messenger for services such as text chat, and, if you have Kinect, video chat.

## Account Management

Selecting Account enables you to manage all of your transaction-based account options.

Once within Account Management, you can redeem a code from a prepaid card, manage your payment options, add Microsoft Points, and view your download history, as well as transfer ownership licenses from another console. You can also see information on your existing memberships and upgrade options; your existing Windows Live ID with the option to change it; your present billing information and security details with the option to change them; and the ability to set a four-button Xbox LIVE pass code that restricts access to the current profile.

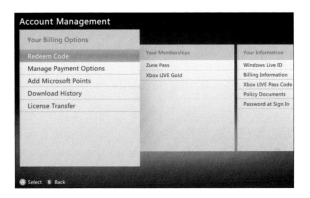

## Setting a Pass Code

After you set a pass code for your profile, anyone who wants to use that profile must enter the pass code before signing in to Xbox LIVE. To set an Xbox LIVE Pass Code, follow these steps:

1. From the Account Management screen, select Xbox LIVE Pass Code from the Your Information blade.

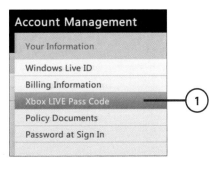

2. Using your controller, enter a four-button code by pressing X, Y, Left Trigger, Right Trigger, Left Bumper, Right Bumper, or the D-pad.

3. Enter your code again to confirm it. To reset your pass code, repeat this procedure at any time.

**Set Pass Code**

Use X, Y, triggers, bumpers, and the D-pad to enter your 4-button pass code.

To clear your pass code, press A.

| 1 | 2 | 3 | 4 | 5 |
|---|---|---|---|---|
| 6 | 7 | 8 | 9 | 0 |

### Forgot Your Pass Code?

If you forget your Xbox LIVE account pass code, you can recover your account by following the steps in Chapter 3 under "Recovering Your Gamertag from Xbox LIVE."

## Privacy Settings

Selecting Privacy enables you to customize and manage your family's access to games, movies, and television content, and the console and Xbox LIVE. This customization includes which games can be played, which movies and TV shows can be watched, how long each family member can use the console on a daily or weekly basis, and whether someone can access Xbox LIVE.

When you select Change Settings, you have the choice of three presets: Adult, Teen, and Child, and one Custom option, which is selected by choosing Customize.

| Adult | | Current Settings |
|-------|---|------------------|
| Teen | | Allowed |
| Child | | Voice and Text |
| ● Custom | | Video Communication |
| Customize | | Profile Sharing |
| | | Kinect Sharing |
| | | Game History |
| | | Online Status |
| | | Video and Music Status |
| | | Friends List |
| | | Voice Data Collection |
| | | Standard Programming |
| Save and Exit | | Profile Viewing |
| Cancel | | |

Selecting Customize provides access to 17 different areas of customization organized into four main sections: Activity, Privacy, Content, and Contact Preferences.

| Activity | Current Setting |
|---|---|
| Voice and Text | Everyone |
| Video Communication | |
| Privacy | Decide who to communicate with using voice and text on Xbox LIVE. |
| Profile Sharing | |
| Kinect Sharing | This includes voice and text chat, messaging, and game invites. |
| Game History | |
| Online Status | |
| Video and Music Status | |

You can customize these options down to specific levels of access, such as Allowed or Blocked, Standard or Family, or Everyone, Friends Only, and Blocked, as shown in the Voice and Text example.

| Everyone | Current Setting |
|---|---|
| Friends Only | Everyone |
| Blocked | |
| | Everyone: Communicate with anyone on Xbox LIVE using voice or text. |
| | Friends Only: Communicate only with friends. |
| | Blocked: Prevent communication with everyone. Friend requests will still be received. |

When satisfied with your selection, choose Save and Exit from the Online Safety Settings screen to save your settings.

# Understanding and Enabling Media Sharing

You can stream video, music, and pictures to your console from any Windows XP or newer PC on your network. Use your choice of the Zune software or Windows Media Player 11 (or newer) to stream content to your console.

### Want to Access Media on Other Devices?

The Digital Living Network Alliance (DLNA) is a global collaboration of hundreds of different companies that create products that are cross-compatible to do things such as send and display photos, and find, send, and play music and videos. DLNA-certified products include televisions, Network-attached storage (NAS), digital cameras, and other consumer electronics devices. If you have a DLNA-certified device on your network and it contains media, there's a good chance your Xbox 360 lists it as an accessible streaming source.

## Media Sharing with Zune

The free Zune software is a visual hub where you can access everything in your personal collection of music, videos, pictures, apps, and podcasts from your Windows PC. To stream media from Zune on a Windows PC, follow these steps:

1. If the Zune software is installed on your Windows PC, proceed to step 2. Otherwise, download and install the Zune software from http://www.zune.net/en-us/products/software/download/default.htm.

2. Launch Zune on your Windows PC.

**3.** Within Zune, click Settings, Software, and then Xbox 360.

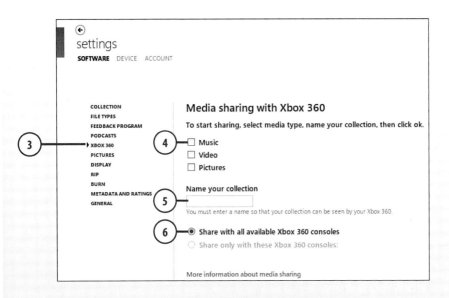

**4.** Select the media types you want to stream to your Xbox 360 console by clicking in the desired check boxes.

**5.** Provide a name for your collection. This name appears in the media source list on your Xbox 360.

**6.** Choose whether to share with all available Xbox 360 consoles on your network or just specific systems. Click OK after making your choice. If a User Account Control (UAC) prompt appears, select Yes.

**7.** On your Xbox 360, whenever you select a video, music, or picture source, you see your Zune collection name listed as one of the sources.

## Media Sharing with Windows Media Player

Like Zune, Windows Media Player is a hub where you can access everything in your personal collection of music, videos, pictures, apps, and podcasts from your Windows PC. The major difference between Windows Media Player and Zune is that Windows Media Player features a more traditional interface for accessing media and controlling sharing options, and is more directly integrated into Windows. To stream media from Windows Media Player on a Windows PC, follow these steps:

1. If Windows Media Player 11 or later is installed on your Windows PC, proceed to step 2. Otherwise, download and install the latest version of the software from http://windows.microsoft.com/en-US/windows/downloads/windows-media-player.

2. Launch Windows Media Player on your Windows PC.

3. Within Windows Media Player, click Stream and select Automatically Allow Devices to Play My Media.

4. At the screen that asks "Do you want to automatically allow devices to play your media?," select "Automatically allow all computers and media devices."

5. Click Stream again and select More Streaming Options.

6.  Provide a name for your media library. This name appears in the media source list on your Xbox 360.

7.  Choose whether to allow or block the available Xbox 360 consoles on your network. If you want to stream content from a specific Xbox, you need to allow that traffic here.

8.  You can further customize the Xbox 360's access by clicking Customize or remove the Xbox 360 from the list completely by clicking Remove. Remove works only if the console is powered off.

## Customize

If you select Customize, a "Customize media streaming settings" screen appears, which enables you to choose what is streamed to your Xbox 360. You can opt to make all of the media in your library available on your Xbox, or you can set streaming based on a particular media's star or parental rating.

9.  When finished, click OK.

10. On your Xbox 360, whenever you select a video, music, or picture source, you see your Windows Media Player collection name listed as one of the sources.

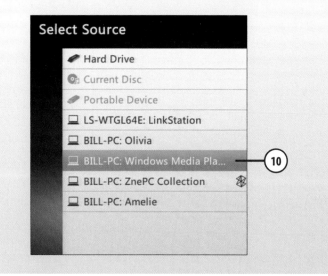

## Accessing Your Media Libraries

Your Xbox 360 is a multimedia powerhouse. In addition to the expected Game library, your Xbox 360 has a Video library, Music library, and Picture library, enabling you to stream videos, music, and pictures to your console as long as your console is connected to the Internet or your network is using a wired or wireless connection. See Chapter 2, "Networking Your Xbox," to learn how to establish an Internet or network connection.

### Watching Your Video Library

To view your profile's associated Video library, which is all your downloaded or streaming Zune videos, video files on your various storage devices, a DVD in your console's disc tray, and videos from a computer on your network, select Video Player under My Video Apps in the Video channel. The Video Player can also be found under My Apps under the Apps channel. For more information on the Video library, refer to "Checking Out Your Video Library" in Chapter 6, "Viewing the Video Channel."

## Getting Down with Your Music Library

To view your profile's associated Music library, which is the CDs you ripped to your hard drive, the music on an attached portable device or media player, and music from a computer on your network, from the Music Channel, select My Music Apps and then Music Player. Music Player can also be found under My Apps under the Apps channel. For more information on the Music Library, refer to "Checking Out Your Music Library" in Chapter 7, "Tuning into the Music Channel."

## Viewing Your Picture Library

To view pictures on your Xbox 360 from a connected digital camera, disc, portable device, or computer on your network, follow these steps.

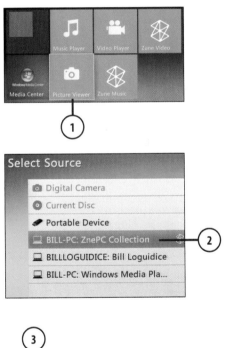

1.  Select Picture Viewer under My Apps from the Apps channel.

2.  Select from one of the available sources or plug in a new source, such as a digital camera, and select that.

3.  After selecting a source, you have the option to play a slideshow of all available images or select an individual folder or subfolder. Playing a slideshow begins an automated slideshow that applies various transitional effects to your images. Highlighting an image and pressing Y on your controller enables you to apply the image as your dashboard's background, overriding any background presently in place, including a background that's part of a theme.

## Interacting with Images in Your Picture Library

After selecting an image, or from within a slide show after moving the Left Stick or D-pad, the following commands are available:

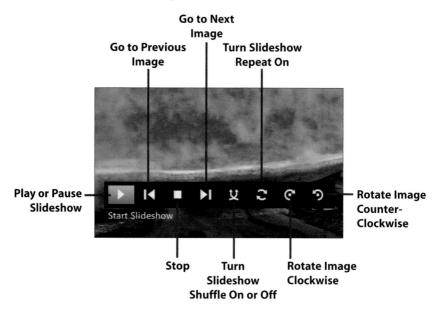

- **Play or Pause Slideshow**—Plays a slideshow or pauses an active slideshow. The A Button on your controller performs the same function.

- **Go to Previous Image**—Goes back to the prior image. The Left Bumper on your controller performs the same function.

- **Stop**—Stops the active slideshow.

- **Go to Next Image**—Skips to the next image. The Right Bumper on your controller performs the same function.

- **Turn Slideshow Shuffle On or Off**—Places the images in a random order when a slideshow starts. Selecting the option again turns this feature off.

- **Turn Slideshow Repeat On**—Endlessly loops the slideshow until you choose Stop. Select the option again to turn this feature off.

- **Rotate Image Clockwise**—If your image displays in an incorrect orientation, flip it clockwise using this option.

- **Rotate Image Counter-Clockwise**—If your image displays in an incorrect orientation, flip it counter-clockwise using this option.

# Connecting with Windows Media Center

Microsoft's Windows Media Center is a digital video recorder and media player application that enables Windows XP Media Center Edition, Windows Vista, and Windows 7 computer users to view and record live television, and organize, stream, and play music, pictures, and videos. Your Xbox 360 can act as a Windows Media Center Extender, which remotely enables use of the media center's features. The Media Center can be accessed by up to five such extenders at once.

## Adding Your 360 to Windows Media Center

You can easily add your Xbox 360 to your existing Windows Media Center by following these steps:

1. On your PC, go to the Windows Media Center start screen, scroll to Tasks, and click add extender. The Extender Setup screen appears.

2. On your Xbox 360, select Windows Media Center from My Apps in the Apps channel. Select Continue. Your 8-digit setup key appears.

3. Enter the 8-digit setup key that you get from your Xbox 360 and click Next to proceed.

4. Click Next. The Media Center begins configuration on both your PC and your Xbox 360. You are now done. Click Finish on your PC. Your Xbox 360 shows the Windows Media Center screen.

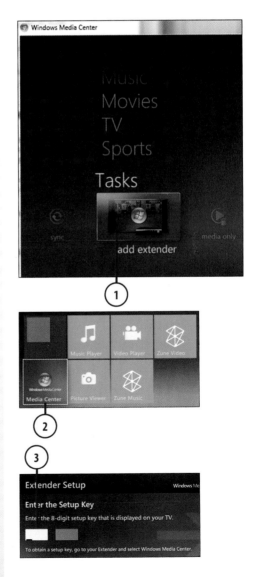

### Navigating Windows Media Center

You can move between the Windows Media Center menu options by using the Left Stick or D-pad on your controller. To select an item, press A. To exit Windows Media Center, go to Tasks and select Close.

### Where's the Play Button?

As with all the other ways to access and play media on your Xbox 360, a superior alternative to using a controller with Windows Media Center is a compatible remote control. Turn to Chapter 3 and "Accessorizing Your Xbox" for some suggestions.

# Adjusting Family Settings

If you have children, you may want to ensure that they have access to only age-appropriate content. You can do this by using Family settings to control which games they can play, which movies and TV shows they can watch, who they can talk to, how long they can use the Xbox 360 on a daily or weekly basis, and whether they can access Xbox LIVE.

## Turning on Parental Controls

When Console Controls are turned on, explicit and unrated content won't be accessible on your Xbox 360. What will be allowed are any games with a rating of T, which stands for "teen" and may not be suitable for those younger than 13 years of age; movie rating of PG-13, meaning parent discretion is strongly encouraged for children younger than 13 years; and TV rating of TV-14, meaning parental discretion is strongly encouraged for children younger than 14 years. Xbox LIVE access and Xbox LIVE Membership Creation are enabled. The Family Timer is Off.

To turn Content Controls on, follow these steps.

1. Select Family from the Settings channel.

2. Select On under Console Safety.

3. Select Save and Exit.

4. Select Create Pass Code.

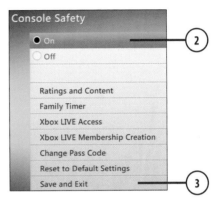

5. Select Set Pass Code.

6. Enter your four-button pass code by pressing the areas on the controller that corresponds with the numbers you want. As you enter your code, the gray circles turn black.

7. At the Verify Pass Code screen, confirm your four-button pass code by entering it again.

8. You are returned to the Set Pass Code screen. Select your pass code reset question.

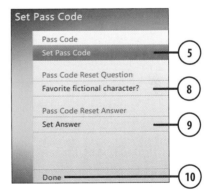

9. Select Enter Reset Answer and enter your answer when the virtual keyboard appears.

10. Your answer to the reset question now appears at the Set Pass Code screen. Select Done.

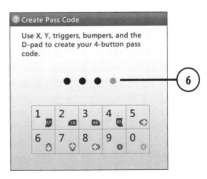

**11.** At the Content Controls screen, select Save and Exit.

After you turn on Content Controls, you can further customize the settings, including Ratings and Content, Family Timer, Xbox LIVE Access, and Xbox LIVE Membership Creation.

**Content Controls**

- ● On
- ○ Off

Ratings and Content

Family Timer

Xbox LIVE Access

Xbox LIVE Membership Creation

Change Pass Code

Reset to Default Settings

Save and Exit

⑪

## Setting Ratings and Content

This feature enables you to restrict access to content based on its rating and set whether unrated or explicit content can be played. Select each of these options to make your selections.

**Ratings and Content**

Game Ratings
Game Exceptions
Movie Ratings
TV Ratings
Explicit Content
Unrated Content

Current Setting

Game ratings help you decide which games can be played on this console.

Only games with the selected rating level and lower can be played.

Ⓐ Select   Ⓑ Back

- **Game Ratings**—Enables you to set game access to either All Games; M, mature (17 years and older); T, teen (13 years and older); E10+, everyone 10 years and older; E, everyone 6 years and older; and EC, everyone 3 years and older.

- **Game Exception**—Enables you to enter up to 25 games that may be played on the console, regardless of their rating.

- **Movie Ratings**—Enables you to set movie access to All Movies; R, parental guidance suggested for those under 17 years; PG-13, parental guidance suggested for those under 13 years; PG, parental guidance suggested; and G, OK for all ages.

- **TV Ratings**—Enables you to set TV access to All TV Shows; TV-MA, may be unsuitable for those younger than 17 years; TV-14, may be unsuitable for those younger than 14 years; TV-PG, parental guidance suggested; and TV-G, OK for all ages.

- **Explicit Content**—Enables you to select if explicit content is Allowed or Blocked on the console.

- **Unrated Content**—Enables you to select if unrated content is Allowed or Blocked.

## Setting the Family Timer

When this feature is enabled, notifications pop up indicating how much time is left, starting 1 hour before time runs out and then again at 30 minutes, 15 minutes, and 5 minutes.

1. Under the Content Controls menu, select Family Timer.

2. Click either Daily or Weekly timer, depending on if you want to limit daily hours or weekly hours.

3. Move down to the time period, and then use the left stick to adjust to the wanted time. The Daily timer moves in 15-minute increments and the Weekly timer (shown in the figure) moves in 1-hour increments.

4. Select Continue.

5. At the Content Controls screen, select Save and Exit.

---

**Find That You Need More Time?**

You can always add additional time. When a Family Timer notification appears, press the Xbox Guide button to see the Family Timer Options, enter your pass code with your controller, and choose to add more time. You can also opt to suspend the timer or turn your console off.

---

## Setting Xbox LIVE Access

This feature enables you to enable or disable your family's ability to connect to Xbox LIVE from the console. Select Allowed or Blocked.

## Setting Xbox LIVE Membership Creation

This feature enables you to control whether new Xbox LIVE memberships can be created from your console. Select Allowed or Blocked.

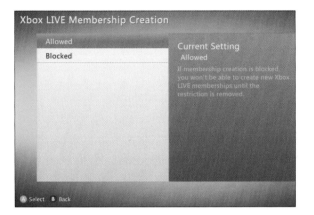

# Tweaking System Settings

The final important selection for tweaking options is System under the Settings channel, which is like the master control for key system, accessory, and network settings.

When selected, you have access to the following eight system settings options:

The eight options follows:

- **Console Settings**—Changes your console's settings, which include Display, Audio, Language and Locale, Clock, Startup and Shutdown, Auto-Play, Remote Control, and System Info.

- **Kinect Settings**—Changes Kinect sensor, chat microphone and speech recognition settings, and access to the Kinect Tuner. Refer to Chapter 10, "Getting to Know Kinect," and Chapter 11, "Using Kinect," for specifics on Kinect.

- **Storage**—Moves or deletes saved games, profiles, and other data on or from all your storage devices. You can also rename and format the storage devices and clear their caches.

- **Network Settings**—Connects to Xbox LIVE or your home network, sets up wireless connections, and tests all your network settings, including your PC and Windows Media Center connections.

- **Computers**—Manages your connection to Windows Media Center if one were already established.

- **TV**—Changes your live TV provider.

- **Xbox LIVE Vision**—Modify its Room and Lighting settings if you own the Xbox LIVE Vision camera.

- **Initial Setup**—Restarts the original system setup process described in Chapter 1, "Getting Started."

# Searching with Bing

Bing is Microsoft's powerful Web search engine converted for use on the Xbox 360 as the Bing channel. Bing can find content such as movies, music, apps, and games both on the Xbox LIVE Marketplace and on your Xbox 360 console.

To search with Bing, follow these steps:

1.  Under the Bing channel, select the search box and press A.

2.  Start selecting letters in your search term by moving the D-pad or left stick left or right. Press A to enter each letter in the search box.

3.  When you see the result you want, move the D-pad or left stick down and press A to select it.

4. Filter your results by selecting the green filter box.

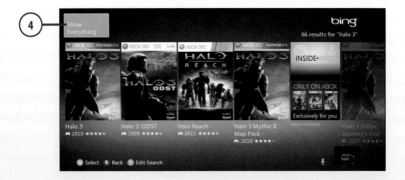

5. Select between applicable Movies, TV, All Video, Games, Apps, and Music results.

## Coming Up Empty?

If you find your results lacking, try to shorten your searches to one or two key words. If the content is new, it may not be indexed yet, so also try browsing for content in the respective Games, Music, Video, or Apps marketplaces.

# Using Cloud Storage for Game Saves

If you have more than one Xbox 360 or want to play games at a friend's house, you can store your saved games in the Cloud on the Xbox LIVE servers. As long as you make your Xbox LIVE profile available on the other console (see "Moving, Deleting, and Recovering a Gamertag" in Chapter 3), you can continue playing right where you left off. Enabling Cloud Storage is easy if you follow these steps:

1. Go to the Settings channel, select System, and select Storage.

2. Select Cloud Saved Games.

3. Select Enable Cloud Saved Games.

4. Cloud Saved Games now shows up as an available storage device.

## It's Not All Good

If you no longer have an Xbox LIVE Gold membership, you will not be able to select your roaming profile or a Cloud Saved Game. Your files are still stored in the cloud and can be moved out of cloud storage to a local storage device. You can do this even if the file does not exist in the console's memory cache.

Get quick access to all the games
and demos you've downloaded.

Search for games, try demos, and
locate game add-ons and extras.

In this chapter, you learn about the Games channel, which features your game library and a substantial selection of downloadable games and demos, ensuring there is something for everyone to play.

→ Browsing the Marketplace
→ Finding Games
→ Trying Out Demos
→ Grabbing Add-Ons and Extras
→ Scoping Out the Specialty Shops
→ Checking Out Your Game Library
→ Transferring Game Licenses

# Playing on the Games Channel

The Games channel is your gateway to access both your library of existing games and a huge selection of new games for one of the best videogame playing consoles ever made. After you sign into any of your Xbox LIVE accounts, you can access the Game Marketplace, where you have access to free games, demos, and trailers, and hundreds of downloadable titles available for purchase. In this chapter, you learn all about the Games channel and its wares, including how you can use it to find new games and give them a test run before purchasing, locating add-ons for games that you own, and finding specialty items (for example, a pet for your avatar and music for *Rock Band*).

# Getting to Know the Games Channel

When you scroll to the Games channel, you see five content boxes. The center box and the two boxes on the far right feature advertisements for new games, add-ons, or demos that Microsoft wants you to be aware of. The most important boxes are the two on the far left: My Games, which is your game library, and the Game Marketplace, which allows you to expand your game library through downloads and purchases. Move to any box to highlight one, and then press A on your controller to select it.

**My Games is another name for
your library of previously
downloaded games and demos.**

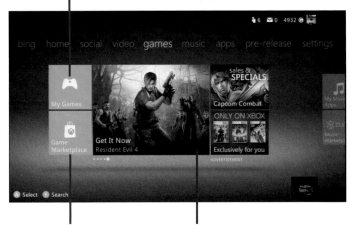

**The Game Marketplace lets
you download and purchase
games and related items.**

**Middle boxes are promotional,
highlighting new games,
add-ons, or demos.**

# Browsing the Game Marketplace

After you enter the Game Marketplace, you see six horizontal blades. You start out in the Featured blade, which you know because the category name "featured" is highlighted in white. The available sections are as follows:

**Featured is highlighted in white, indicating it is the active blade.**

**The white outline indicates New Releases is highlighted. Pressing A selects it.**

- **Picks**—This provides quick access to 10 highlighted games. Titles may consist of sale games or other select new releases worth highlighting.

- **Featured**—This area basically serves as an advertising portal, highlighting various games, especially recent releases, and add-ons. This section includes a Game Showcase, which features some of the most popular Xbox 360 games (for example, *Halo* and *FIFA 12*), enabling users to access demos and add-ons for these games, watch game-related videos and trailers, win items to enhance the game experience, and more; and Kinect Games, which shows a full line-up of Kinect-related Games, items, and add-ons.

- **Games**—This area of the Marketplace shows categorized listings of all games available on demand. This includes new Xbox LIVE arcade games, games that were previously available only at retail stores, independently produced games, and games released for the original Xbox console. All games are purchased using Microsoft Points, except for the previously retail-only games, which are priced in dollars and purchased conventionally. As with most of the other blades, Games features advertising blocks.

- **Add-Ons**—This area is where you can find and obtain game add-ons, such as new characters or map packs, purchase subscriptions to game-specific services known as *season passes*, view videos, access themes (these are applied to your dashboard), and get gamer pics (these are the pictures that anyone viewing your profile sees). For more on themes and gamer pics, turn to Chapter 4, "Getting to Know Your Xbox."

- **Extras**—This area provides access to the Avatar Marketplace and themes and gamer pics, which are outlined in Chapter 3 "Personalizing Your Xbox Experience," and Game Hubs, which is a selection of portals designed around and to enhance specific game experiences.

- **Demos**—Here you can search for demos to download and play for the latest Xbox 360 and Kinect retail games. It's the perfect way to try before you buy.

The Game Marketplace has an intuitive interface, making it easy to peruse the available digital content. Whether you have a particular title or genre in mind or are open to anything that strikes your fancy, you can locate content in many ways, including using the built-in Bing search feature, which is accessible by pressing Y on your controller at almost any time. Games, demos, add-ons, and other content are also sorted in multiple ways, enabling you to locate a game by its title, genre, or general category, depending on which blade you investigate. In addition, if a title is new to the Game Marketplace or popular, it will likely also appear under the New Releases and Game Showcase blocks, respectively. Keep in mind that not all games listed on the Game Marketplace will be available for purchase; some may just enable you to download a demo, watch a video, or obtain add-ons. When you find a game you're interested in, simply press A to select it and see the available options. If you want to go back to a previous screen, press B.

# Searching Among the Marketplace Selections

Now look at an example of how a search may be conducted by trying to locate a good fighting game from the Game Marketplace.

1. Scroll to Games blade and select Genre since this block provides the easiest way to locate a specific type of game. Because the only current criterion here is to locate a title that enables kicking some virtual booty, it can serve your needs nicely.

2. Under Featured, scroll down to Fighting, and press A to select it.

3. By default, the available games are listed by release date, from newest to oldest. By selecting the green Sort by box, you can change the sort order from Release Date to Top Downloads, User Rating, or, alphabetically by Title. When you see a game that interests you, press A to get more info on it.

## Game Type

Pay attention to the top of the game cover thumbnails. They outline the game type (for example, Kinect, Arcade, whether it is Xbox LIVE-enabled), which may help you make a decision. For example, some titles are marked as Xbox 360 Platinum Hits, which are games that sold considerable units in the 9 months following their release and now generally retail for approximately $19.99 USD. If you want something less expensive, an Arcade title may be more up your alley.

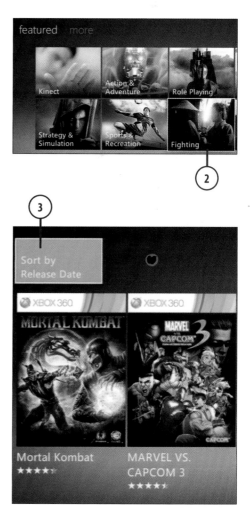

4. The default title-specific blade is an overview screen that outlines the game's price, star rating based on consumer input, classification (for example, Fighting), whether it is multiplayer and/or co-op, and its ESRB rating (for example, Teen or Mature) and details. You can also Get a Trial of the game (demo) and Rate the game yourself. If you want to see related games, scroll to the left and access the Related blade; otherwise for additional information on the selected game, scroll right to access the Details screen.

5. The Details screen provides additional information on the game, including its Developer, Publisher, Online Capabilities, and a description that also outlines additional resources, such as where to get the game's manual. If the description is larger than fits on the screen, the text can be scrolled with the right and left triggers. If you want to find out about any add-ons, scroll right to get to the Extras screen.

6. The Extras screen provides you with another opportunity to purchase the game, download the demo, and buy any available add-ons. To see some screenshots of the game, scroll right to access the Gallery screen.

7. The Gallery screen cycles through a slide show of screenshots of the game, enabling you to get a better sense of the game environment and its graphics. Press A to get a full-screen view. When in this view, use the A button to pause the slide show. You can also use the D-pad or Left Stick to scroll through the pictures. Press B to return to the Gallery screen.

>>> Go Further

## NEED AN EASIER WAY TO NAVIGATE THE GAME MARKETPLACE?

If you find it time-consuming and cumbersome to navigate the Game Marketplace Channel via your Xbox 360, you can access the Game Marketplace on the Xbox website via your computer at http://marketplace.xbox.com/en-US/Games/All.

On the website, you can see more titles simultaneously, and after you select the game type, genre, or game rating you are interested in, you can do a more comprehensive sort of the applicable titles.

Sort options include Release Date, Best Selling Today, Best Selling All-Time, Top Rated, and Title (alphabetical, starting with titles that start with numbers first). The website also features a much more comprehensive list of titles than the Game Marketplace on your console; although, some blockbuster titles still need to be purchased through online retailers or brick-and-mortar stores.

## Purchasing Selections

Now that you've found the game you want, you can either try a demo or purchase the full game. For more on testing demos, turn to "Trying Out Demos" later in this chapter. If you want to purchase the game through your console, follow these steps:

1. Go to the Overview screen for the game you want, make sure Purchase is highlighted, and press A if you are OK with the price, whether dollar amount or number of Microsoft Points. If the game is free, you see Download instead of Purchase.

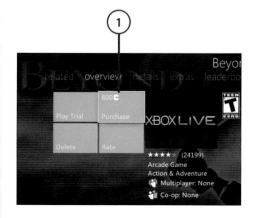

## Dollars and Points

Games that retail for a dollar amount on the Game Marketplace are games that are also available from other retailers. Microsoft often does not have the best deal on these titles, so it is wise to shop around to get a good price and the complete game package (game disc, box, game manual, and any extras), unless you want the game immediately.

**2.**  Select Confirm Download to make the purchase. If the title requires Microsoft Points and you don't have enough to complete the transaction, turn to "Adding Microsoft Points to Your Account" in Chapter 2, "Networking Your Inbox," for guidance on purchasing Microsoft Points.

**3.**  After the download finishes, the game is now under My Games, which is the first box in the Games channel or on the Games blade of the Xbox Guide.

## It's Not All Good

**Watch That Space!**

If you purchased an Xbox 360 4GB and have not added additional storage to your console, whether by purchasing the optional stand-alone hard drive or some other removable storage, you may find that downloading a full game or a few demos quickly takes up all your console's available storage space. If this occurs, you either need to purchase additional storage or remove extraneous downloads (for example, demos you've already played or free games that did not appeal to you) from your game library. See Chapter 1, "Getting Started," and "Checking Out My Games" in this chapter, respectively, for more on these options.

If you suspect a game's storage requirement exceeds your console's storage capacity, check your console's available space before proceeding with a download. To do this, go to the Settings channel, select System, and then select Storage. The amount of space on your console's storage devices is displayed for each available option.

## Downloading Content from the Game Marketplace Website

If you are away from your console, you can still purchase digital content from the Game Marketplace, which can then download to your console the next time you turn it on. Follow these steps:

1. Go to the Game Marketplace Website at http://marketplace. xbox.com/en-US/Games/All and sign in to your Xbox LIVE account.

2. Click the game you want to purchase or download.

3. Click Buy Game.

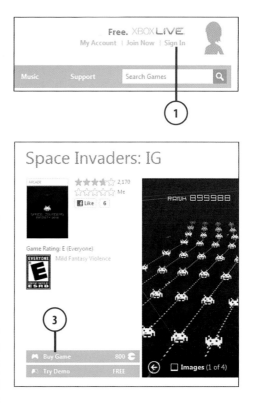

4.  At the Confirm Purchase screen, select Confirm Purchase.

5.  When the Purchase Complete screen appears, you can opt to Go to Queue or select Done. If you want to manage or check on items in your queue, select Go to Queue. Otherwise, select Done. The next time you turn on your Xbox 360 and log into your account, the game automatically downloads and is available under My Games.

### Accessing Your Download Queue

You can access your Download Queue anytime. Simply select Xbox 360 Download Queue from under My Account at the Xbox LIVE website (www.xbox.com/en-US/live).

## It's Not All Good

### Downloading to the Appropriate Console

If you purchase any games from the Xbox LIVE Website and have any pending games in your Download Queue, be sure to log into the console that you want them to be downloaded to first. Otherwise you may have to perform a transfer content license, described later in this chapter, to move the game to the appropriate console. If you receive an "Other Console" error message when you log into your Xbox 360, you need to set your new Xbox as the default console on Xbox.com. If you don't, this error message appears every time you set a download from the Xbox LIVE Website and initiation of the download becomes a manual process, requiring you to sign into your profile on your Xbox, selecting Active Downloads from the main profile screen, and selecting the conflicted title to download it.

# Finding Arcade Games

According to the Xbox LIVE Arcade page on Wikipedia, as of November 30, 2011, 449 Xbox LIVE Arcade titles have been released for the Xbox 360. Produced by both major publishers and independent game developers, these titles tend to be smaller downloadable games than their retail counterparts. As such, they are often cheaper, generally costing between 800 and 1,200 points, or $10 and $15, respectively. Another feature that these games share is that they have leaderboards, encouraging competition among players.

The best place to peruse Arcade Games on your Xbox 360 is under Game Type on the Games blade under the Game Marketplace, where it is the first option. Other options include Games on Demand, Indie Games, and Xbox Originals. After you select one of these categories, you can further refine your search by using the Release Date, Top Downloads, User Rating, and Title sort options.

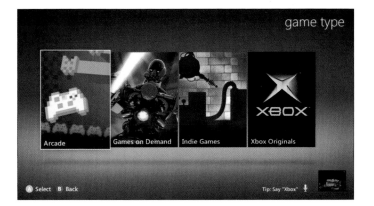

If you are not sure which Arcade Games are worth investing in, consider starting with the following five, which have all received high marks:

- **Braid** (Microsoft Game Studios, 2008)—In this beautifully rendered platform puzzle videogame with a profound storyline, you play Tim, who is on a quest to rescue a princess from a monster. Throughout the game, Tim runs, jumps, and climbs across game levels, stomping on enemies and collecting keys to unlock doors or operate levers to trigger platforms. A key feature of the game is Tim's ability to reverse time and "rewind" his actions, even after dying. As you move Tim along, you find and assemble jigsaw puzzle pieces, which help the story unfold and provide clues into

Tim's relationship with the princess. This is a single-player game. If you like this game, you may also like *Limbo* (Playdead, 2010).

- **Castle Crashers** (The Behemoth, 2008)—This action, adventure, role-playing, side-scrolling game immerses you in a world of magic and mystery as you battle your way across various terrains to find your kidnapped princess. The game features 20 unlockable characters and 40 customizable weapons plus countless combos and magical attacks that you can use to defeat your enemies. Numerous add-ons are also available for download. The game supports up to four players on the same console or over Xbox LIVE. If you like this game, you may also like *Teenage Mutant Turtles: Turtles in Time Re-Shelled* (Ubisoft Singapore, 2009).

- **Pac-Man Championship Edition Dx** (NAMCO BANDAI Games Inc., 2010)—No game better represents the arcade experience than PacMan. This version introduces a new variety of ghost, which sleep until Pac-Man moves past them, after which they begin to follow him. After passing several sleeping ghosts, they form a large rainbow-colored trail. If Pac-Man can reach power pellets during this time and eat them, you earn massive bonus points. This version features enhanced graphics, sound, and an increased number of mazes. If you like this game, you may also like *Pac-Man Championship Edition* (NAMCO BANDAI Games Inc., 2007), which is this game's predecessor.

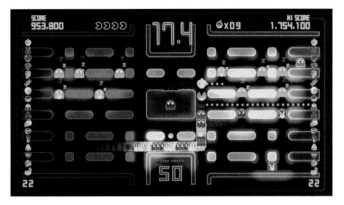

- **Peggle** (PopCap Games, 2009)—This highly addictive puzzle game features 55 levels with different arrangements of blue and orange pegs. The objective is to clear each board of the orange pegs by using a ball launcher located at the top center of the screen to strike one or more of these pegs. Any pegs hit light up and are removed after the ball falls through the bottom of the screen or is caught by the ball catcher. You can face off against four of your friends on Xbox LIVE or test your skills in 75 Grand Master Challenges. Several add-ons are available, including a Peggle Nights Content Pack, which features a nighttime dreamscape world with 60 new Adventure levels and 75 new challenges. If you like this game, you may also like *Zuma* (Oberon Media, 2005).

- **Uno** (Microsoft Game Studios, 2006)—This classic card game, which comes to life on the Xbox 360 through the use of avatars, can be played as a single-player game or on Xbox LIVE with up to four players. The game features three different game modes, including Standard Uno, which follows standard Uno rules; Partner Uno, which enables players to join forces to become a team, with a win by either player representing a win for the team; and House Rules Uno, which enables players to customize the rules to meet their preferences. If you like this game, you may also like *Hasbro Family Game Night* (EA Bright Light, 2009).

### Freebie but Goodie

*Doritos Crash Course* (Wanako Games/A2M, 2010) is a free game sponsored by Doritos that has received good ratings. This fast-paced, silly game features obstacle courses in which your avatar competes against your friends and family over Xbox LIVE. There are 15 platformer levels to complete.

# Finding Games on Demand

Xbox Games on Demand includes the titles that were previously only available in retail stores. You usually won't find the newest games here because these still need to be purchased from stores or online vendors; however, a large number of titles are available, so unless you want a newly released game, chances are good that you'll find what you are looking for here.

The best place to find Games on Demand is under Game Type on the Games blade under the Game Marketplace, where it is the second option. You can then further refine your search by using the Release Date, Top Downloads, User Rating, and Title sort options.

Looking for a few good Games on Demand? Consider these:

- **Alan Wake** (Microsoft, 2010)—In this critically acclaimed, story-driven psychological thriller and third-person shooter, you control Alan Wake, a best-selling writer whose wife Alice disappears while they are on vacation in Bright Falls, Washington. A major element of the game is the optional discovery and collection of manuscript pages from *Departure*, Alan's latest novel, which he does not remember writing. However, the book starts coming to life around him as a dark presence pushes him to the brink of sanity as he works to solve the mystery and save his wife. If you like this game, you may also like *Resident Evil 5* (Capcom, 2009).

- **Borderlands** (2K Games, 2009)—This addictive, action-packed game has been described as a "role-playing shooter." In the game, you play a mercenary searching for a legendary stockpile of powerful alien technology known as "The Vault," which is located on Pandora, a lawless planet that has largely been abandoned after a failed xenoarcheology mission. Throughout the game, you have to defeat bandits, dangerous alien wildlife, bosses, and other riffraff. You can select between four characters, each with their own special skill set. Although a first-person shooter, the game supports four-player co-op and is best enjoyed in this mode. After all, if you found yourself in your character's shoes in real life, wouldn't you rather have one to three other people working with you toward a shared objective? If you like science fiction, role-playing, and shooters, this is the game for you. Not sure about the fast pace of this title but would like something similar? Consider *Fallout 3* (Bethesda Softworks, 2008).

- **Civilization Revolution** (2K Games, 2008)—Sid Meier's *Civilization* has been dubbed the "greatest strategy game of all time," and with *Civilization Revolution*, you can now experience this legendary game on your Xbox 360. In this addictive, turn-based game, you select one of 16 nations to guide as you make your way through history on a quest to conquer the world. As you build your empire, you wage war against history's greatest leaders, conduct diplomacy, and discover new technologies. The game is Xbox LIVE–enabled, enabling multiplayer competitions, and multiple add-ons keep gameplay fun and engaging. If you like this game, you may also like *Tom Clancy's EndWar* (Ubisoft, 2008).

- **Dead Rising 2** (Capcom, 2010)—In this sequel to *Dead Rising*, you play Chuck Greene, a professional motorcycle racer who participates in a controversial game show where contestants win money by killing zombies. Chuck needs to win the prize money so that he can provide his daughter, Katey, with a medication that prevents zombification. However, the game show does not go as planned, and your actions as the story unfolds determine the game's ultimate ending. Can't get enough of *Dead Rising 2*? Check out *DR2: Case Zero* (Capcom, 2010), a full-featured prologue to *Dead Rising 2*.

- **Viva Piñata** (Microsoft Game Studios, 2006)—The objective of this bright, fun, family-friendly game is to turn a neglected plot of land into a beautiful garden that attracts piñata residents, each of which has special requirements. Everything in this game can be personalized, from the grass in your garden to the hat on your piñata's head. You cannot win or lose in this game because you are free to determine your own goals, such as cultivating your land to attract your favorite species of Piñatas (there are more than 60 to choose from) or taming one of the troublemaker piñatas that makes an appearance every now and again. Can't get enough of your virtual piñatas? Then check out its , *Viva Piñata: Trouble in Paradise* (Microsoft Game Studios, 2008).

# Finding Indie Games

Indie Games are videogames created by individuals or small teams without financial assistance from a videogame publisher. The games are developed using Microsoft's XNA Game Studio and the game's developers are registered with the App Hub, which has the final product reviewed by other videogame creators to determine whether the title should be included on the Xbox LIVE Marketplace.

The best place to check out Xbox LIVE Indie is under Game Type on the Games blade under the Game Marketplace, where it is the third option. You can then further refine your search by using the Release Date, Top Downloads, User Rating, and Title sort options.

Xbox LIVE Indie Games generally cost considerably fewer Microsoft Points to download than other Xbox LIVE Arcade titles, with titles ranging from 80 to 400 points. Although the selection has been a bit of a mixed bag, it has gotten considerably better over time, and there are definitely some gems to be discovered. Here are five that you may want to check out:

- **FortressCraft Chapter 1** (ProjectorGames, 2011)—One of the fastest selling indie titles on the Xbox LIVE Marketplace, this game has you build the landscape around you by putting 32 different cube-shaped polygons at your disposal. How you build your surroundings is limited only by your imagination. In addition, you can search for relics that provide bonuses, such as the ability to blow up blocks. A particularly nifty feature of the game is that it makes use of your Xbox LIVE avatar by pulling him or her into the game.

- **I MAED A GAM3 W1TH Z0MBIES 1N IT!!!1** (ka Studios, 2009)—This quirky shooter is one of the most popular and highest rated Xbox LIVE Indie Games. The game controls are simple, requiring use of the Xbox controller's left and right sticks to shoot droves of attacking zombies while collecting power-ups. A rock-style song is sung in the game's background by the game's creator, James Silva, which has also garnered some attention for this title.

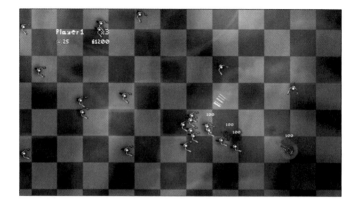

- **Lumi** (Kydos Studios, 2010)—This high-rated, action-based, platform puzzle game was the grand-prize winner of Microsoft's Dream.Build.Play 2010 Challenge. In this game, you control Lumi, a small magnetized creature who is charged with the big task to bring the universe, which has been plunged into darkness, back to life.

- **The Avatar Legends** (BarkersCrest Studio, 2011)—A Kotaku favorite, this game enables you to slay monsters and cast spells using your own avatar. In addition, you can create and share your worlds over Xbox LIVE using the game's role-playing game builder. Up to six players can play the game on Xbox LIVE.

- **What The?! Party Trivia Game** (Social Loner Studios, 2009)—This top 20 finalist of Microsoft's Dream.Build Play 2009 Challenge transports your avatar to the set of a 1970s game show where you face off against your friends in a trivia battle to win virtual cash and prizes. The game, which supports up to four players offline and features hundreds of modern trivia questions, can help keep your party guests entertained for as much as a pack of balloons costs from the dollar store.

# Finding Xbox Originals

Xbox Originals are games that were originally released for the first Xbox system and are now emulated for play on the Xbox 360. Although it's hard to think of games released only as far back as 2001 as vintage, this is still a great way to experience some Xbox history without the hassle of tracking down a boxed copy of a game and worrying about whether or not it's compatible. (See "Understanding Backward Compatibility with the Original Xbox" later in this chapter.)

The best place to check out Xbox Originals is under Game Type on the Games blade under the Game Marketplace, where it is the fourth and final option. You can then further refine your search by using the Release Date, Top Downloads, User Rating, and Title sort options.

Xbox Originals games generally cost 1200 points. Although the downloadable selection of games from the original library is relatively small, here are five that you might want to check out:

- **Crash Bandicoot: The Wrath of Cortex** (Traveller's Tales, 2002)—The seventh game in the popular *Crash Bandicoot* series, which started in 1996, this platformer game tasks the player with traveling the world to gather special crystals to ultimately defeat the superweapon of longtime nemesis Doctor Neo Cortex. Challenging at times, the wacky characters and diverse environments and vehicles all make it worth a go for fans of games with lots of running and jumping.

- **Dreamfall: The Longest Journey** (Funcom, 2006)—There have been several popular adventure games released in recent years, but few have attempted the type of dramatic storytelling that *Dreamfall* has. As a comatose 20-year-old resident of Casablanca in 2219 named Zoe Castillo, the player controls four different characters to explore various locations, gather and combine items, and solve puzzles in an attempt to uncover exactly what happened.

Bad things are happening, and everyone who knows the truth is either dead or has vanished off the face of the Earth.

- **Grabbed by the Ghoulies** (Rare, 2003)—In this game, players take control of Cooper Chance, who needs to rescue his girlfriend Amber from Ghoulhaven Hall. If the names haven't already clued you in, this beat 'em up adventure platformer doesn't take itself particularly seriously and offers a fun alternative to more traditional survival horror games.

- **Jade Empire** (BioWare, 2005)—With its inspired mix of Chinese mythology, mature themes, action-based combat, and accessible controls, BioWare, who has made some of the most popular role-playing games in recent memory, created just such a game in *Jade Empire*. When you play, you will quickly see why it delighted long-time fans of the genre and newcomers alike.

- **Sid Meier's Pirates!** (Firaxis Games, 2004)—A reimagining of a 1987 classic, this game took all the best elements of the original and gave them a makeover for a new generation of gamers with tongue planted firmly in cheek. Players swashbuckle their way around the Caribbean islands, sailing, trading, battling, and even dancing their way to becoming an infamous pirate. Equal parts action, strategy, and adventure, *Sid Meier's Pirates!* has a little something for everyone.

# Trying Out Demos

Demos are available for the majority of games listed in the Game Marketplace. In some cases, you might find that only the demo is available. This is often the case for more recent releases or games not yet released. For example, if you look in the Featured section of the Game Marketplace and select Game Showcase, you'll likely encounter demos for quite a few games currently only available from outside retailers.

Although there is a Demos blade under the Game Marketplace, the only demos included there are for retail games. Game Demos for Xbox LIVE Arcade titles and Indie games are accessible from their respective sections.

## Downloading a Demo

Regardless of how you browse for games, you can typically access a demo for the game you are interested in by clicking the title and selecting Get Trial from the game overview screen. Now look at an example.

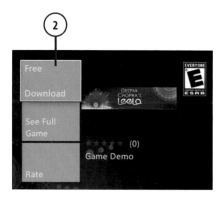

1. Select the game you are interested in.

2. At the game's overview screen, make sure Free Download is highlighted, then press A to select it. Pay attention to how much storage space the demo requires.

3. At the next screen, make sure Confirm Download is selected, and press A to continue.

4. At the first Active Downloads screen, press A to continue. The download status is shown by the tracking bar. Depending on your connection and the size of the demo file, it may take a while for the download to complete. Since the Xbox 360 supports background downloads, it is not necessary to remain at the Active Downloads screen if there are other activities you want to perform on your system.

5. Once the download completes, at the second Active Downloads screen, press B to get out of the screen.

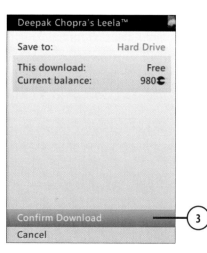

6. The game demo is now available in your game library under My Games. For more information on your game library, fast-forward to "Checking Out My Games" later in this chapter.

### Demos Can Be Large!

Although demos do not have the same storage requirements as full games, they can still require a substantial amount of space. Retail game demos tend to be especially large, with some taking 1GB or more. If all you have is a 4GB Xbox 360, downloading a few demos can quickly drain your console's storage capacity. See "It's Not All Good" under "Purchasing Selections" in this chapter for guidance on checking your system's available space and what to do if you find it to be maxed out.

# Grabbing Add-Ons and Extras

Game add-ons help keep games interesting by enabling you to download new in-game digital content (for example, songs, maps, levels, themes, characters, and weapons) to expand and enhance your gaming experience. Of course, the available add-ons vary by title, with some games featuring none and others featuring numerous free and paid options; paid options require Microsoft Points. In addition to add-ons, you can also download extras, including videos/trailers, gamer pics, and themes.

You can access Add-Ons and Extras from several places in the Game Marketplace. They may receive their own block, appear under the extras screen when you make a game selection, or appear under the Add-Ons or Extras blades, which are your best sources for a specific type of content. From either of those blades you can further narrow down your search to specific

Add-Ons, Videos, Themes, and Gamer Pics. Now examine these categories in the two blades more closely:

- **Map Packs**—This section includes new online multiplayer maps for popular first-person shooters like *Halo 3* and *Call of Duty: Black Ops.*

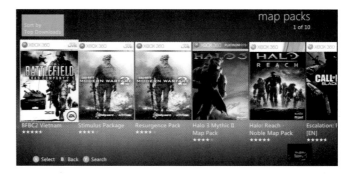

- **Subscriptions**—Purchase what are called Season Passes from this section, which provides blocks of content for a specified time period for a specific game or group of games. For instance, if you own *Forza Motorsport 4* and you purchase its Season Pass, you receive a subscription good for six packs of 10 new cars released monthly from November 2011 to April 2012.

- **Avatar Gear**— Features a diverse range of items you can purchase for your avatar, from the latest fashion items, silly costumes, and game-themed garb to new moves (for example, jumps and gestures), pets, props, and more. For more information on the Avatar Marketplace, see Chapter 3.

- **Videos**—The videos available in this section are usually game-specific and must be downloaded. In contrast, in other areas of the Game Marketplace, you can generally stream videos; although, those tend to be lower quality. After you download a video, it is accessible from your video library. See Chapter 6, "Viewing the Video Channel," for more on your video library.

- **Game Hubs**—This block features a selection of downloadable game portals that include Halo Waypoint, which is designed to track your Halo career; Game Room, which serves as a virtual arcade of classics, including arcade and console games; Kinect Fun Labs, which are simple software toys specific to the Kinect accessory; Rockband and Guitar Hero VIP Pass, both of which have add-ons specific to their respective music-based series; Hasbro Family Game Night, which focuses on the company's digital board games; and EA Sports Season Ticket, which provides early access, among other features, to the company's popular sports games.

- **Themes and Pics**—Themes are the equivalent of wallpaper for your computer. In this section, you can download game-specific themes for your dashboard. These generally cost approximately 240 Microsoft Points. To access a downloaded theme, go to the Social channel, select your avatar, pick Change Theme, and then select the theme that you want to use. Gamer pics are small thumbnail images associated with your gamer tag. Although you can use a personal picture or a picture of your avatar for free (see Chapter 3 for more on this), you can also use game-specific gamer pictures, which you can download from this section. Single gamer pictures generally cost 15 to 20 Microsoft Points, but often only bundle packs of four or more gamer pictures are available for purchase, which generally range in price from 80 to 160 Microsoft Points. To access a downloaded gamer pic, go to My Xbox, select your avatar, pick Profile, select Edit Profile, choose Gamer Picture, pick Change Gamer Picture, and then select the gamer picture that you want to use.

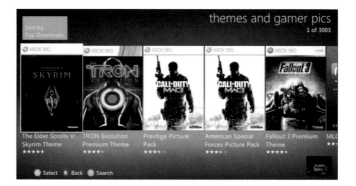

# Checking Out My Games

You can find all videogames and videogame demos and trials that you download from Xbox LIVE in your game library, which is known as My Games, located under the Games channel.

My Games defaults to show all your downloaded games. You can filter this view by selecting Show, which lets you sort games into more specific categories, including Demos, Arcade, Indie, Kinect, Recently Played, and Recently Downloaded. If you score Gamer Points in any game, it indicates how many you have out of the total number available for that particular game when it's shown in the list.

## What Are Gamer Points?

On Xbox LIVE, every achievement has a predetermined number of Gamer Points. As you gather achievements and Gamer Points, your Gamerscore increases. The Gamerscore is your overall ranking, which you can easily use to see how you measure up against your friends. Most Xbox LIVE Arcade games enable up to 200 Gamer Points to be earned, whereas most full videogames enable up to 1,000; however, game add-ons can enable additional points to be earned. Unlike Microsoft Points, you cannot use Gamer Points to make any purchases, but they can give you bragging rights. If you get into Gamer Points, websites such as www.xbox360achievements.org can provide guidance on how to get achievements to maximize your Gamerscore.

If you select any games in your Game Library, you have the option to play the game or delete it. Other game information is listed under the other headings as normal.

# Understanding Backward Compatibility with the Original Xbox

The Xbox 360 can play many of the games made for the original Xbox, which was released way back in 2001. For these games to work, you need to have an official Xbox 360 hard drive and need to download a patch for each original Xbox game from Xbox LIVE. To do this, simply insert the original Xbox game disc that you want to play into your Xbox 360 and follow the prompts. The game upscales to 720p if your display device supports it, but there is no guarantee even with the patch that the game can run smoothly. To see a list of original Xbox games that are playable on the Xbox 360, visit http://support.xbox.com/en-us/pages/xbox-360/how-to/play-original-games.aspx.

Xbox LIVE functionality for original Xbox games has been discontinued, but you can still directly link your original Xbox with your Xbox 360 to enable system link play. For more on this, visit http://support.xbox.com/en-us/Pages/xbox-360/troubleshoot/kb/xbox-kb.aspx?kbid=910583.

# Transferring Content Licenses to a New Console

If you have an older Xbox 360 to which you downloaded content and want to move that content to your new console, you can use the license transfer tool at www.xbox.com/en-US/Support/LicenseMigration/Home. You can use this tool once every 121 days. After you follow the instructions on the website, follow these steps to download the licenses to your new Xbox 360 to complete the process:

1. Turn on your new Xbox 360.

2. Sign in to Xbox LIVE with the gamer profile used to download the content to the old console.

3. Press the Xbox Guide button on your controller to open the Xbox Guide.

4. Go to Settings and select Account Management.

5. Select License Transfer.

6. At the License Transfer screen, select A to continue with the transfer. If you want more information first, select Y. To abort the process, select B to go back.

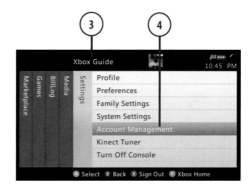

Access various video services
to watch TV shows, movies,
Web clips, and sports events.

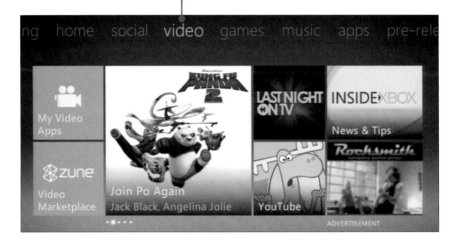

In this chapter, you explore all the video offerings and related playback functionality the Xbox 360 offers. The topics include the following:

→ Finding and watching video content, including movies, TV shows, and sports
→ Exploring your video library
→ Playing DVDs

# Viewing the Video Channel

Your Xbox 360 is a great way to enjoy different types of video, including movies, TV shows, and sporting events. As long as you have a decent high-speed Internet connection, you can enjoy almost instant HD-quality video streams. You can also purchase, download, and keep selections from a huge content library and play your own DVDs upscaled to HD resolutions.

## Taking Control of Video Playback

Though optimized for gaming, your controller has uses far beyond blasting aliens. Although using a compatible remote control (refer to Chapter 3, "Personalizing Your Xbox Experience") with your console to control video playback is far more intuitive, you'll likely use your controller more often than not for convenience.

The general controls for using your Xbox 360 controller for video playback are outlined below. Keep in mind that these controls are different from those used to control video playback in the Windows Media Center.

Open onscreen display    Play or Pause

Skip forward one chapter

Skip back one chapter

Fast Forward/ Page Up

Rewind/ Page Down

- **Play or Pause**—Start button.

- **Skip back one chapter**—Left Bumper.

- **Skip forward one chapter**—Right Bumper.

- **Fast Forward**—Right Trigger.

- **Rewind**—Left Trigger.

- **Page up through a list of items**—Right Trigger.

- **Page down through a list of items**—Left Trigger.

- **Open the onscreen display playback controls**—A button. Depending upon the application, you may also use the B button, X button, Y button, or Back button.

## Understanding Display Modes

You console's display mode specifies the size, or aspect ratio, that the video content displays at. The default display mode is Auto. If you change a display mode in a particular area, such as for DVDs, the next time you use that particular function, it continues to use that display mode until you change it again.

To access different display modes while watching a video, press A on your controller to open the onscreen display playback controls, and then select Display.

**Display mode**

The display mode options follows:

- **Auto**—Automatically determines the optimal viewing experience. The aspect ratio of the original content is retained.

- **Letterbox**—Displays the image full screen while retaining the aspect ratio of the original content.

- **Full-screen**—Displays the image full screen with a 4:3 aspect ratio. This can be helpful for older content that may have this aspect ratio with black bars encoded into the image.

- **Stretch**—Displays the image full screen and stretches content with a 4:3 aspect ratio horizontally to fill a 16:9 screen.

- **Native**—Displays content at its original resolution. This is useful for content that has an extremely low resolution or quality, or you simply want to see something the way it was shot.

## THE SCOOP ON ASPECT RATIOS

*Go Further*

At the dawn of cinema in the late 19th century, movie screens were square, typically with a 4:3 aspect ratio. When home TVs with this aspect ratio became popular in the 1950s, movies began appearing in rectangular widescreen formats, typically with a 16:9 aspect ratio, to differentiate the experiences. If you tried to watch a movie on your TV, either the sides of the picture were cut off or you got black bars on the top and bottom of the screen. It wasn't until HDTVs started gaining popularity in the 2000s that both formats featured content in a rectangular widescreen format. Thanks to over 100 years of dueling formats, we now have content in a range of aspect ratios, which is why your Xbox 360 and modern TVs have so many display options.

# Enjoying TV Shows and Movies with Zune

Zune is a digital media brand owned by Microsoft that includes a line of discontinued portable media players, digital media player software for Windows-based computers and Windows Phone smartphones, a music subscription service known as Zune Pass, and a TV show subscription service known as Season Pass. Although much can be written about all these components, this chapter focuses on how to buy, rent, and watch movies and TV shows using Zune on your Xbox 360. To learn how to access music with Zune, turn to "Enjoying Music with Zune" in Chapter 7, "Tuning into the Music Channel."

## Downloading the Zune Application

Before you can access Zune, you need to download it from the Apps channel or Video channel. Follow these steps to get the Zune software:

1. Go to the Video channel and select Zune Video Marketplace. Zune begins downloading.

2. Once the download is complete, your Xbox places you in the Zune Video Marketplace.

# Navigating Zune

After selecting Zune Video Marketplace from the Video channel, you have access to the following categories and options:

- **Picks for Me**—This category lists three suggestions based on your previous viewing habits, with an option to see another seven suggestions. This is a great option when you just can't decide what you're in the mood for.

- **Spotlight**—This default category has blocks for New Releases, Featured Movies, special offers, Top Rented, Featured TV, and Movie Trailers. Many of these blocks can also be found under the other categories.

- **Movies**—Consists of feature films, documentaries, trailers, and extended clips in a variety of genres from dozens of different studios. Blocks include Featured, New Releases, Top Rented, Top Purchased, Genres, Studios, and A to Z, which lists all available movie viewing options alphabetically.

**Select this category to browse movies.
You can elect to view all movies, or locate
movies by filtering, such as by genre.**

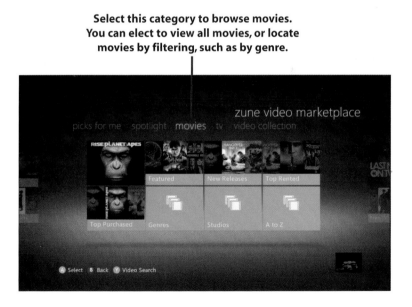

- **TV**—Consists of television shows or TV-related movies in a variety of genres from dozens of different networks. Blocks include Last Night on TV, Featured, New Releases, Top Series, Free TV, Genres, Networks, and A to Z, which lists all available TV viewing options alphabetically.

- **Video Collection**—This category contains all your previously downloaded movies, TV shows, and videos. You also manage your purchase history from here through the Account Management option.

**This category contains your existing video library.**

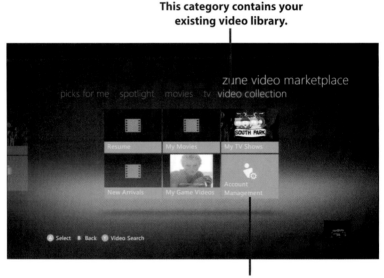

**Manage your purchase history here.**

- **Search**—Pressing Y on your controller enables you to do a keyword search of all videos to find exactly what you're looking for.

  As you select each letter, the search results start to display. The more letters you select, the more the results are narrowed, like in the example used here, which yielded 16 results in the Movies category. When you feel you've sufficiently narrowed your search criteria, move down to the selection of your choice with the Left Stick or D-pad, and press A to select it.

**Indicates how the search results are being filtered.**

**Term being searched for appears here.**

**This symbol works as the space key.**

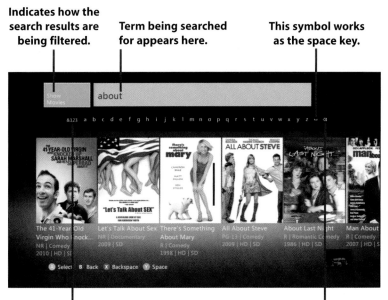

**Selecting this displays the rest of the keyboard for titles with numbers or special characters in the name.**

**The arrow with the x inside it works like a delete key.**

You can also select the green Show block to change the category for the matching criteria. In the example used here, there are also four TV Series matching the keyword "about."

**Selecting the green Show block lets you change categories, as shown.**

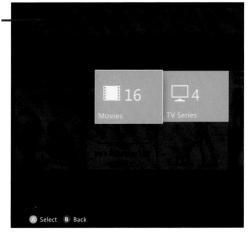

The Left Stick or D-pad moves between the various selections, and the Left and Right Bumpers work as left and right quick scroll buttons for long lists. Selections are made by pressing the A Button on your controller. Pressing B takes you to the previous screen. For most categories, you can also press X to browse the featured selections with previews. For instance, in the example shown here, X was pressed in the TV Previews category listing, which was sorted by Top Selling, and the details for the *Mythbusters* series were displayed as the video started to play, shortly before going full screen.

If nothing is pressed on the controller after the first preview video plays, the next preview video from the list starts. The previews continue playing in this manner until you press B on your controller to go back to the Zune blades or you press left or right on the Left Stick or D-pad to move between the prior or next video preview, respectively. Pressing A or Start while a preview is playing stops the preview and displays the available purchase, stream, and download options for the video, and displays a summary and other details, such as Cast & Crew, as applicable.

# Renting and Purchasing Media

When inside the Zune Video Marketplace, you can rent or purchase most of the available content using Microsoft Points. After an item is selected and you choose the green Purchase or Rent block, you typically see the following options; however, not every option is selectable for every content type:

**Change the video quality, which also adjusts
the rental or purchase options for this title.**

**Confirm purchase or add Microsoft Points
to make up for any gap between available
points and the purchase price.**

- **Confirm/Add Points**—Proceed with the rental or purchase using the presently selected options for the specified number of Microsoft Points. If you do not have enough points, the option instead says Add Points, which allows you to purchase a block of Microsoft Points. When enough points are added to your account, the block changes to Confirm.

- **Change Options**—Changes the video quality between SD (such as 480p and stereo) and HD (up to 1080p and 5.1 audio). HD video has higher streaming and storage requirements and may also be priced at a premium over SD.

- **Cancel Purchase**—Cancels the transaction. Pressing B performs the same function.

Selecting Rental starts immediate playback, and you have 24 hours to watch before it expires. Select Purchase if instead you want to buy and keep the video in your Video Collection. Select Stream to start immediate playback; select Download to store the content on your console in your Video Collection, which is particularly useful if you have a slower Internet connection and want to maximize playback quality. When a certain percentage of the video is downloaded, a Play button appears on the download progress and you can start watching the video. Some purchased content has an expiration date regardless of whether or not you download it.

# Watching Videos on Netflix

Netflix is a popular video rental service that provides DVDs and Blu-rays by mail, and offers a streaming option for computers and set top boxes such as the Xbox 360. There are two requirements for Netflix streaming on your Xbox 360. The first is that you're an Xbox LIVE Gold member. The second is that you have an unlimited streaming Netflix account, which, if you don't already have one, you can sign up for one on your console, though you'll still need access to a computer to activate it.

## Downloading the Netflix App

After confirming you meet all the requirements, you need to download and activate Netflix. Follow these steps to start:

1. Go to the Apps channel and select Netflix from the Apps Marketplace. The app starts downloading.

2. If you're already a Netflix member, select Yes, I Am. If you're not a Netflix member, follow the onscreen instructions to set up a free Netflix trial.

**3.** Write down the activation code that appears on the screen.

**4.** On your computer, go to www.netflix.com/xbox. Sign in to your Netflix account. Enter the activation code and click Activate. Your Xbox 360 console automatically registers the code so that you can instantly stream movies from Netflix.

## Navigating Netflix

After selecting Netflix from My Video Apps in the Video channel, or from My Apps in the Apps channel, a vertical listing of categories displays. Genre-based categories change based on your viewing history. Selecting Recently Watched displays a listing of your most recently viewed videos. Pressing Y for search enables you to search Netflix's entire streaming catalog. Instant Queue displays all the videos you added to your queue.

**Use the Left or Right Bumper to fast scroll through these lists.**

You can move between each of the vertical categories by pushing up and down on the Left Stick or D-pad. Pushing left and right on the Left Stick or D-pad enables you to move between horizontal lists, or to move in larger chunks, by pressing the Left or Right Bumper. Pressing A plays an option, where standard video controls apply. Press X to Add or Remove an item from your Instant Queue. Use the Right Stick to scroll video details up and down. Pressing B gives you the option to exit Netflix.

## Enjoying a Movie or TV Show

Netflix gives you unlimited access to a large selection of movies and TV shows. Follow these steps to launch a movie or TV show from Netflix:

1. Highlight a movie or show you are interested in watching and press A to play it.

**2.** As the video queues, you see the Overview panel and have a brief opportunity before the video starts playing to select More episodes, if they're available; change the Audio and subtitles options; Rate the title; or, by moving right, see more videos like your selection.

**3.** As the video plays, press A or Start, or push down with the Left Stick or D-Pad, to display the onscreen playback controls. From here, you can also push down with the Left Stick or D-pad to display the Overview panel from step 2 and select any of the options.

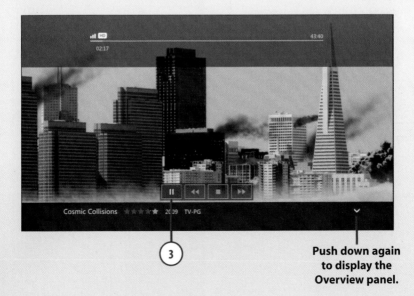

**Push down again to display the Overview panel.**

---

## Tip

On the Overview panel for any title is also an option to Rate it. Taking a few seconds to rate movies and TV shows you have viewed improves Netflix's ability to
recommend other titles that you may like.

---

# Watching Video on Hulu Plus

Hulu Plus is a subscription service that offers ad-supported, on-demand
streaming of TV shows, movies, and other videos, including trailers and Web
shows. Hulu Plus has two requirements for your Xbox 360. The first is that you
must be an Xbox LIVE Gold member. The second is that you must have a Hulu
Plus account, which, if you don't already have one, you can sign up for one on
your console; although, you still need access to a computer to activate it.

## Downloading the Hulu Plus App

After confirming you meet all the requirements, you need to download and
activate Hulu Plus. Follow these steps to start:

1. Go to the Apps channel and
   select Hulu Plus from the Apps
   Marketplace.

2. If you're already a Hulu Plus member, select Log In. If you're not a
   Hulu Plus member, select Try It
   Free to set up a free Hulu Plus
   trial. Proceed to the next step. If
   instead you'd like to see the service's selection before deciding
   upon a membership option,
   select Browse Shows and Movies
   First.

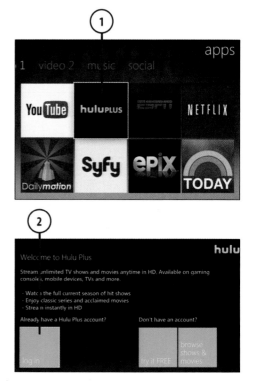

**3.** Write down the activation code that appears on the screen.

**4.** On your computer, go to www.hulu.com/plus/xbox. If prompted, register or sign in to your Hulu Plus account. Enter the activation code and click Activate or Sign Up.

Your Xbox 360 console can now play all Hulu Plus content.

Try Hulu Plus FREE

1. On your computer, go to www.hulu.com/plus/xbox.

2. To activate your Xbox 360 for Hulu Plus, enter the following code registration.

**ZJZ27UK**

Additional Information

In order for us to provide personalized recommendations and advertising as well as relevant content (meaning we'll filter mature videos if appropriate), please share some information about the primary user of this account.

Birth Year * 1992 ▼

Gender * ● Male ○ Female

If you have a referral or device activation code, please enter it here.

Referral or Activation Code   ZJZ27UK                What is this?

Don't have a code? Sign up without it.

☑ I agree to the Terms of Use and Privacy Policy. *

Sign Up ▶

* Required Information

## Navigating Hulu Plus

After selecting Hulu Plus from My Video Apps in the Video channel, or from My Apps in the Apps channel, a horizontal listing of categories displays. Main includes the most popular and recently aired shows, as well as your favorites, which is a way to keep up with your favorite shows and movies, and queue, which displays all the videos you added to your queue. Recommended lists recommendations based on ratings by other Hulu users. Recent Activity displays your recent viewing history. TV displays categorized TV shows, while Movies does the same for movies. Settings lets you log out, displays Hulu support contact information, and provides access to the Kinect Tuner if a Kinect is connected. Pressing Y for search enables you to search Hulu Plus' entire video catalog.

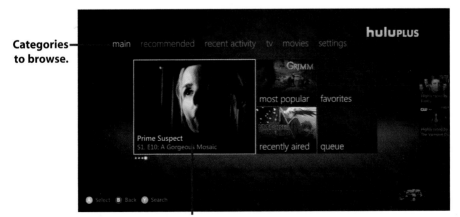

**Categories to browse.**

Featured items for the currently selected category.

You can move between each of the horizontal categories by pushing left and right on the Left Stick or D-pad, or to move in larger chunks, by pressing the Left or Right Bumper. Pressing A selects an option. Press B to return to the previous screen. Press X to return to Hulu Plus Home.

## Enjoying Hulu Plus Content

A Hulu Plus subscription gives you access to hundreds of movies, documentaries, and TV shows, including classic shows and recent episodes of popular shows. Follow these steps to launch a TV show or movie on Hulu Plus via your Xbox 360:

1. Scroll to an item you want to watch and press A on your controller to select it. If it is a single episode, it will begin playing immediately. If it is a series, you are brought to the Show Overview menu item.

2. At the overview screen, you can play the latest episode, add the series to your Favorites, view and play individual episodes, select a different season, see clips and highlights, or view other related shows.

   When playing content, standard playback controls apply. To access the video overlay, press A or Start. To close the overlay, press B. To return to the Hulu Plus Home screen, press X.

# Watching Video on YouTube

YouTube features a mass of original videos on nearly every subject imaginable uploaded by both amateurs and professionals. Although a YouTube account is not a requirement to start watching videos, you do need an Xbox LIVE Gold membership.

## Downloading and Signing in to the YouTube App

To download and activate YouTube, follow these steps:

1. Go to the Apps channel and select YouTube from the Apps Marketplace. The app starts downloading. Your Xbox 360 console can now play YouTube videos.

### Setting Up a YouTube Account

If you already have a free YouTube account, you can access your YouTube subscriptions and playlists directly within the YouTube app by signing in. If you don't have an account, go to www.youtube.com and create one.

2. To sign in to your YouTube account on your Xbox 360, go to the Video channel and select YouTube from My Video Apps.

3. Go to Settings.

4. Select YouTube Sign In.

5. Select Get Started.

6. Write down the code that appears onscreen.

7. Go to www.youtube.com/activate and enter the code.

8. Select Allow Access. Your YouTube account is now synchronized with your Xbox 360.

Get full access to YouTube with your account

1. On your computer, go to www.youtube.com/activate

2. To activate your Xbox 360 console for YouTube, enter the following code on your computer during registration.

**b k i e e f x c**

( 6 )

( 7 )

**Google**

A device is requesting permission to connect with your account.

Enter the code displayed by your device:

After clicking continue, you'll have a chance to approve or deny the request.

[ Continue ]

**YouTube on Xbox Live** is requesting permission to:

▸ Manage your Youtube account

▸ Perform these operations when I'm not using the application

[ Allow access ]  No thanks

( 8 )

# Navigating YouTube

After selecting the YouTube app from My Video Apps in the Video channel, or from My Apps in the Apps channel, a horizontal listing of categories displays. My YouTube features your recommended videos, anything you've flagged to watch later, and your playlists. Featured contains YouTube trends and what's most liked and most popular on the service. Discover groups' popular videos by categories, such as Animation, Beauty & Fashion, Celebrities & Gossip, Comedy, and more. Settings lets you sign out, displays YouTube support contact information, lets you change YouTube's Safety Mode, and provides access to the Kinect Tuner if a Kinect is connected. Pressing Y for search enables you to search YouTube's entire video catalog.

**Press Y on your controller to search all the available content.**

You can move between each of the horizontal categories by pushing left and right on the Left Stick or D-pad, or to move in larger chunks, by pressing the Left or Right Bumper. Pressing A selects an option. Press B to return to the previous screen.

## Playing YouTube Content

When playing YouTube content, standard playback controls apply. To access the video overlay, press A or Start.

Selecting More Actions on the overlay lets you see Related videos, shows Captions, flags the video to Watch Later, and enables you to Like or Dislike the video, Flag the video for inappropriate content, or see the video's details.

**These are the options in the
More Actions menu.**

To close the overlay, press B. To return to the YouTube Home screen, press X.

## It's Not All Good

Due to content licensing restrictions, not every YouTube video is available on your Xbox 360. This restriction is not unique to your console, but rather any device that enables videos to be played away from a computer.

## Changing YouTube Safety Mode

Unlike most of the other video services, YouTube's options for filtering potentially objectionable material are set separately from the Xbox 360's Family Settings, though Family Settings can be used to restrict access to the app itself. To change YouTube's Safety Mode settings, which by default are set to Moderate, do the following:

1. Go to the Video channel and select YouTube from My Video Apps.

2. Go to Settings and select Safety Mode.

3. Select the Safety Mode you want.

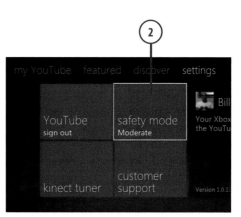

# Watching Sports on ESPN

Like the Zune, Netflix, Hulu Plus, and YouTube examples described previously, ESPN on Xbox LIVE (one of the earliest available video apps on the Xbox 360) demonstrates the potential of other, similar services, several of which are described later in the section "Watching Other Video Services." ESPN on Xbox LIVE delivers thousands of live and on-demand global events from ESPN3.com, including out-of-market programming and daily clips from ESPN.com, and clips from ESPN-specific programming such as Sportscenter. You can also view scheduled match-ups, get real-time score information from ESPN.com's score feed, and then seamlessly jump into other games. Finally, you can predict the winners of games and watch the game with others in the Xbox LIVE community to see if your predictions come true.

ESPN on Xbox LIVE has two requirements. First, you need an Xbox LIVE Gold membership. Second, you need an ESPN3.com affiliated broadband provider. To see if your broadband provider is on the list, refer to this link: http://espn.go.com/espn3/affList?device=null.

## Downloading the ESPN App

After confirming you meet all the requirements, you need to download ESPN for the first time. From the Apps Marketplace on the Apps channel, select ESPN. After the app is downloaded for the first time, it automatically starts. On subsequent use, simply select ESPN from the Video Marketplace or Apple Marketplace again to begin.

**Select this to access ESPN.**

## Navigating ESPN

After the ESPN app starts, press Y on your controller to bring up the Full Guide, which is the content guide. You then can browse the available content, including Live Events, Highlights, and Replays. Press A to watch the content of your choice.

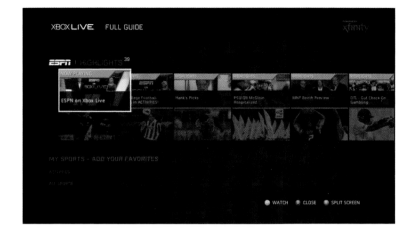

Standard video controls apply to all ESPN content. When viewing content, press A to bring up the video controls overlay.

Press X for a split screen view of two different ESPN video feeds. Switch between each screen's audio by highlighting either the left or right feed. You can change each of the video feeds by highlighting either one and then pressing Y for the Mini-Guide and selecting another source for it. While in the split screen, press X again for the scoreboard, which can be changed with the Left and Right Bumpers.

Press Start to change various settings, including Ticker, Live Alert, Score Overlay, and Controller Layout. Press B to go back to the previous screen.

# Adding Favorites

You can add your favorite sports, leagues, teams, and shows that matter most to you, so you can quickly and easily access them. To add a favorite, try the following from within the ESPN app:

1. Go to My Sports in the Content Guide.

2. Select Add Your Favorites!

3. Pick your favorite sports, leagues, teams, and shows to add them as favorites.

4. Select Manage Favorites to remove a favorite or change its order in the favorites listing.

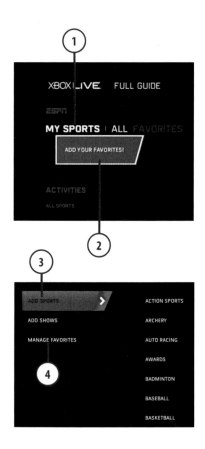

# Watching Other Video Services

Along with a major update to the look, feel, and functionality of the Xbox 360's dashboard and interface in December 2011 came the first of a new wave of video apps that make your console one of the best set top boxes on the market. As you might expect, each app has its own set of subscription requirements and needs to be individually downloaded from the Apps Marketplace. Like the other video apps, after download, each app appears under Video Apps in the Video channel and under My Apps in the Apps channel. Other apps, such as Verizon FIOS TV, appear instead in the TV channel and under My Apps in the Apps channel. While each app's interface and theme features unique elements, they still function roughly the same as the apps detailed earlier in this chapter. What follows are short descriptions of a representative sampling of this ever-growing list of video apps.

**As the video offerings continue to expand, they will be added to the Video categories on the Apps Marketplace.**

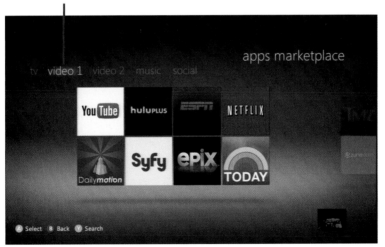

- **Dailymotion**—Similar to YouTube, Dailymotion features original videos uploaded by both amateurs and professionals. The only requirement is Xbox LIVE Gold, but use of a registered user name is recommended to keep track of preferences.

- **Epix**—Epix is a video-on-demand service featuring thousands of hit movies. You must subscribe to both Xbox LIVE Gold and the Epix network on an affiliated cable or satellite provider to use the service.

- **MSN with MSNBC.com**—MSN with MSNBC.com features news, sports, and entertainment videos from the cable news channel and Website. The only requirement is an Xbox LIVE Gold membership.

- **Syfy**—Syfy provides access to the science fiction–centric network's digital series, as well as Webisodes, clips, and behind-the-scenes video. Since the Syfy app does not provide direct access to all the network's content, the only requirement is an Xbox LIVE Gold membership.

- **TMZ**—TMZ features the latest celebrity news and gossip from the popular Website and television series. The only requirement for using the TMZ app is an Xbox LIVE Gold membership.

- **TODAY**—The TODAY app provides the latest headlines and lifestyle news, tips, and advice from the NBC News TODAY morning news program. The only requirement is an Xbox LIVE Gold membership.

- **Verizon FIOS TV**—The Verizon FIOS TV app allows several channels of live television and other selected content to be streamed straight to the Xbox 360. Although not a direct replacement for a cable box, it does provide an alternative for Verizon FIOS TV and Internet subscribers who are also Xbox LIVE Gold members to watch select content from an additional location.

- **Vudu**—Vudu delivers full length, streaming movies and TV series in standard definition (480p), high definition (720p), and enhanced high definition (1080p) formats. An Xbox LIVE Gold membership is required to access Vudu, while each movie or TV series requires a separate rental or purchase price, depending upon desired streaming format.

# Checking Out Your Video Library

Your Video library includes every connected media source on your network, such as your home PC, any portable device connected directly to one of your Xbox 360's USB ports, a data disc in your disc tray, and any downloaded videos stored on your console. To access your Video Library, select the Video Player from My Video Apps on the Video channel, or Video Player from the Media blade on the Xbox Guide.

**Select this to access your
video library.**

Although all your downloaded videos from the Zune Video Marketplace are always in a playable format, the same cannot be said for video files from your other sources. Your Xbox 360 can play videos in the following popular formats: AVI (.avi, .divx); H.264, MPEG-4 Part 2, MPEG-4, and QuickTime (.mp4, .m4v, .mp4v, .mov, .avi); and WMV (VC-1) and ASF (.wmv). While not all files in those formats will always work due to recording variables, when in doubt, simply give it a try—your Xbox 360 will let you know when it can't play a file.

After selecting a source and a folder with compatible files in it, you have the option to press A to select the file to get more details and have the option to select Play. Pressing X enables you to sort by Type or Title. Pressing Y immediately plays your selection. Press B to go back.

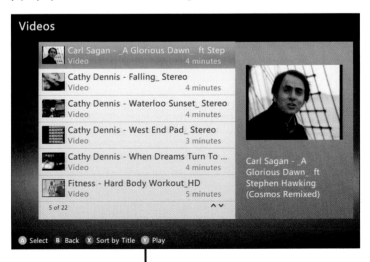

**Press Y on your controller to
immediately play your selection.**

After selecting a source and compatible file to play, standard video playback controls apply.

# Playing DVDs

You don't need to do anything special to play DVDs on your Xbox 360. Simply insert a DVD into the disc drive, and it should automatically start playing, unless you have auto-play disabled (refer to "Playing a Game Disc" in Chapter 4, "Getting to Know Your Xbox," for more on auto-play).

If auto-play is disabled, go to the Home channel, and select Play DVD. Your DVD will now start playing.

**Press A on your controller to start playing your DVD.**

If you stop a DVD and eject it before the feature ends, your Xbox 360 console remembers, or bookmarks, the point where you stopped. When you insert the DVD again, the DVD continues automatically from that point. If the DVD is bookmarked, it starts playing automatically where it was stopped the last time you viewed it.

## Using the Playback Menu Options

When a DVD is playing, bring up the onscreen menu by pressing A, B, X, Y, or Back on your controller. Use either the Left Stick or D-pad to move between each option, and then press A to select it.

The basic onscreen menu follows:

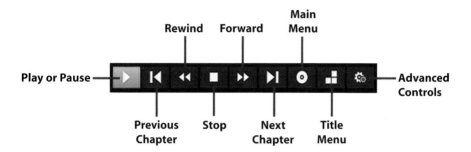

- **Play or Pause**—Play or pause the DVD.

- **Previous Chapter**—Move to the previous chapter on the DVD. When the DVD is paused, selecting this option moves back one video frame.

- **Rewind**—Rewind the DVD.

- **Stop**—Stop DVD playback.

- **Forward**—Fast-forward the DVD.

- **Next Chapter**—Move to the next chapter on the DVD. When the DVD is paused, selecting this option moves forward one video frame.

- **Main Menu**—Move to the main menu for the DVD.

- **Title Menu**—Move to the title menu for the DVD.

- **Advanced Controls**—Select the advanced onscreen menu.

The advanced onscreen menu is as follows:

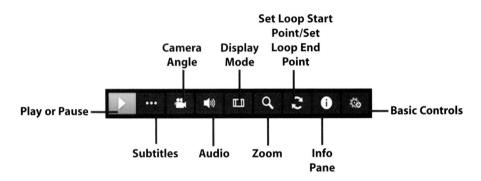

- **Play or Pause**—Play or pause the DVD.

- **Subtitles**—If the option is available on the DVD, enable subtitles.

- **Camera Angle**—If the option is available on the DVD, change the camera angle.

- **Audio**—Change the audio channel or format.

- **Display Mode**—Set the display mode.

- **Zoom**—Zoom in on the picture up to 10 levels.

- **Set Loop Start Point/Set Loop End Point**—Set an A-B looping repeating point. Selecting this option the first time sets the loop start point. When you play your video to the wanted loop endpoint, select this option again.

- **Info Pane**—Display an onscreen information pane, which provides details on elapsed time, title, chapter, and time remaining.

- **Basic Controls**—Return to the basic onscreen controls.

Pressing B on your controller closes either onscreen menu.

Discover Last.fm
and iHeartRadio.

Learn how to play music and
locate and stream audio content
from a variety of other sources.

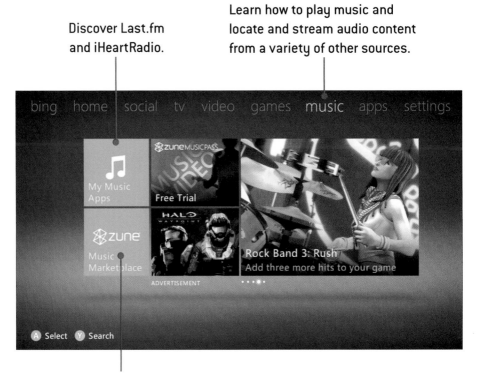

Learn about the Zune
Music Marketplace.

In this chapter, you learn how to play music through your Xbox 360 console.

→ Finding and playing audio content
→ Exploring your music library
→ Playing and ripping audio CDs
→ Listening to music from a portable device

# Tuning into the Music Channel

Although most people consider their Xbox 360 to be a visual powerhouse—and it certainly is—it is also capable of some amazing audio feats, which include playing and storing music. When it comes to playing music, the Xbox 360's versatility can't be beat. You can listen to music by connecting a portable media player, inserting a CD, or playing music stored on your console's hard drive (that is, your music library). You can also purchase an unlimited streaming music subscription through Zune or turn your Xbox 360 into your own personal radio station through Last.fm or iHeartRadio. In this chapter, you learn how to tap the full potential of your console's musical capabilities.

## Taking Control of Music Playback

Although the term *controller* may be synonymous with *gaming*, your Xbox 360 controller is also your ticket into the music arena. Although not the most intuitive way to control music playback on your Xbox 360, it's hard to beat the controller's all-in-one convenience.

Now examine the general onscreen controls for using your Xbox 360 controller to play music. As expected, the Left Stick or D-pad moves between the various options, and the Start button or A button selects a highlighted option.

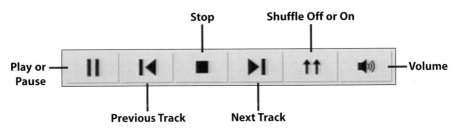

- **Play or Pause**—Play or pause the current song.

- **Previous Track**—If there's a previous song, go back one song; otherwise, restart the current song.

- **Stop**—Stop the current song.

- **Next Track**—Go to the next song if one is available.

- **Shuffle Off or On**—Play your selections in random order. Default is off.

- **Volume**—Adjust the music playback volume.

*Go Further*

## LOOKING FOR BETTER CONTROL OVER YOUR MUSIC?

If your controller is too cumbersome for playing music, you can purchase a compatible remote control. By using a remote control, you can use its dedicated buttons to independently Play, Pause, Stop, and go to the Next and Previous tracks, all without interrupting your current game or other activity by having to call up the Xbox Guide. Turn to "Accessorizing Your Xbox" in Chapter 3, "Personalizing Your Xbox Experience," for more on remote controls.

# Playing Music in the Background from the Xbox Guide

A unique feature that the Xbox 360 has over other consoles is its capability to play your own music in the background while browsing the Dashboard or playing most games, the latter of which replaces that game's own background music with yours. The only way to begin music playback while a game runs is by calling up the Xbox Guide. Follow these steps to play your own music while playing a game:

1. After starting a game, press the Xbox Guide button on your controller.

2. Go to the Media blade, scroll to Select Music, and press A on your controller to select it. NOTE: This option is disabled when any in-game cutscene or movie is playing.

3. Select the location of the music you want to hear from Music Sources and then select the music you want to play.

4. Press the Xbox Guide button again to return to your game. Your music now plays in place of the game soundtrack if the game supports custom music. You can adjust the in-game volume mix of sound effects, music, and voice from the game's options or settings menu.

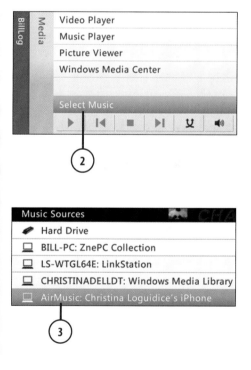

## The Silence Is Deafening

Unfortunately, no music apps, namely Zune, Pass, Last.fm, or iHeartRadio, enable background play (cue the stereotypical sound of a needle being ripped from a record album). When you exit any service, the music stops!

## Want to Stream Music From Your iOS Device?

You can download the AirMusic app by Plutinosoft from the Apple Store for approximately $2.99. The app enables you to stream your iPhone, iPad, or iPod Touch Music Library directly over Wi-Fi to your Xbox 360 or any other compatible DLNA device; DLNA stands for Digital Living Network Alliance, an organization spearheaded by Sony that ensures end-to-end interoperability among digital devices that enable storing, playing, and sharing of digital content. More information on AirMusic can be found at http://itunes.apple.com/us/app/airmusic/id409782234?mt=8.

## Restoring In-Game Background Music

To restore the in-game background music or soundtrack, follow these steps:

1. Press the Xbox Guide button and go to the Media blade. Scroll to the currently playing song and press A to select it.

2. At the Music Sources screen, press X on your controller to restore Game Audio. Press the Xbox Guide button again to return to your game. The game's soundtrack now plays like usual.

# Enjoying Music with Zune

Unless you subscribe to Zune Pass, there's not much you can do with the music side of Zune on your Xbox 360 other than purchase music videos or browse through music titles and listen to 30-second previews. With Zune Pass, you can stream the full versions of millions of songs on your Xbox 360 console. Your subscription also includes unlimited streaming and paid downloads to your PC and Windows Phone (and the discontinued Zune HD media player).

You can sign up for a Zune Pass within Zune on Xbox LIVE (see the "Getting a Zune Pass" section), on your computer with the Zune software (refer to "Media Sharing with Zune" in Chapter 4, "Getting to Know Your Xbox," for more information), or on www.zune.net. A 14-day trial is available, and 1-month and 12-month subscriptions.

## Getting a Zune Pass

Before you can access Zune, you need to download it from the Music channel or the Apps channel. After it finishes downloading, you'll be brought directly to the Zune Music Marketplace. If you just want to browse the service, proceed to "Navigating Zune." Otherwise, follow these steps if you want to get a Zune Pass account:

1. Go to the Music channel and select the Zune Music Marketplace block.

2. From the Zune Music Marketplace screen, select the Zune Pass block.

3. At the Pick Your Pass screen, select one of the Zune Pass purchase options and confirm your purchase on the screen that follows. At the Congratulations! screen, press A to complete the process.

Zune Music Pass gives you unlimited access to millions of songs you can stream or download and play on your Xbox 360, PC, and Windows Phone.

Note: Your free trial will convert to a monthly Zune Music Pass subscription after 14 days. To

| 14-day free trial | 1-month subscription | 12-month subscription (best value) |
|---|---|---|
| $0.00 | $9.99 | $99.90 |

## Navigating Zune

After you enter Zune from the Music channel, you have access to the following blades:

- **Picks for Me**—Consists of Artist Picks, Album Picks, and Song Picks. As you play music, Zune recommends artists, albums, and songs you may like based on your music playing history.

Zune recommends artists, albums, and songs you may like based on your music preferences.

- **Spotlight**—This is the default category. From here, you can access blocks highlighting various featured content, such as new music videos, top songs, seasonal music, and popular picks.

- **My Collection**—Here you can find all of your previously downloaded music and personalize your Zune music listening experience through features such as Smart DJ, Smart VJ, My Queue, and My Downloads.

**Creates a personalized playlist for you based on your music history.**

**Streams instant playlists of videos based on artists of your choosing and includes related artists.**

**When you pin music or a music video, it appears here for easy access.**

**Serves as a repository of your purchased music videos.**

zune music market

picks for me    spotlight    m / collection    music videos    music

Smart DJ    Smart VJ    My Downloads

My Pins    My Queue    Social    Account Management

**Your music queue.**

**See what your Xbox LIVE friends with a Zune Pass are listening to.**

**Manage your Zune music pass, see your purchase history, and adjust privacy settings, which may enable a more personalized music experience.**

- **Music Videos**—Here you can find music videos in various ways, including browsing the New Releases, Featured, and Most Popular blocks. You can also conduct a search by Genre, which yields 17 categories (Rock, R&B/Soul, Electronic/Dance, Reggae/Dance, Country, Jazz, Comedy/Spoken Word, Soundtracks, More, Hip Hop, Pop, Latin, World, Classical, Blues/Folk, Christian/Gospel, and Kids), and by A to Z, which as you likely surmise lets you sort alphabetically. If you like a particular artist or his or her music video, selecting the Smart VJ Artists block presents you with music videos of comparable artists.

- **Music**—Here you can locate music by searching the New Releases, Top Artists, Top Songs, and Featured Music blocks. You can also access and browse a series of playlists via the Playlists blocks, or search for music by Genre (the same 17 categories are featured as in the Genre block under the Music Videos section).

The Left Stick or D-pad moves between the various selections; the Left and Right Bumpers work as left and right quick scroll buttons for long lists; and the Left and Right Triggers bring you to the previous and next song in your queue, respectively. You make selections by pressing the A button on your controller. Pressing B takes you to the previous screen, whereas pressing Y from any of the main menus (Picks for Me, Spotlight, My Collection, Music Videos, and Music) launches a search bar with a keyboard from which you can conduct a Music Search; when this search bar launches, the X button serves to move the cursor back and the Y button functions as a space bar. In submenus, you can press X to add a selected album, artist, or song to your queue. This may all sound incredibly confusing, but your available options are always clearly indicated at the bottom of the screen, so there is no need for concern.

## Managing Your Zune Account

Managing your Zune account on your Xbox 360 is easy. Simply go to the My Collection blade and select Account Management. When selected, the following three options display:

**You can manage all of the details of your Zune account.**

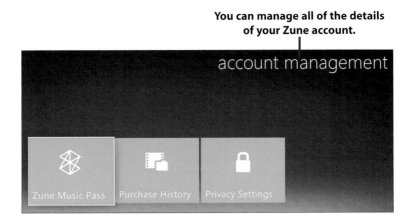

- **Zune Music Pass**—Buy, change, and view details of your Zune Pass subscription.

- **Purchase History**—View the titles and dates of your purchases and rentals.

- **Privacy Settings**—Change your privacy settings.

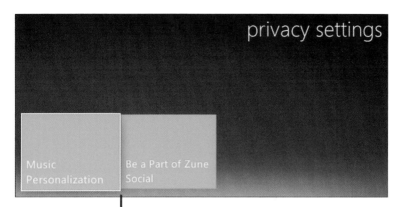

privacy settings

**The two options under Privacy Settings determine whether you want to allow Microsoft to track your listening habits to better personalize your experience, and also whether or not you want your Xbox LIVE friends to see your activity.**

Selecting Music Personalization sends Microsoft your music playing and rating data, which is used to tailor your listening experience to your interests.

Selecting Be a Part of Zune Social enables others to see your recent music plays, favorites, most played artists, and other musical preferences via the Social blade. You can choose between Everyone, which shares with the entire Zune online community; Friends Only, which shares only with those on your friends list; or Blocked, which shares nothing.

## Playing Music

Once your music plays, you can take control of it by selecting the cover thumbnail at the bottom of the screen, which launches a control and options panel. If in screensaver mode, press the B button on your controller to go back to the menu, where you can access the thumbnail. The control and options panel consists of the following options:

**Selecting the cover thumbnail pulls up the control and options menu.**

**Control and options menu showing the song title, artist, seek bar, and available options.**

- **Play or Pause**—Plays or pauses the current song.

- **Previous**—Plays the previous song on the album or in your playlist.

- **Next**—Plays the next song on the album or in your playlist.

- **Now Playing**—Shows a larger thumbnail of the album cover. Pressing A lets you pause the song and also launches an Edit block. The Edit block shows everything that is in your queue and enables you to Turn Shuffle On (it is off by default) and Clear Queue.

- **Pin Track**—Selecting this block pins the music to your My Pins block for easy access in the future.

- **Artist Details**—Pulls up the following options: Play Top Songs; Smart VJ; Pin Artist, enabling you to pin the artist to My Pins; Smart DJ; and Play Music Videos.

The screensaver mode kicks in a few seconds after a song starts to play if there is no activity. The screensavers show artist photos as an animated slide show, along with the song number, title, and artist keywords. If you press A, you are brought to your queue, where you can access the edit block and move between items in your queue.

# Personalizing Radio with Last.fm

If you don't want to go with a Zune Pass subscription and you're an Xbox LIVE Gold member, you can get an experience similar to Zune Pass through Last.fm for free, albeit peppered with ads and with a bit less control over exactly what you listen to.

Think of Last.fm as a multiplatform streaming radio station that plays more of the type of music you like and less of what you don't like. Of course, Last.fm does offer a subscription option, which, as of this writing, is set at $3.00 per month, which includes uninterrupted and ad-free browsing and streaming. However, even without a subscription, the ad-supported version of the site still offers a wealth of options.

## Tuning in to Last.fm

Last.fm can initially be found in the Apps Marketplace on the Apps channel. To get Last.fm, follow these steps:

1. Go to the Apps Marketplace, scroll to Music, and select Last.fm.

2. After Last.fm finishes downloading, select Create a FREE Last.fm Account in Seconds.

**3.** At the Last.fm Terms of Use screen, select Accept. Enter your information into the Create a Last.fm account fields and then select Continue.

**4.** Decide whether you want to automatically log in, show artist photos while a particular song plays, and allow "scrobbling." *Scrobbling* is the Last.fm term for creating a detailed profile of your musical tastes by recording the details of the songs you listen to and is at the heart of the service. Like the other two options, it's best to keep scrobbling checked.

## Navigating Last.fm

When you enter Last.fm, you have access to the following blades, many of which are just different ways to play the same type of personalized music:

- **Your Recent Stations**—Includes up to 13 blades of your most recently played stations. The blade with your username represents an overall mix.

**Your Recent Stations includes up to 13 blades of your most recently played stations for quick access.**

- **Your Library Radio**—Displays station blades of scrobbled artists, mixed in with a few recommendations. The first blade represents an overall mix.

- **Your Mix Radio**—Displays station blades of scrobbled artists, mixed in with a few recommendations from the latest music. The first blade represents an overall mix.

- **Your Recommended Radio**—Displays station blades of new recommendations based on your preferences. The first blade represents an overall mix.

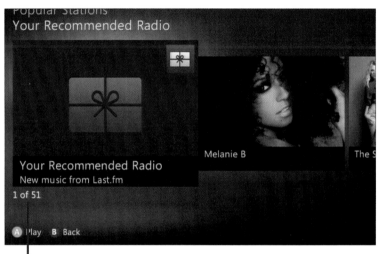

**Your Recommended Radio displays a large
selection of station recommendations
based on your preferences, with the first
blade representing an overall mix.**

- **Popular Stations**—Displays 50 of the most popular station blades from the overall Last.fm community.

- **Tag Stations**—Displays station blades grouped by keyword, such as acoustic, ambient, blues, and emo.

Gamer Stations
Tag Stations

Jack Johnson
City and Colour          Boards of Canada          Tom W
Kings of Convenience     Moby                      The Bl
John Mayer               Brian Eno                 Eric Cl
Elliott Smith            Sigur Rós                 B.B. Ki
José González            Aphex Twin                Mudd
                         Biosphere                 John L

                         ambient                   blues

acoustic

1 of 27

Ⓐ Play   **B** Back

**Tag Stations displays groupings by common keywords, providing a nice alternative for finding new music that's compatible with your preferences.**

- **Gamer Stations**—Displays station blades targeted to videogame players.

- **Start a New Station**—Start a new station either via artist name or keyword tag through the standard virtual keyboard interface.

- **Your Last.fm Profile**—Switch between Last.fm User Accounts and Modify Your Xbox 360 Last.fm Settings. The latter represents the same three check boxes from step 4 under "Tuning in to Last.fm."

The Left Stick or D-pad moves between the various selections; the Left and Right Bumpers work as left and right quick scroll buttons for long lists; and the Left and Right Triggers work as up and down quick scroll buttons. Selections are made by pressing the A button on your controller. Pressing B takes you to the previous screen. When given the option, pressing Y displays artist information, which provides the artist's play stats, photos, biography, similar artists, and related tags.

## Playing Music

After selecting the perfect station, it's time to take control and play. Though other buttons work, simply press A to bring up the following control panel:

- **Information**—Selecting this option displays artist information, which provides the artist's play stats, photos, biography, similar artists, and related tags.

- **Favorite**—Selecting this favorites the song and helps to guide future recommendations.

- **Dislike**—Mark as disliked and play the next song, guiding future recommendations. In the free version of Last.fm, you have a limited number of skips per session.

- **Stop**—Stop the current song, and return to the Last.fm main menu.

- **Next**—Skip to the next song. You have a limited number of skips per session in the free version of Last.fm.

In addition to working the control panel, the controller provides other functionality. Pressing the Back, B, or X buttons returns you to the Last.fm main menu, but continues playing your music, minimizing the control panel to the bottom of the screen, as shown in the example.

**With the control panel minimized to the bottom of the screen, you can continue to listen to your music while you perform other activities in Last.fm.**

To shift focus between the control panel and the Last.fm main menu, press X. When the control panel is highlighted, highlight and select the artist name and song title, and press A to return to the playback view.

# Getting iHeartRadio

The iHeart Radio app is your ticket to a customizable digital listening experience that includes access to more than 800 of the most popular live broadcast and digital-only radio stations from 150 cities across the United States. In addition, you have access to a host of user-created custom stations.

iHeartRadio is one of a new breed of an ever-growing list of audio apps, each of which has its own set of subscription requirements and needs to be downloaded. In the case of iHeartRadio, an Xbox LIVE Gold membership and a minimum of 75 MB of storage space is required. Like the other music apps, after download, each app appears under Music Apps in the Music channel and under My Apps in the Apps channel. Although each app's interface and theme has unique elements, they all function roughly the same, as described in the iHeartRadio subsections that follow.

## Downloading the iHeartRadio App

To download the iHeartRadio app, navigate to the Apps Marketplace and do the following:

1. At the Apps Marketplace, scroll to music and select iHeartRadio. After the iHeartRadio finishes downloading, you are free to explore its interface, though activation is required to access most features.

## Activating iHeartRadio

The first time you access features that require an iHeartRadio user account, including My Stations, Recent Stations, Listen History, or the social features of the app, you are prompted to activate iHeartRadio. Navigate to the Music channel and follow these steps to associate the iHeartRadio app with your iHeartRadio account:

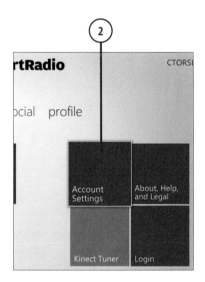

1. From the My Music Apps page, select iHeartRadio.

2. Select Profile from the main menu and then the Account Settings block.

3. Select Log In and, at the terms of services screen that follows, select Accept.

4. Record the activation code that displays on your console and visit http://www.iheart.com/activate to activate your account. You can elect to activate with your email address or Facebook account, with the latter offering a more quick process.

5. Sign in with (or create) your iHeartRadio account. Enter the activation code, and select Activate. Your Xbox 360 console is now activated as an iHeartRadio device.

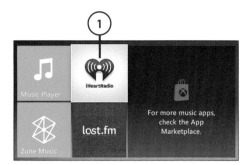

# Examining iHeartRadio Content and Features

After you activate iHeartRadio, you can enjoy its many offerings and features. The following options are available to you:

- **Search**—Selecting Search gives you access to the Find Station and Create Station options. Selecting Find Station launches an onscreen search bar that can be used to locate live stations by name or zip code. If you select Create Station, the same search bar launches, but serves as a tool to locate songs and artists.

**A search bar is used to help you locate stations, artists, or songs.**

- **Stations**—This option is the default when you enter iHeartRadio and is where much of the action occurs. Here you can access the following blocks: My Stations, which is where the stations you save can be easily accessed in the future (it acts like the My Pins block in Last.fm); Browse Live, which enables you to Browse by City, Browse by State, Browse by Genre, and Browse by Station Name to locate a station of interest; Near Me, which locates and lists stations near you; and Create Custom, which enables you to Create Station From Artist, Create Station From Song, and access the More Hottest Stations by Genre block.

**All of your saved stations are accessible here.**

**The middle and right blocks serve to highlight content iHeartRadio wants you to be aware of.**

**All of your saved stations are accessible here.**

**Locate live radio stations across the United States.**

**Shows what station, artist, or song is currently playing.**

**Available controller options are always clearly indicated.**

**Create your own station.**

- **Featured**—This section serves to highlight various stations and/or artists. You can also access the More Hottest Stations by Genre here.

- **Social**—Here you can discover what your friends, who are also iHeartRadio subscribers, are listening to. If you do not have any friends subscribed to iHeartRadio, you encounter a suggestion here to invite your Facebook friends to join iHeartRadio.

- **Profile**—This option shows your iHeartRadio history, including information on Recent Stations, Listen History, and Likes. In addition, you can adjust your Account Settings; access more information on iHeart Radio via the About, Help and Legal block, the latter of which contains About Us, Terms of Use, Support, Help/FAQ, Privacy Statement, and Music Intelligence Provided by the Echo Nest blocks; and access the Kinect Tuner if your system is Kinect-enabled.

**Selecting any of these blocks launches associated submenus that show various information regarding your music listening history on iHeartRadio.**

**Adjust your account settings, learn more about iHeartRadio, access the Kinect Tuner, and Log in to your account via these blocks.**

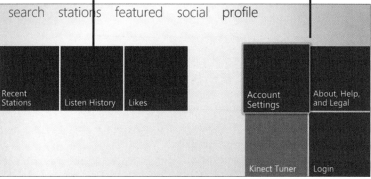

# Working with Stations

Once you select the perfect station, artist, or song there are several actions you can take:

Radio station currently playing.

Toggles between station and artist covers.

Lets you share radio stations discoveries with Facebook friends.

Other recently played stations are listed here.

Serves as the equivalent of turning the dial on the radio.

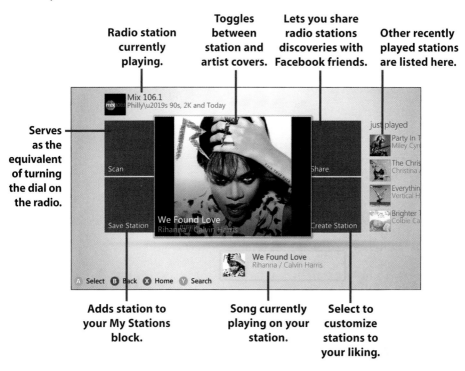

Adds station to your My Stations block.

Song currently playing on your station.

Select to customize stations to your liking.

Depending on if you are listening to a radio station, song, or particular artist, additional options become available when you select the block showcasing what you are listening to. Some options include:

- **Pause**—As you may expect, this pauses the music.

- **Remove Station**—This option removes the station from your My Stations block and causes playback of the title to be stopped.

- **Like and Dislike**—Lets iHeartRadio know what to play and what not to play.

- **Lyrics**—Provides you with the Lyrics to the song that is playing; however, this option may not be available for all songs.

- **Skip**—Brings you to the next song.

Your controller operates much the same as in other music apps and available controls are always clearly indicated at the bottom of the screen you are on. In brief, the basic controls are as follows:

- **A Button**—Use this to select items.

- **B Button**—Brings you to the previous screen or enables you to Exit iHeartRadio.

- **Y Button**—Enables you to conduct a search for Live Stations or Artist and Song Stations. When the search bar is launched, it can be used to close the search bar.

- **X Button**—Brings you to the Home screen if you are not in the main menu. When the search bar is launched, it serves as a Backspace button.

- **Back Button**—Functions like the B Button.

- **Start Button**—Functions like the A Button.

- **Left Stick and D-pad**—Moves items left and right.

- **Left and Right Bumper**—Serves as a quick scroll button, moving items left and right.

- **Left and Right Trigger**—No functionality.

## Checking Out Your Music Library

Your music library includes every connected media source on your network, including your home PC, any portable device connected directly to one of your Xbox 360's USB ports, and any music CD in your disc tray. To access your Music library, select the Music Player from the My Music Apps block on the Music channel, or the Media blade from the Xbox Guide. When there, simply select your source and start playing using the standard controls.

The Music Player is your one stop source to access all your networked and USB-connected devices that contain audio.

## Playing a CD

Just like with DVDs, your Xbox 360 is equipped to play music CDs by default. Simply insert the CD into the disc drive, and it should automatically start playing, unless you have auto-play disabled (refer to "Playing a Game Disc" in Chapter 4 for more on auto-play).

If auto-play is disabled, go to the Settings channel, select the System block, then select Console Settings, and then scroll to Auto-Play to ensure it is enabled; if it disabled, select Auto-Play and then select Enable from the next screen. You can also select Play CD from the profile blade of the Xbox Guide. Your CD should now start playing and you should see a screen like this one on your console.

If you put in a commercial CD and you're connected to the Internet, there's a good chance the CD's contents will be automatically identified.

Standard playback controls apply, with one cool exception: visualization. Visualization is, as the name suggest, a music visualizer that presents a series of different special effects that automatically react to the audio input. You can switch between visualizations by pressing the Left Bumper or Right Bumper on your controller. However, the music visualizer built into the Xbox 360 does even more and can actually be controlled by you and up to three other friends. The first step is to make the Visualization full screen by pressing Y on the first controller.

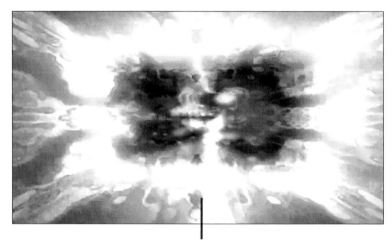

**This is one of the many visualization effects built in to your Xbox 360 that you and up to three of your friends can take control over.**

Trippy! Now that your Visualization is full screen, you can use the D-pad on the controller to cycle through more than 100 different effects by moving it up, down, left, and right. When you start changing effects, the auto change mode disengages and you'll be in full control, only changing the effect when you want it changed. You can use nearly every button, stick, and even the D-pad on the controller to do something interesting, except for the Left and Right Triggers, which remain dedicated to going to the previous or next song in the playlist, respectively, and B and Back buttons, which exits out of the full screen visualization and returns you to the Now Playing screen.

As mentioned, this does not have to be a solitary undertaking, so try to get your friends and family involved. Controller one controls the camera and effects, controller two controls speed and light, controller three controls the amount of objects on screen, and controller four controls the spinning of tunnels.

Go Further

## LLAMAS AND LIGHT SHOWS

The Xbox 360's trippy music visualizer, also known by its project name, Neon, was created by Llamasoft, which has been creating zany videogames since 1982. Check out http://minotaurproject.co.uk/x360manual.php for the only detailed Neon manual available. When finished, be sure to check out some of the other site links for information on the company's previous music visualizers, and, of course, its many llama-based videogames.

## Ripping a Music CD

One of the most reliable methods for playing background music on your Xbox 360 is by first storing and then streaming the music locally on a hard drive. Unfortunately, the only music you can store on your hard drive is that which you rip from a CD. On the plus side, the process is straightforward:

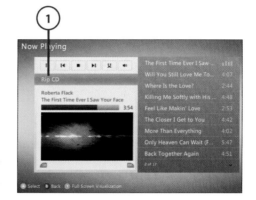

1. From the Now Playing screen, select Rip CD.

2. By default, all songs on the CD will be selected for ripping. You can deselect all songs by pressing Y on your controller or manually deselecting each song. When satisfied with your selections, highlight Rip CD, and press A on your controller.

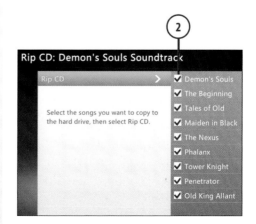

3.  Your Xbox 360 begins ripping the selected songs. If you ripped the CD while offline or the Xbox was unable to identify the songs, you can edit the song information by highlighting the title and pressing A on your controller.

4.  When finished ripping, select Done. Your music is now on your hard drive and selectable from your Music Player.

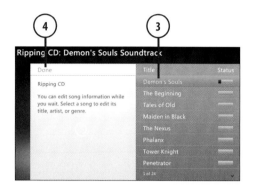

View your friends' profiles, add and subtract friends, send messages, and chat.

Compare your Gamerscore with that of your friends.

See which of your friends are online.

Set and view beacons.

In this chapter, you learn how to add or remove friends and various ways in which you can interact with your friends using your Xbox 360.

8

→ Managing Your Friends
→ Viewing Your Friends' Profiles
→ Inviting Your Friends to a Party
→ Sending Messages
→ Managing Beacons
→ Chatting With Your Friends
→ Mobilizing Xbox LIVE

# Getting Social with Friends

Your Xbox 360 is a great way for you to connect with friends and family, people from your favorite gaming forums, and other gamers from all over the world. Through your Xbox 360, you can play games together, send messages back and forth, chat via a headset, or video chat using an Xbox LIVE Vision Web camera or Kinect. (For more on video chatting with Kinect, turn to Chapter 11, "Using Kinect".)

In this chapter, you learn how to expand your social circle via your Xbox 360. You also learn the many ways you can use this platform to communicate and interact with your contacts.

# Managing Friends

As you might expect, the friend-making action on your Xbox 360 occurs on the Friends block in the Social channel. Before you add any friends, a note to the right of your avatar encourages you to make friends on Xbox LIVE. After friends are added, up to three of your friends' avatars join yours in this space when your friends are online. Alternatively, you may visit any of your friends' avatars anytime by going to the Friends block. When your friends' avatars are awake and alert, it signals that your friend is online. When your friends' avatars are asleep or counting sheep, your friends are offline. Through your friends' avatars, you can pull up their profile information and interact with them in various ways, such as inviting them to chat privately or play a game. However, before you start adding every Tom, Dick, and Harriet to your account, keep in mind that you are allowed no more than 100 friends. If you have Windows LIVE Messenger set up on Xbox LIVE, these contacts are automatically added to your Xbox LIVE friends list. Now that the briefing is out of the way, you can start building your friend pool.

## Sending Friend Requests

Adding friends on Xbox is easy, but just as you must know someone's address if you send them snail mail, you must know your friend's Gamertag to send them the friend request. Unlike with popular social networking sites such as Facebook, you cannot conduct searches for individuals on your Xbox 360. You must know who you're looking for. When you have your friends' Gamertags, follow these steps to add them:

1. Go to the Social channel and select the Friends block.

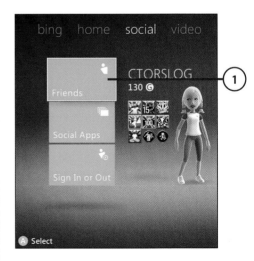

2.  At the Friends screen, select the Add Friend block.

3.  Enter the Gamertag of the recipient of your friend request and select Done.

4.  At the Friend Request screen, select Edit Recipient if you made a mistake and need to edit the Gamertag you entered; select Add Voice if you want to include a voice message with your request (steps for this are outlined under "Incorporating Voice Mail"); or select Send Request if the Gamertag is correct as entered and you are happy sending just the text message, which appears on the right. After the message is sent, you cannot take further action until the recipient accepts your friend request.

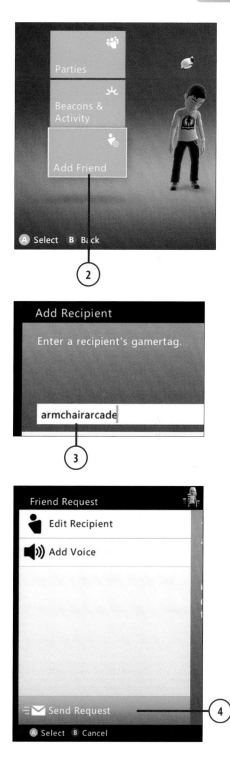

5. After your friend request is accepted, the next time you access Xbox LIVE, your friend's avatar appears under your Friends block.

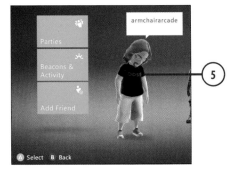

## Incorporating Voice Mail

You can personalize your friend request by attaching a 15-second voice mail to it. If a friend is unlikely to recognize your Gamertag, it is advisable that you include one. To incorporate a voice mail, you need either a headset or a Kinect sensor to record your message. If you opt to use a Kinect sensor, turn to Chapter 11 for more details. If you use a headset, follow these steps:

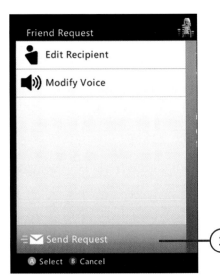

1. Select Add Voice at the Friend Request screen.

2. At the Voice Mail screen, press A to start recording your message, and press A again when you finish recording. Press B to cancel the recording and start over. Scroll to the triangle to review your voice mail. When you are happy with your voice mail, select Done.

3. At the second Friend Request screen, select Edit Recipient if you need to change or revise the Gamertag; select Modify Voice if you want to record a new message; or select Send Request to put your message in your friend's mailbox.

## Playing Voice Messages

Voice messages can only be played on your console or in a Games for Windows LIVE game. You can't play them via the Xbox 360 website.

# Managing Friend Requests

When someone sends you a Friend Request, the request appears in your mailbox. Follow these steps to manage friend requests that are sent to you:

1. Go to the Social channel and select your avatar.

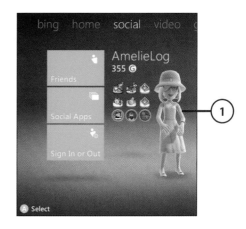

### Quicker Friend Access

You can also access Friend requests by pressing the Xbox Guide button on your controller and then selecting Friends.

2. Select the Messages block from your profile screen.

3. Scroll to a friend request and press A to select it.

4.  Select Accept Friend Request to accept the request; Decline Friend Request to reject the request; Reply to send a message to the requestor; View Profile if you want more details before taking action; and Block Communications if you don't want the person to contact you again.

5.  After you accept a request, your friend's avatar appears under your Friends block.

| Friend Request |
| --- |
| Message Received<br>12/10/2011<br>10:40  AM<br>5 minutes ago |
| Accept Friend Request  ──④ |
| Decline Friend Request |
| Reply |
| View Profile |
| Block Communications |

## Want to Manage Your Friends While Away from Your Console?

To check up on your friends while away from your Xbox 360, visit http://live.xbox.com/en-US/Friends. Here you can find a friend by inputting a Gamertag; manage pending friend requests; send friend requests; view your friends' profiles; send messages; compare games; and access the Xbox LIVE community, where you can find gaming events, sweepstakes, promotions, a weekly Gamer Spotlight that includes a short interview with someone from the Xbox LIVE community, and an archive of past Gamer Spotlights.

# Removing a Friend

Sometimes, the need may arise to remove a friend. Maybe you're no longer friends with that person, or maybe your Friends list has gotten out of control. If you find either to be the case, follow these steps:

1.  Go to the Social channel and select the Friends block.

2.  Scroll to the avatar of the friend you would like to remove.

3.  At your friend's profile screen, scroll to the right and select the Friend Options block.

4.  At the Profile screen, select Remove Friend. After you make this selection, this contact is removed from your friends list; there is no confirmation screen.

## Remove Friends
If you inadvertently remove a friend, you can send them a friend request again.

## Viewing Your Friends

Your friend's information is contained in a Gamercard and in a personal profile, as is the case with your information. The Gamercard includes the following tidbits:

- **Gamertag**—This is your friend's username on Xbox LIVE. Upon joining Xbox LIVE, everyone is given a preassigned Gamertag, which can be changed once for free. For more on this, turn to "Changing Your Preassigned Gamertag" in Chapter 2, "Networking Your Xbox." If your friend's Gamertag appears in a silver bar, it indicates he or she has Xbox LIVE Free, which was previously called Xbox LIVE Silver. If it appears in an orange bar, it means he or she has Xbox LIVE Gold. The number of years your friend has been an Xbox LIVE member also appears in the bar, unless he or she has had the account for less than 1 year.

- **Gamer Picture**—This is generally an image of your friend's avatar or a picture he or she purchased or downloaded for free from the Game Marketplace. If your friend has elected to take a personal picture using an Xbox LIVE Vision Web camera or Kinect, you see this instead when viewing his or her profile.

- **Reputation**—Indicated by stars, with five stars being the highest rating, this measure shows how other Xbox LIVE players perceive your friend; it is based on positive or negative feedback. The default rating is three stars. Although you can see your friend's reputation, you can't see what went into its making.

- **Gamerscore**—This shows the number of achievement points your friend has accumulated under the profile you are reviewing. These points are awarded for completing game-specific challenges.

- **Gamer Zone**—Although originally intended to match players with like-minded players online, in practice this selection just represents your general gaming preference and does not affect online gameplay. The four Gamer Zones include *Recreation*, for those who appreciate a relaxed casual game environment; *Pro*, for advanced gamers who enjoy competition but play fair; *Family*, for gamers who want a zone where they don't have to worry about their children being exposed to inappropriate talk or content; and *Underground*, for more aggressive gamers whose motto is "take no prisoners."

- **Recent Games**—At the bottom of your friend's Gamercard, you see their most recent activity and the four most recently acquired achievements in that activity.

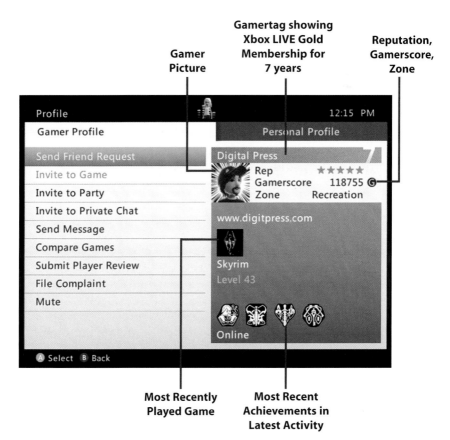

**Gamer Picture**

**Gamertag showing Xbox LIVE Gold Membership for 7 years**

**Reputation, Gamerscore, Zone**

**Most Recently Played Game**

**Most Recent Achievements in Latest Activity**

## Displaying a Friend's Profile and Gamercard

Follow these steps to pull up your friend's details:

1. Go to the Social channel and select the Friends block. If you want to view the profile of a friend who is online, his or her avatar may be accessible directly from the Social channel.

2. Scroll to the friend whose profile you want to see and press A.

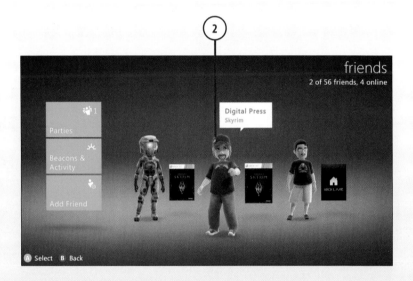

3. Scroll to the right and select Friend Options. You now see your friend's Gamer Profile, including his or her Gamercard.

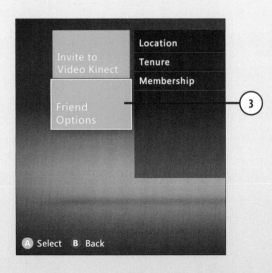

## Gamer Profile

Your friend's Gamer Profile shows your friend's Gamercard and enables you to take additional actions. What follows is a brief description of these actions, most of which are outlined in greater detail later in this chapter:

- **Invite to Game**—Enables you to invite up to seven people to join in a game with you.

- **Invite to Party**—Enables you to communicate online with up to seven friends simultaneously while everyone can do other activities, such as watching movies or playing games.

- **Invite to Private Chat**—Enables you to communicate privately with one of your friends. You can conduct up to four private chats simultaneously.

- **Invite to Video Kinect**—Enables you to video chat with a friend using Kinect. Turn to Chapter 11 for more on this.

- **Send Message**—Enables you to send your friend a text message with or without a picture or voicemail.

- **Compare Games**—Compares your Gamerscore with that of your friend and shows the Gamer Points achieved in each game you and your friend have played. For games you have not played, you receive no Gamer Points and vice versa.

- **Submit Player Review**—Enables you to rate your friend. When you select this option, you can choose Prefer This Player or Avoid This Player, increasing or decreasing the odds, respectively, that you will be paired together when playing games online. Your rating also factors into your friend's reputation. Additionally, you can select What Is Rep? to receive a description of how Reputation works on Xbox LIVE.

- **File Complaint**—Enables you to file a complaint with Xbox LIVE if you feel your friend has violated the Xbox LIVE Code of Conduct (www.xbox.com/en-US/legal/codeofconduct). Complaints are reviewed by the Xbox LIVE Team, and action is taken if deemed necessary; however, it is probably wise to discuss any grievances directly with your friend before filing a complaint.

- **Mute**—Enables you to block your friend's voice if you are playing a game together and you no longer want to hear him or her.

- **Remove Friend**—As outlined earlier in this chapter, this option deletes your friend from your My Friends list.

## Bio

Your friend's profile may also contain more detailed information, including his or her motto, real name, location, and bio, depending on which information your friend has added.

# Enabling Chat and Xbox LIVE Parties

To chat with other Xbox LIVE members and participate in Xbox LIVE Parties, you first need to make sure that your voice, text, and video settings allow these features. Alternatively, if you do not want to chat with anyone or participate in any Xbox LIVE parties, you can also block these features.

## Changing Your Online Safety Settings

Follow these steps to check on and adjust your online safety settings to reflect your preferences:

1.  Go to the Settings channel and select the Privacy block.

2.  At the Privacy & Online Settings screen, select Change Settings.

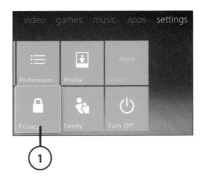

3. At the next Privacy & Online Settings screen, select Customize.

4. At the Custom Privacy & Online Settings screen, select Voice and Text.

5. At the Voice and Text screen, select Everyone if you are fine communicating with anyone on Xbox LIVE using voice or text; Friends Only if you want to communicate with just your friends; or Blocked if you do not want to communicate with anyone. If you select Blocked, it does not prevent you from receiving friend requests.

6. Select Video Communication from the Custom Privacy & Online Settings screen, and then select Everyone, Friends Only, or Blocked. If you opt for Blocked here, you can't communicate with anyone using video.

7. Press B on your controller to return to the Privacy & Online Settings screen, and select Save and Exit. If your settings have changed, this is noted under the Current Settings box, and after you select Save and Exit, Xbox LIVE may sign you out and then sign you back in to ensure your settings are updated.

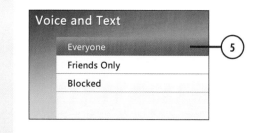

# Managing Xbox LIVE Parties

When you host an Xbox LIVE party, you can invite up to seven people to communicate online while you are each engaged in separate activities or in the same activity. To partake in an Xbox LIVE party, you and your guests must have an Xbox LIVE Gold membership and either an Xbox 360 headset or a Kinect sensor; although, individuals who don't have either of these options can still listen to the party over their speakers. As in real life, only one party can be attended at a time, and after the maximum attendance is reached, someone must leave the party before another person can join.

## Inviting Friends to a Party

To start a party, follow these steps:

1. Press the Xbox Guide Button in the middle of your controller to pull up the Xbox Guide and then select Party from the main menu.

2. At the first Community screen, select Start a Party.

3. At the second Community screen, select Invite Players to Party.

4. At the Select Gamertag screen, select friends from your list, or choose Enter Gamertag to invite an individual you are not currently friends with. After you invite a friend, an invite notice appears at the bottom of the screen, and the friend disappears from the list.

| Select Gamertag |
| --- |
| Enter Gamertag ──────── ④ |
| AmelieLog |
| armchairarcade |
| BillLog |
| Kude 46 |
| RAYLE |
| SlippingFuture8 |

## >> Go Further

## NUMEROUS WAYS TO START THE PARTY

As is typical with the Xbox, there are many ways to accomplish the same task. If you prefer, you can also start a party via the Friends block in the Social channel. Upon entering the Friends block, you are immediately able to see which of your friends are online, enabling you to send invitations to the individuals who are most likely to accept your invitation. Simply select the avatar of the friend you want to invite and then select the Invite to Party block from their Profile screen. Alternatively, you can select the Parties block immediately upon entering the Friends block, and then select the Invite to Party block, which pulls up the same Select a Gamertag screen as is encountered if you use the Xbox Guide button to launch a party. Regardless of how you get your party going, you are limited to inviting seven individuals.

## Inviting Friends to a Game

You can use parties to invite an entire group of people to play a game, instead of inviting them individually. Only players who have the game can participate in the game, but they can still chat with party members while doing a different activity on Xbox LIVE. In addition, any party you set up remains active even if you put in a new game disc or start a new activity on Xbox LIVE, so you can keep the party going even after the gaming portion ends. To launch a game party, follow these steps:

1. Follow steps 1 through 4 in "Inviting Friends to a Party."

2. Select an online multiplayer game to play with your friends; each of your friends needs to own the game to participate.

3. After you enter the game lobby, which is the area where players wait for a game to start, press the Xbox Guide Button and select Party.

4. Select Invite Party to Game.

---

### Different Games, Different Lobbies!

Is the Invite Party to Game option inaccessible to you? Different games have different Game Lobbies, or areas where you must go to invite your friend or party to play a game. In some cases, you may have to create a mission or event before you can proceed with the invitation. If you run into difficulty, consult your game manual or try to send the invitation from different areas of the game.

---

## Accepting Party Invitations

After you build your pool of friends, you'll undoubtedly be invited to Xbox LIVE parties. Follow these steps to manage these invitations.

1. When you receive a party invitation, as noted at the bottom of your screen, select your avatar from the Social channel.

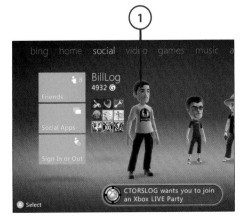

2. Select the Messages block.

3. Select the party invitation from the Messages tab.

4. At the Party Invite screen, select Join Party.

### Late to the Party or No Invitation?

Don't worry! There are several ways to join a party in progress. You can select the avatar of a friend who is in the party, and then choose Join Party. Or, you can press the Xbox Guide button, select Friends, choose a friend in the party you want to join, and then select Join Party.

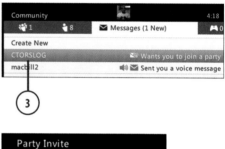

# Working with Messages

You can send messages to your friends via your Xbox 360 console or through your computer by visiting http://live.xbox.com/en-US/MessageCenter/Compose. If you anticipate sending many text messages to your friends or other individuals via your console, you should consider investing in a keyboard to facilitate the process. For more on keyboards, see "Accessorizing Your Xbox" in Chapter 3, "Personalizing Your Xbox Experience."

# Sending a Message

To send messages to your friends, follow these steps:

1. Press the Xbox Guide Button on your controller and then select Messages.

2. Select Create New.

3. At the Create New screen, select Message.

4. Select a Gamertag from your list, or select Enter Gamertag to send a message to someone you are currently not friends with.

5. Select Add Text.

6. Enter your message and select Done.

7. Select Send Message if you are ready to mail your message, or select Edit Text if you need to revise your message before sending it out. To tack on a voicemail, select Add Voice, or to include a photo, select Add Picture.

### Another Way to Send a Message

You can also send a message by selecting your friend's avatar and then selecting the Send Message block from their profile screen. Thereafter, follow steps 6 to 7 from "Sending a Message."

## >>> Go Further
## VOICE MESSAGES AND PICTURES

You can also send voice messages or include pictures in your text message. Adding voicemail requires a headset or a Kinect sensor. At the Voice Mail screen, press A to start recording your message, and press A again when you finish recording. Press B to cancel the recording and start over. Scroll to the triangle to review your voice mail. When you are happy with your voice mail, select Done.

You need the Xbox LIVE Vision camera to attach a photo to your message. You can't use Kinect, and if you have Kinect hooked up, you need to disconnect it first. At the Message screen, select Add Picture. Move your Vision camera to the desired position, and press A to take the picture. At the Picture Options screen, select Accept Picture if you are happy with your photo; Add Effect if you want to apply any special effects to your photo; or Take Picture Again if you want to take a new picture.

## Accessing Received Messages

To access received messages, follow these steps:

1. Press the Xbox Guide Button on your controller and select Messages.

2. Scroll to the message you want to view and press A to select it.

3. You now see your received message and can reply to it, view the sender's profile, delete the message, or block communications with the sender. The received message will be stored for a maximum of 29 days.

---

### Another Way to Access Your Messages

Select your avatar from the Social channel and then select the Messages block. Thereafter, follow steps 2 and 3 from Accessing Received Messages.

---

## Playing Voice Messages

Follow these steps to listen to your voice messages:

1. Press the Xbox Guide Button on your controller and select Messages.

2. Select the voice message you want to view; the message contains a speaker icon next to it.

3. Select Play Voice.

4. Your voice mail now automatically plays. Because the voice mails are so short, the bottom controls are not terribly useful, except for the right facing arrowhead, which plays back the message if you need to listen to it again.

# Comparing Games

Want to see how you stack up against your friends? Select the friend whose Gamerscore you want to see from the Friends block of the Social channel, and then select the Compare Games block from their profile screen. This pulls up a listing that shows your total Gamerscore and that of your friend, all the games that you both have played, and the Gamer Points awarded in each game to both of you. You receive no points for games that you have not played, and - - appears next to that particular title. If you've played a game but haven't gotten any achievements in it, a 0 appears next to that title. For a game you've earned achievements in, you see the number of Gamerpoints acquired for that particular title.

**Your friend's**       **Your**
**Your**   **Gamerscore**   **Gamerscore.**
**Gamer**   **and Gamer**
**Picture.**   **Picture.**       **Gamer Points**
**achieved in**
**each game.**

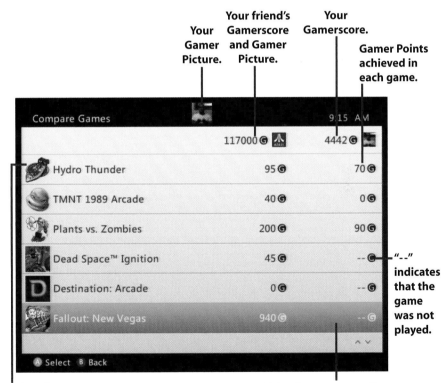

"--" indicates that the game was not played.

**Games played by you and/or the gamer you are comparing yourself with.**

**Selecting a game pulls up a screen that shows each achievement, giving a breakdown of how you and your friend earned your points and which achievements have yet to be obtained.**

# Managing Beacons

"Beacons" enable you to let your friends on Xbox LIVE and social networks know which games you're currently playing, those you'd like to play, or those you will be playing in the near future. Beacons appear as text bubbles that say "I want to play [*Name of Game Here*]" above your avatar. They indicate to your friends that it is OK to ask you to play the game in your beacon, even if you are currently occupied with another activity on your console. You can set up to three beacons.

**2/2 indicates that this is the second beacon out of the two that were set.**

**Beacons appear as voice bubbles above your avatar on Xbox LIVE. You can set up to three beacons.**

## Setting a Beacon

Follow these steps to set a Beacon:

1. Press the Xbox Guide button on your controller and scroll to Beacons & Activity.

2. Go to the My Beacons tab and select Set Beacon.

3. On the Beacons screen, choose the game you want to play from the list of your recent activities.

4. If you don't want to share your beacon on Facebook, select Share to social networks to remove the check mark before you select Set Beacon. Your beacon is now set and you can disregard all the other steps in this list. If you want to announce your beacon on Facebook, make sure the check mark appears next to Share to social networks and then select Set Beacon.

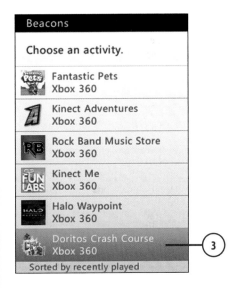

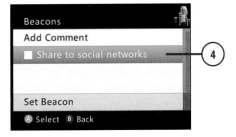

5. At the Facebook screen, select Share if you want to alert your Facebook friends to your beacon; select Add Message if you want to include a personalized note with your beacon on Facebook; or select Cancel if you decide you don't want to announce your beacon on Facebook after all.

6. If you haven't shared something from your Xbox 360 to Facebook before, you have to first log into your Facebook account. Enter your Facebook email or username and password and then select Sign In. This is achieved by selecting the empty ruled areas designated for each item and using the virtual keyboard to enter your information. You will only have to do this and steps 7 and 8 the first time you set a beacon.

7. At the You're Connected screen, select OK.

8. At the Share on Facebook screen, select Allow.

9. At the Share on Facebook screen, which is the same screen as in step 5, select Share. Your Beacon now appears on Facebook.

## Reposting a Beacon

If you don't get enough action from your beacons, you may consider updating your beacon periodically. Select the Beacon you want to update and then select Update Beacon. Finally, select Share. This reposts your beacon to Facebook.

# Removing a Beacon

Follow these steps to remove a beacon:

1. Press the Xbox Guide button on your controller and select Beacons & Activity.

2. Scroll to the My Beacons tab and select the beacon that you want to remove.

3. Select Remove Beacon.

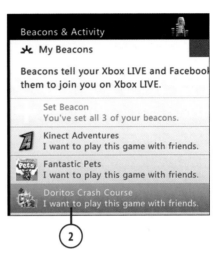

# Live Chatting with Your Friends

You can chat with your friends and other Xbox LIVE Gold members in real time on Xbox LIVE using a headset to voice chat or the Xbox LIVE Vision Camera or Kinect to video chat (turn to Chapter 11 for details on the latter option). You can also be selective in who you chat with and whether you opt to have a private conversation with someone, decide to communicate with select friends only, chat only with party members, or keep the lines of communication open with everyone while playing a multiplayer game.

## Conducting a Private Chat

The Private Chat option enables you to converse with one other person so that no one else can hear or participate in the conversation. This type of chat can be conducted whether you and your friend participate in the same activity or undertake separate endeavors. Four private chat channels are available to you, enabling you to have up to four private chats going on simultaneously while hosting an Xbox LIVE party or during an Xbox LIVE multiplayer game, even if you elect to maintain public in-game communication. Follow these steps to initiate a Private Chat:

1. Connect your Xbox 360 headset or Kinect sensor, and sign into your Xbox LIVE account.

2. Press the Xbox Guide Button on your controller and select Chat & IM.

3. Select an available Private Chat channel.

4. Select the Gamertag of the friend you want to invite to a private chat, or select Enter Gamertag if you want to extend the invitation to an individual you are currently not friends with.

5. Select Send Invite.

6. The Gamer Picture of the friend you invite to chat now appears in the channel you selected, and he or she has 5 minutes to accept your invitation. As an extra measure, you can press Y on the controller to page your friend, resulting in a message appearing on his or her screen indicating that you want to chat. If your friend does not respond, Xbox LIVE assumes that your friend is unavailable and cancels the invitation.

## Adjusting Your Chat Channel

Sometimes, members of your party may not want to play the same game as you. You can elect to continue talking to these people or can opt to talk exclusively with those playing the game. Follow these steps to adjust your chat channel to reflect your preference:

1. Press the Xbox Guide Button on your controller and select Party.

2. Select Party Options: Party Chat.

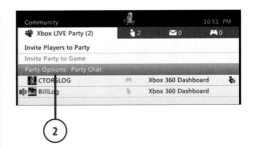

**3.** Select Chat Channel, and then move your D-pad left or right to select Game Chat or Party Chat. If you want to talk only to players in your game, select Game Chat. If you want to talk to only members of the party, select Party Chat.

# Getting Mobile with Xbox LIVE

In the not so distant past, people needed to be tethered to their consoles to engage in the activities their systems enabled. Xbox has revolutionized that aspect of gaming by offering increased portability and functionality via various apps, including My Xbox LIVE for iOS device owners and Xbox Companion for Windows Phone users.

## My Xbox LIVE for iOS Owners

The My Xbox LIVE app for iOS owners is a free universal app designed for all iOS devices, including the iPhone and iPad. This app enables you to stay connected to the Xbox LIVE community when you are away from your Xbox 360. Notable features include the ability to read and send messages to friends, manage your current friends list and add new friends, edit your Xbox LIVE profile and avatar, and view and compare your achievements with that of your friends. For more information on this app, visit http://itunes.apple.com/us/app/my-xbox-live/id480914036?mt=8.

## Xbox Companion for Windows Phone

Xbox Companion  is a free app that enables Windows Phone users to search for their favorite movies, TV shows, music, and games on Xbox Live using their phone. They can also play the content on their Xbox 360 via their phone; however, several app reviews have noted that traditional remotes are still more effective for playing the content. In addition to needing a Windows Phone, an Xbox 360 console and Xbox LIVE membership are prerequisites. The app can be downloaded from http://www.windowsphone.com/en-US/apps/b057fbe2-ceb1-470f-a7fe-09c862ca6dd9.

Learn about Halo Waypoint, a game-based social app not found under the Social channel.

Access your Facebook account to connect with your contacts and find out what they are up to.

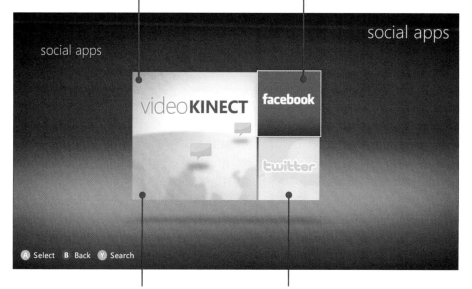

Look for coverage of this social app in Chapter 11.

Connect with the world and share thoughts and information via Twitter.

In this chapter, you discover how to use Facebook and Twitter on your Xbox 360 and learn about Halo Waypoint, a prime destination for *Halo* fans.

→ Installing and Using Facebook
→ Using Twitter
→ Enlisting with Halo Waypoint

# Exploring Social Apps

The Social Apps block under the Social channel provides access to services and features intended to enhance your sense of community. It is your portal to the two largest social networking services in existence: Facebook and Twitter. You can access Video Kinect here as well, which is discussed in Chapter 11, "Using Kinect." Although not housed under the Social channel, Halo Waypoint serves as an example of a game-based social app that can be used to access the extensive Halo community. If you are a fan of the *Halo* games, Halo Waypoint is your central hub for content related to this franchise. In this chapter, you learn how to use Facebook and Twitter on your Xbox 360, and, as a representative example of an alternative social app, the various features of Halo Waypoint.

# Connecting and Sharing with Facebook

Facebook is the big kahuna among social networking services, with approximately 800 million active users as of December 2011. If you have an Xbox LIVE Gold membership, you can access your Facebook account through your Xbox 360. This access enables you to see your friends' photos, post your gamer scores, invite friends to play games, update your status, and comment on your friends' updates.

## Setting Up Facebook

Before you can access Facebook, you must download the application that enables it to run on your Xbox 360. Follow these steps to set up Facebook on your console:

1. Select the Social Apps block from the Social channel.

2. At the Social Apps screen, select Facebook.

3. When the download completes and the Active Downloads screen appears, press the B button on your controller, and then select Facebook from the Social Apps screen.

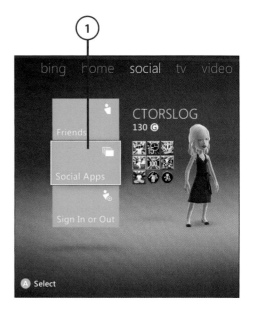

**4.** At the Welcome to Facebook on Xbox LIVE! screen, press A to log into your account. When prompted, enter the username or email address and password for your Facebook account and select Log in To My Facebook Account when your information is complete.

**5.** Choose how you want to set Display My Xbox LIVE Info: If you select Yes, your Gamertag appears next to your name on Facebook, but only when your profile is accessed through Xbox LIVE.

**6.** Choose how you want to set Automatically Log In: If you select Yes, you can automatically sign into your Facebook account when you start Facebook on your Xbox 360 console. If you opt not to log in automatically, you need to go through steps 4–6 of this process each time before you can access your account. Therefore, automatic log in is recommended.

**7.** After you make your selections, scroll to Save Settings and press A to select it.

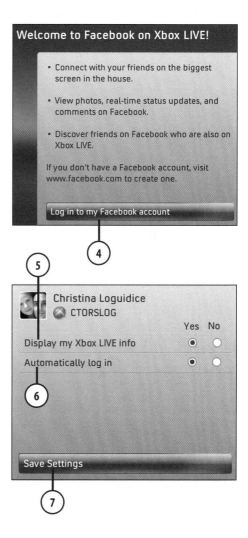

## Want to Change the Settings?

If you want to change these settings, you can do so by going to your Facebook Profile, selecting Settings, and then tweaking your selections to suit your preference.

## General Controls

When you are on any of the main Facebook menus (that is, Home, Photos, Friends, or Profile), the controller options are as follows, as shown at the bottom of the screen:

- **A button**—Selects a highlighted option
- **B button**—Takes you back to a previous screen
- **X button**—Enables you to update your status
- **Y button**—Enables you to log out of Facebook

After you make a selection from any of the main menus, the functionality of the X and Y buttons changes. When a selection under the Photos menu is made, pressing the X Button launches a slideshow. When selecting News Feed – Photos from the Home menu, the X button enables you to comment on a photo by launching the onscreen keyboard. In submenus, the Y button takes you to Facebook Home, so if you are deep into submenus, pressing this button transports you back to the main menu, whereas pressing the B button just takes you back to the previous screen. The function of all buttons is always clearly indicated on the bottom of the screen, so you are never left wondering what will happen if you press a particular button.

## Exploring the Menus

There are four main menus: Home, Photos, Friends, and Profile. Unlike on a computer, all items display horizontally, which is in keeping with Xbox LIVE menu navigation, but may take some getting used to. Now explore each of the menus more closely:

- **Home**—The Home menu has three main options: News Feed, Status, and News Feed – Photos. In addition, if you are subscribed to any specific news feeds on Facebook (such as that of an employer, alma mater, or company you like to keep tabs on), there are blocks enabling access to each of those feeds as well. Select News Feed to view your Facebook News Feed and comment on someone's status. Choose Status to update your own status. Select News Feed – Photos to view and comment on posts from your Facebook News Feed that include photos.

• **Photos**—The Photos menu has two options: [Your Name Here] Photos and Friends Photos. Whether you choose to view your photos or those of your friends, you can opt to have them display in a slideshow. When the slideshow launches, a slideshow navigation bar briefly appears. If you want to get it back during the slideshow, press anywhere on your D-pad. Basic slideshow controls are outlined in the figure.

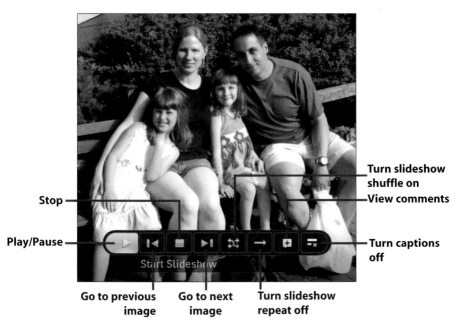

- **Friends**—The Friends menu has three options: Friends, Facebook Friends on Xbox LIVE, and Xbox LIVE Friends on Facebook. Selecting Friends enables you to scroll through your Facebook Friends. After you make a selection, you can then elect to view your friend's Status, Photos, Wall, Mutual Friends, and Info. Selecting Facebook Friends on Xbox LIVE pulls up your Friends on Facebook who have an Xbox LIVE account, whereas the Xbox LIVE Friends on Facebook pulls up your Xbox LIVE friends who have a Facebook account. Individuals who you are friends with on only one platform can be invited to become your friend on the other. You can view the Facebook or Xbox LIVE Profile for any individuals you are friends with on both platforms, as demonstrated in the figure; however, only your Xbox LIVE friends can be invited to play games.

- **Profile**—The Profile menu has five options: Status, [Your Name Here] Photos, Wall, Info, and Settings. Selecting Status enables you to update your status by launching the onscreen keyboard. Choosing [Your Name Here] Photos is another entry point to view your photos, which are sorted the same way as under the Photos menu, enabling you to view all your photos, just your profile pictures, mobile uploads, Webcam photos, wall photos, and special albums or collections. Selecting Wall enables you to view your Facebook Wall and Like or Comment on any posts, as shown in the figure. Choosing Info pulls up your profile information; however, you can only view it, not edit it. Selecting Settings enables you to adjust how you log into Facebook on Xbox LIVE and whether your Xbox LIVE

Gamertag appears in your Facebook profile information (see steps 6 and 7 in "Setting Up Facebook").

---

**Christina's Wall**                                                                **face**

Christina Loguidice
CTORSLOG

Testing Facebook on Xbox...let's see what happens. will my brain explode because I am overwhelmed by all this wonderful technology?

1 hour ago

Like                                                                                        1 👍

Comment                                                                                     0 💬

Charlott

Charlotte Gebel-
16 hours ago

Like

Comment

Christina
We will m

1 of 21

Ⓐ Select    Ⓑ Back    Ⓧ Comment    Ⓨ Facebook Home

---

## Updating Your Status

Updating your status lets your contacts know what you are up to. Follow these steps to give them the scoop:

1. From one of the main Xbox interface screens, press X on your controller to update your status.

2. At the Update Status screen, enter your update and select Done.

3. Your status is now updated and can be viewed under Status in the Profile blade.

## Launching a Slideshow

You can launch a slideshow of your photos or your friend's photos. Follow these steps:

1. Scroll to Photos.

2. Select whether you want to view your photos or your friends' photos. Proceed to step 3 if you select your photos, or step 4 if you select your friends' photos.

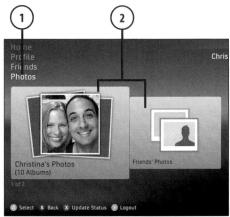

3. **Your Photos:** Scroll to the blade that contains the photos you want to see in a slideshow and press X on your controller to launch the slideshow. See "Exploring the Menus" earlier in this chapter for slideshow controls.

4. **Friends' Photos:** Select the friend whose photos you want to view (see figure) and press A on your controller to access his or her photo repository. On your friend's Photos page, scroll to the blade that contains the photos you want to view in a slideshow and press X on your controller to launch the slideshow. See "Exploring the Menus" earlier in this chapter for slideshow controls.

# Adding Facebook Friends to Xbox LIVE

Follow these steps to add Facebook Friends to Xbox LIVE:

1. Scroll to Friends.

2. Select the Facebook Friends on Xbox LIVE block.

3. On the Friend Linker page, scroll to the Facebook Friend you want to add to your Xbox LIVE friends and press A to add him or her.

4. At the Friend Request screen, select Send Request. You can attach an optional voice message. Turn to "Incorporating Voice Mail" in Chapter 8, "Getting Social with Friends," if you need assistance with adding a voice message. Once your friend accepts, he or she is added to your Xbox LIVE friends and you can find his or her avatar on the Friends block in the Social channel.

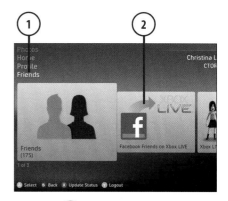

# Enabling Facebook Sharing

Facebook Sharing enables you to brag about your achievements to your Facebook friends using direct posts. This action occurs outside of the Facebook app—you cannot yet share achievements in real-time; the game must be exited first. Follow these steps to share your achievement(s):

1. Select your avatar from the Social channel to access your profile.

2. Select the Achievements block from your profile screen.

3. Scroll to the block for the game that has the achievement you want to share and press A to select it.

4. At the Achievements screen, scroll to the achievement you want to share and press X to share it.

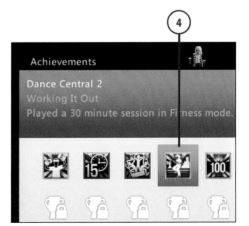

5. At the Facebook screen, select Share. If you select Add Message, you can personalize your post before sharing your achievement with your Facebook friends.

6. Your post now appears on your Facebook page.

**f** Share on Facebook

CTORSLOG

Dance Central 2 - Working It Out
Achievement unlocked for 20G
Played a 30 minute session in Fitness mode.

Share

Add Message

Cancel

⑤          ⑥

Christina Loguidice

Dance Central 2 - Working It Out
Achievement unlocked for 20G
Played a 30 minute session in Fitness mode.

Like · Comment · Visit Xbox.com · 3 minutes ago via Xbox LIVE

# Sharing and Discovering with Twitter

Twitter is another social media powerhouse, with approximately 300 million users. You can use Twitter on your console to post updates and communicate with those you follow. Unlike with Facebook or Halo Waypoint, you don't need to download an app to access it, but you do need to have an Xbox 360 hard drive or storage device with at least 5 megabytes of available space (not very much), an Xbox LIVE Gold membership, and an existing Twitter account to log into. You should also consider getting a keyboard or the Xbox Chatpad, like the one discussed in Chapter 3, "Personalizing Your Xbox Experience," to facilitate entering text. Now feel free to get your tweet on!

# Signing Into Twitter

Before you can start tweeting via your Xbox 360, you have to sign into your Twitter account on your console. Follow these steps for the initial sign-in and for subsequent sign-ins if you opt not to have Xbox LIVE automatically log you into your account upon launching the Twitter application on your console (see step 5).

1. Select Social Apps from the Social channel.

2. Select Twitter from the Social Apps screen.

3. Enter your Twitter username or email address and password and select Sign In.

4.  Choose how you want to set the Display My Xbox LIVE Info. If you select Yes, your Gamertag appears next to your name on Twitter—but only when your profile is accessed through Xbox LIVE.

5.  Choose how you want to set Automatically Sign In. If you select Yes, you are automatically signed into your Twitter account when you start Twitter on your Xbox 360.

6.  After you make your selections, scroll to Save Settings, and press A.

## Getting a Handle on the Interface

Now that you have accessed the Twitter interface, explore the key functions and options.

### Setting a Status

Besides viewing other tweets, setting a status is probably the number one thing you do on Twitter. To let the world know what you're up to, follow these steps:

1.  When on the main Twitter page, press X on your controller or select What Are You Doing? from the left menu.

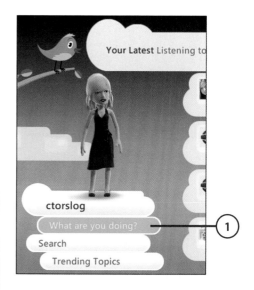

2.  At the New Tweet screen, enter your status. After you reach 140 characters, you can no longer enter text and need to pare down your status. Select Done when you're finished.

## Tweeting URLs

If you plan to post a long link, there is no easy way to do this using Twitter on Xbox because there is no built-in URL shortener.

# Searching for Topics and People to Follow

To look for tweets on a particular topic, conduct a Search. This enables you to locate recent tweets on that topic from the Twitter community on Xbox LIVE, not just individuals you currently follow. It can also help you locate new individuals to follow.

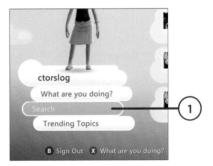

1.  From within the Twitter app, select Search.

2.  At the Search Tweets screen, input what you want to search for. Using a keyword instead of a string of words generally yields the best results. Select Done to see your search results.

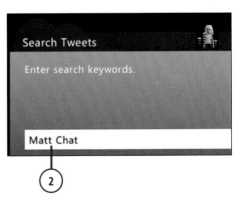

## Updating the Search Results

After the results are provided, you can press Y on your controller to refresh the findings, which pulls up additional tweets on that topic if any others are posted since the search was first conducted. To quickly scroll up and down through the pages of tweets, use the left and right trigger buttons, respectively.

**3.** If you find an interesting post from someone you want to follow, you can do so from the Search Results for [*Your Key Word*] screen. Select the post from the individual/entity you're interested in following.

**4.** At the next screen, select the Profile for that individual/entity.

**5.** At the final screen, select Follow.

Search Results for "Matt Chat"

gnomeslair: Matt Chat and a brilliant 22 minutes on Stonekeep http://t.co/ut5Hw8db (About 8 hours ago)

IgorHardy: RT @mattbarton: Wahooka! It's time for Matt Chat 128: Stonekeep http://t.co/A3dho9vY via @youtube (About 9 hours ago)

mattdallasworld: Hi @jaquelinedallas - Does this help? http://t.co/vjJ3uv8M If not, please let us know and we'll try to walk you through it. #ChatWithMatt (About 9 hours ago)

mattbarton: Wahooka! It's time for Matt Chat 128: Stonekeep http://t.co/A3dho9vY via @youtube (About 9 hours ago)

③

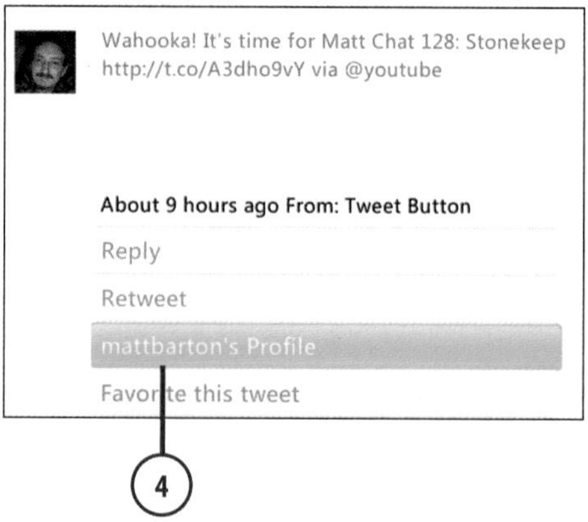

Wahooka! It's time for Matt Chat 128: Stonekeep http://t.co/A3dho9vY via @youtube

**About 9 hours ago From: Tweet Button**

Reply

Retweet

mattbarton's Profile

Favorite this tweet

④

Matt Barton                                    AirtightLeaf0

St. Cloud, MN
English professor, videogame historian, wiki enthusiast, Matt Chat producer

259 Following                    1623 Updates

501 Followers                    Send direct message

Follow mattbarton                User Lists

Xbox LIVE Profile                Favorites

⑤

# Replying to or Retweeting Posts

Whether you want to reply to and/or retweet a post by someone you are following or an individual who turns up in a search result, follow these steps:

1. Select the post you want to reply to or retweet and then follow steps 2 to 4 for the former or steps 5 to 7 for the latter.

2. From the next screen, select Reply.

3. At the Reply to Tweet screen, enter your message and select Done.

4. After a Reply Successful screen appears, your reply is posted.

5. Select Retweet.

6. At the Retweet screen, add to or modify the post to suit your fancy and select Done.

7. A Retweet Successful screen appears and your retweet is now posted.

---

## Mind the D-pad!

When you select a post, be careful with your D-pad because pressing to the left and right moves through posts. So, if you select a post to comment on, but inadvertently press the D-pad to the left or right instead of down or up to access the Reply, Retweet, Profile, and Favorite This Tweet options, you'll be taken away from the post you want to take action on.

---

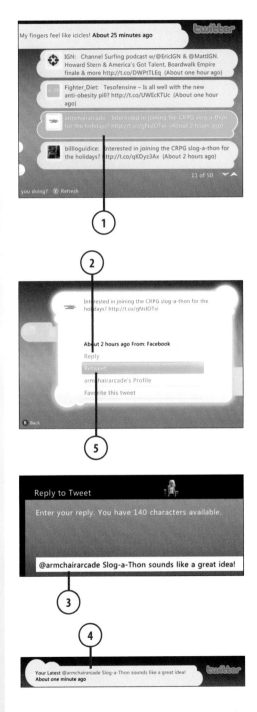

## Make a Tweet a Favorite

When you make a tweet a favorite, it bookmarks that tweet for you, enabling you to view it in the future. You can favorite any tweet, whether it is your own, those of individuals/entities you follow, or those from accounts who come up in a general or trending topics search. To favorite a tweet, select the post you want to favorite and follow these steps:

1. From the screen that appears, select Favorite This Tweet. A star then appears next to the prior Favorite This Tweet option. If you want to undo the action, just select Unfavorite This Tweet. (This menu option appears in place of the Favorite This Tweet item.)

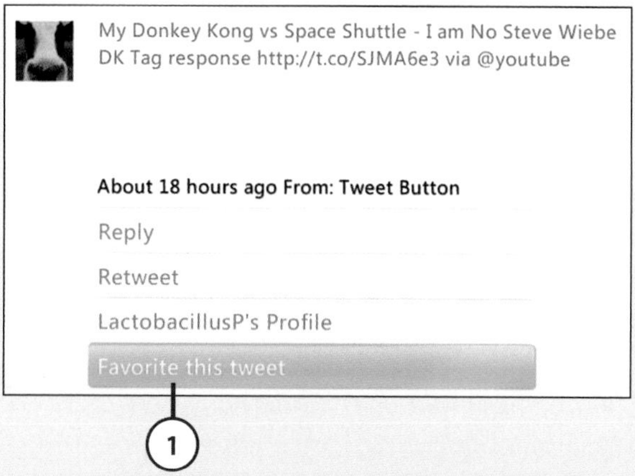

2. To view your favorite tweets, select your Twitter username from the main interface.

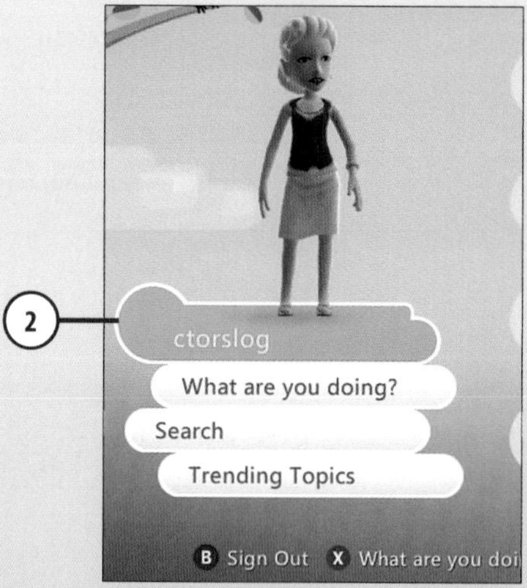

**3.** At your profile screen, select Favorites.

> ### Christina Loguidice
> Burlington, NJ
> Christina is a science, technical, and medical writer and editor. She oversees a clinical journal and is engrossed in various book projects.
>
> | | |
> |---|---|
> | 22 Following | 3 Direct Messages |
> | 18 Followers | @ctorslog |
> | 7 Updates | User Lists |
> | Settings | Favorites | ③

**4.** The next screen shows your Favorites. Selecting any of these tweets gives you all the usual options, such as replying and retweeting.

④
> **ctorslog's Favorites**                                  twitter
>
> LactobacillusP:  My Donkey Kong vs Space Shuttle - I am No Steve Wiebe DK Tag response http://t.co/SJMA6e3 via @youtube  (About 22 hours ago)
>
> ctorslog:  Wish there were an easy way to post links using Twitter on Xbox!  (About 6 hours ago)
>
> feliciaday:  You can send invites if you have Google+ looks like, there's a new sidebar thingie under the mobile graphic. ME -> http://t.co/SrdyG8N  (About 16 hours ago)

## Viewing Trending Topics

Trending Topics is an algorithm built into Twitter that identifies topics that are immediately popular, enabling you to discover the latest news from Twitter users worldwide. Follow these steps to view Trending Topics on your Xbox:

**1.** Select Trending Topics from the main Twitter interface.

2. At the Trending Topics screen, scroll through and select any topic you are interested in seeing tweets on.

### Hashtags

Some topics appear with a hashtag, as demonstrated by a # sign before the word or phrase. The hashtag is specifically added by some users to mark that term as a topic so that people can follow the conversation in a search.

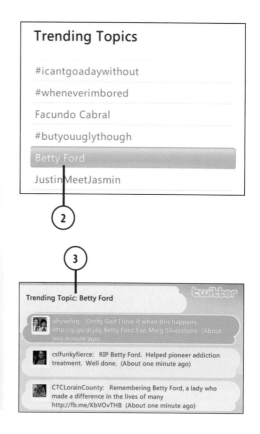

3. After you make a selection, tweets for that particular topic appear. If you select a tweet, all the usual actions become available: Reply, Retweet, access users Profile, and Favorite This Tweet.

# Enlisting with Halo Waypoint

If you're not interested in *Halo* or do not own any of the games, it is futile to enlist with Halo Waypoint, and you're free to take leave of this section. However, if you're a fan of the *Halo* games, you should sign up for Halo Waypoint, which provides access to a plethora of Halo-related content, including Machinima videos, gameplay strategies and tutorials, access to and tracking of your gameplay-related data across *Halo* games, and a host of special weekly features, such as behind-the-scenes previews.

### Machinima?

Machinima videos are animated films produced using software similar to that used to make videogames; to see a famous example, type "Red vs. Blue" as a search term into YouTube. Halo fans will enjoy what they get back.

To access all of Halo Waypoint's features, you need to be an Xbox LIVE Gold member. Halo Waypoint is a free download, and if you have a Windows Phone, iOS device or Android device, you can also enable Halo Waypoint on any of them. Of course, Halo Waypoint is also accessible to anyone online at http://halo.xbox.com/en-us, but downloading the application to your Xbox 360 gives you access to a more comprehensive experience because some content is available exclusively on the console.

## Enlisting Brings Rewards

For downloading and launching Halo Waypoint, you receive an enlistment reward in the form of *Halo* gear for your avatar.

# Downloading Halo Waypoint

Although Halo Waypoint can best be described as a social app with its myriad social features, it is actually located under the Games channel. This is likely because while it is not a game, it is solely dedicated to the *Halo* franchise and enhancing and extending the gaming experience for *Halo* enthusiasts. Follow these steps to accomplish your mission of down-loading Halo Waypoint:

1. Go to the Games channel and select the Game Marketplace block.

2. Scroll to the Games category and select the A-Z block. At the Titles A to Z screen, scroll to H and select it.

3. Scroll to the cover for Halo Waypoint and select it.

4. At the Halo Waypoint screen, select the Free Download block. When prompted, select Confirm Download and select it.

5. After the download is complete and the Active Downloads screen appears, press B to go back, and then select the Play Now block to access Halo Waypoint.

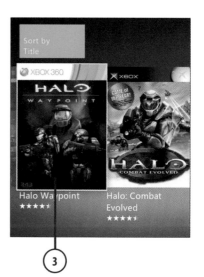

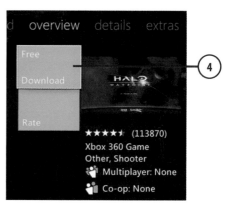

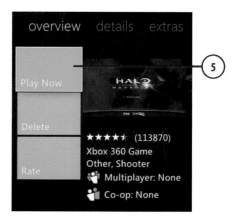

**6.** When the Halo Waypoint screen appears, press the Start or A button on your controller to enter. You are now in Halo Waypoint and are free to explore the terrain.

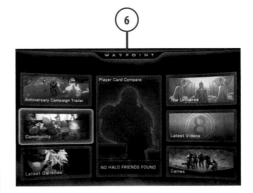

## Accessing Halo Waypoint After Downloading

After you download Halo Waypoint, it is accessible under the My Games block in the Games channel.

## Exploring the Halo Waypoint Interface

When you access Halo Waypoint, an abundance of features are available. These features are constantly changing, some daily and others weekly. In addition to some advertising blocks and access to the Halo Store, the content and features you might encounter on your Halo Waypoint deployment include:

- **Reach Challenges**—Enter this block and you can embark on both a designated weekly and daily challenge. Timelines note how much time is left to complete a particular challenge.

- **What's New**—As the name implies, selecting this block gives you access to the newest content on Halo Waypoint, including videos and screenshots. Although these videos and screenshots also appear in other areas on Halo Waypoint, this portal ensures you don't miss a thing.

- **Community**—This section is devoted to videos and screenshots created by *Halo* fans. In addition, you can learn about various gaming events and access recaps of such events.

- **Your Profile**—When you select your profile, it launches a Career screen. Your achievements, career milestones, awards, and progress on any Reach Challenges are outlined here. As you earn achievements in the series, you unlock Avatar awards.

- **This Week on Waypoint**—This provides a bulleted list outlining the events and featured content on Halo Waypoint for a particular week.

- **Latest Galleries**—This features images created by the *Halo* community, whether of a memorable event during the game or an environment created in Forge, a gameplay mode in some *Halo* games that enables users to play and edit multiplayer maps.

- **Player Card Compare**—This enables you to compare your stats with your *Halo* teammates, but only if they are online and enlisted in Halo Waypoint.

- **The Universe**—This provides an overview of the Halo universe through videos and screenshots. Areas covered include the ships, vehicles, weapons, factions, characters, events, locations, and technology featured in *Halo*.

- **Latest Videos**—Just like the What's New gives you access to the newest content on Halo Waypoint, Latest Videos provides easy access to the most recently posted videos on Halo Waypoint.

- **Games**—This provides an overview of the various Halo games, including *Halo 4*; *Halo: Anniversary*; *Halo: Reach*; *Halo 3: ODST*; *Halo Wars*; *Halo 3*; *Halo 2*; and *Halo: Combat Evolved*.

## Going Mobile with Halo Waypoint

On December 10, 2011, Microsoft launched the Halo Waypoint app for Windows Phone, Android, and iOS devices. This app is free and essentially provides access to the same information as is available on the console, ensuring you have convenient access to all things Halo while you are out and about.

If the Halo Waypoint app does not satisfy your Halo fix, you can consider a premium Halo app dubbed "ATLAS," which stands for Assisted Tactical Assault System. Through ATLAS, Halo gamers can tap directly into their *Halo: Reach* or *Halo: Anniversary* matches, providing them with near real-time data during ongoing games. For example, ATLAS provides access to information such as the locations of health packs, weapons, and vehicles, and it can plot out your and your teammates' location on *Halo* maps; thus, your phone can become another powerful weapon in your *Halo* gaming arsenal. As you move through levels on the console, you can consult your phone for in-game data that can help you devise your next strategy. ATLAS is free for Windows Phone users but costs $4.99 for use on Android or iOS devices.

More information on the Halo Waypoint app can be found for Windows Phone at http://www.windowsphone.com/en-US/apps/79c9f9c8-ace7-df11-9264-00237de2db9e, for Android devices at https://market.android.com/details?id=com.halo.companion, or for iOS devices at http://itunes.apple.com/us/app/halo-waypoint/id468457600?mt=8.

### Still Can't Get Enough of *Halo*?

You can add *Halo* to your social media network. There are numerous official *Halo* groups on Facebook, including a general *Halo* group that has approximately 2 million followers, a Halo Waypoint group with approximately 350,000 followers, and numerous game-specific *Halo* groups. In addition, you can follow Halo Waypoint on Twitter.

Learn how to add this innovative
motion and voice controller to your
Xbox 360 for a more immersive
multimedia experience.

In this chapter, you learn how to set up your Kinect sensor, maximize your play space, and start playing games, including *Kinect Adventures!* You also learn about basic Kinect controls and how to troubleshoot some common problems that may arise.

# 10

→ Unboxing Kinect
→ Setting up Kinect
→ Playing for the First Time
→ Getting into *Kinect Adventures!*
→ Troubleshooting Problems

# Getting to Know Kinect

Steven Spielberg's hit 2002 science fiction film, *Minority Report*, captivated audiences with its iconic depiction of star Tom Cruise as a cop in the year 2054 navigating massive amounts of visual computer data by doing nothing more than donning computerized gloves and making various hand gestures in the air. Amazingly, the vision of what computer interfaces might be like in the year 2054 is already a reality, and not only does away with the movie's gloves, but also gets your whole body and voice in on the action. As such, it's not surprising that when Microsoft's Kinect was first brought to the market in the United States in November 2010, it soon made its way into the *Guinness World Records* for being the fastest selling consumer electronics device of all time.

Kinect is a high-tech motorized sensor that detects and tracks movement, registers spoken commands via built-in micro-phones, and virtually renders you and your environment in various game worlds through its sophisticated video camera and software. In addition, you can use it to chat with friends via Video Kinect (see "Chatting with Video Kinect" in Chapter 11, "Using Kinect"). By making you the controller, Kinect provides a more liberating gaming and navigation experience because you are no longer tethered to your couch or game controller. Gameplay is immersive and can even be physically challenging, aspects which factored into Kinect winning a Parent's Choice Award in spring 2011. The future really is now, and, as a Kinect owner, you get to experience it firsthand.

---

### Don't Yet Have a Kinect?

If you own one of the many Xbox 360 models that preceded the Xbox 360 S, consider purchasing the Xbox 360 4GB or 250GB that comes bundled with Kinect, rather than purchasing the Kinect separately to add onto your system. Overall, this is a better deal, and the upgrade gives you a more powerful system that is optimized to use Kinect, as demonstrated by its dedicated Kinect port. You can then give your old Xbox to the kids or use it to stream Netflix or watch DVDs if you no longer want to play games on it.

---

# Unboxing Your Kinect

If you purchased your Kinect bundled in with an Xbox 360 4GB or 250GB, you should find the Kinect Sensor and a copy of *Kinect Adventures!* in the box. (While other games may be included with special bundles, *Kinect Adventures!* remains the one common denominator.) Inside the *Kinect Adventures!* box is a game manual and a calibration card. If you purchased the Kinect sans console, an additional power supply is included if you need to hook up your Kinect sensor to an older Xbox 360 model, which does not have a dedicated Kinect port.

## Kinect Sensor

The Kinect sensor, which is the obvious star of the show, is a horizontal bar that contains several video cameras and microphones. Its sophisticated software technology makes it highly sensitive for recognizing voices, faces, and gestures. The sensor tracks movements in 3D, and its tracking capability is facilitated by the small motorized pivot that serves as its base, enabling the sensor to follow the subjects in focus. It can recognize up to six players at once; although, it can track only up to four active users at a time.

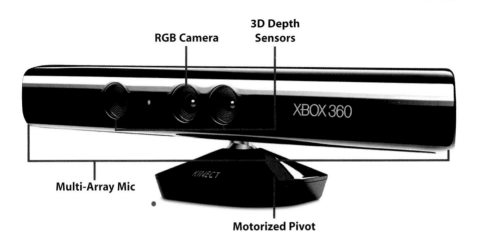

## Kinect Adventures!

*Kinect Adventures!* is the game that comes bundled with your Kinect to show-case its capabilities. The game features five minigames and several game modes that require you to use various bodily actions to successfully complete challenges, such as plugging holes in an underwater shark tank or popping bubbles. It is described in greater detail later in this chapter.

## Calibration Card

The calibration card is exactly what it sounds like: a card that can calibrate your Kinect. It measures 4 1/2 x 7 inches and is printed on heavy card stock. The calibration side features a boxed-out face with eyes and a smiling mouth. If you experience a lag with your Kinect or it is not accurately tracking your movements, it is time to whip out this card and recalibrate your system, which is described later in this chapter.

Don't throw this cute little guy away.

## Power Supply

The power supply is included only if you purchase the Kinect separately, rather than bundled in with the Xbox 360 4G or 250GB. It is used to connect, via USB, the Kinect sensor to older Xbox 360s, which do not have a dedicated Kinect port. Because the Kinect's motorized pivot requires more power to operate than can be supplied by the Xbox 360's USB ports, the additional power supply is needed for older Xbox 360s.

AC Adapter

Kinect Attachment

USB Connector

# Setting Up Your Kinect

Setting up your Kinect is simple, regardless of whether you are attaching it to an older Xbox 360 or an Xbox 360 S with a dedicated Kinect port. However, before you proceed to make any connections, it is best to determine where to place your sensor. You want to make sure that the Kinect's cable or the power supply cords (if hooking it up to an older 360) are long enough to reach your console and, in the latter case, a wall outlet.

Microsoft recommends positioning your Kinect sensor between 2 and 6 feet above the ground and centered just above or below your visual display, whether a TV or a monitor, as demonstrated in the figure. Your Kinect sensor must see you to track you. If you plan to attach your sensor to the top of a flat-panel display, you should consider purchasing a Kinect TV mount clip to ensure it stays secure. Third-party Kinect TV clips are available starting at around $12 at Amazon.com, whereas the official Microsoft Kinect TV Mount Kit (#220828200) retails for $39.99 on the Microsoft Store Online at www.microsoftstore.com/store/msstore/pd/productID.220828200.

 **Each player should ensure sufficient clearance in all directions when playing to avoid contact with objects and other players.**

**Arrows demonstrate approximate placement of the Kinect sensor either directly above or below the center of the display.**

*Image credit: From the Kinect Lifestyle Press Kit*
*www.xbox.com/en-US/Press/PressKits/2010-Kinect-Launch*

**Play space should be about 6 ft away from the Kinect sensor for single players and at least 8 ft for two or more players.**

### Not Sure You Want a TV Mount Clip?

If you don't want to use one of the several TV mounts available, there are numerous other options, including various tripods, wall mounts, and ScreenDeck shelves (http://screendeck.tv) for your TV. It is best to peruse online retailers and read reviews to find out which option may be best suited to meet your needs.

## Clearing Your Play Space

The sensor can see you when you are approximately 6 feet from it; however, playing 8 feet from the sensor is optimal, especially if you play next to someone else. Before you hook up your Kinect and start playing, clear away any furniture or other items that may otherwise occupy your play space (6 feet to 10 feet from the sensor), such as any coffee tables, chairs, or other items. You want to give yourself plenty of space to comfortably move around. You shouldn't need to worry about avoiding anything other than virtual obstacles when you play Kinect.

If you don't have the room to play 8 feet from the sensor and would still like to play with another player, you can play closer to the sensor; however, you and your friend need to take turns. You should also take the time to recalibrate your Kinect before you start playing. Recalibration enables Kinect to get a better sense of your play space, providing you with a more pleasurable gaming experience. Calibration is discussed later in this chapter.

### Kinect Glasses Give You a New Lease on Space

If your space is tiny and you don't have much room to spare, consider buying your Kinect some glasses. Nyko has released Zoom for Kinect (www.nyko.com), which are specially designed optical lenses that fit over the Kinect sensor, reducing the play range required by up to 40%, enabling you to play closer to your visual display. The Zoom's wide-angle lens also enables two people to play in an area normally only suitable for a single player. Because Zoom just snaps onto the Kinect, with nothing to plug in and no additional software or calibration required, installation is a breeze and takes mere seconds. Zoom retails for approximately $30.00, though it is suggested that you carefully read the reviews before purchasing—it is known to reduce Kinect's sensitivity under certain conditions.

# Hooking Up Your Sensor and Console

Connecting your Kinect to your Xbox is quick and easy. Follow these steps to introduce your Xbox 360 to your new high-tech friend, Kinect:

## Instructions for Xbox 360 S

Because you have one of the Xbox 360 S models, hooking up your Kinect sensor is so easy that it doesn't even require a step list. Simply plug the end of the Kinect sensor's cable into your console's AUX port. The AUX port appears directly below the orange line on the sticker that indicates your console's serial number.

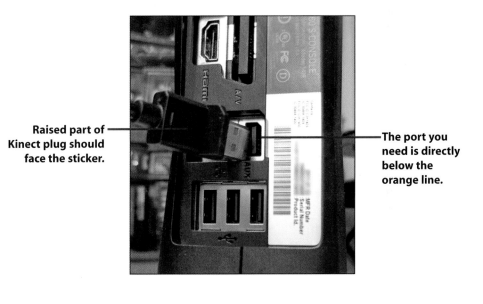

**Raised part of Kinect plug should face the sticker.**

**The port you need is directly below the orange line.**

## Instructions for Older Xbox 360 Models

If you attach your Kinect to an older Xbox 360, you have a few more steps to follow, but it is still a painless process:

1. Unplug any accessories from the USB ports in the back of your console.

2. Plug the end of the Kinect sensor's cable into the Kinect attachment in the middle of the power supply cable.

3. Plug the USB end of the power cable into your console.

4. Plug the AC adapter end of the power cable into a wall outlet.

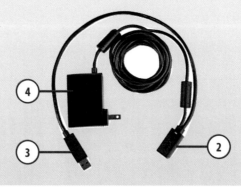

# Installing the Sensor Software

If you are an Xbox LIVE member, after you plug in your Kinect and power your console on, an Update Required screen will likely appear, provided you are signed into your Xbox LIVE account. Select Yes to proceed with the update. When the installation is complete, you can begin setting up your sensor, which is discussed in the next section.

Update Required

To use this device, an update must be applied. If you accept this update and are playing a game, you'll lose any unsaved progress. If you decline the update, you won't be able to use the device.

Do you want to apply the update now?

Yes

No

Select   Back

If you are not an Xbox LIVE member, insert *Kinect Adventures!* The update should install automatically. If not, select the disc tray from the dashboard. After the installation confirmation message appears, remove the disc and begin setting up your sensor.

## Setting Up Your Sensor

After the Kinect software update is complete, you are prompted to set up your Kinect sensor, which reviews and assesses sensor placement, speech recognition and chat, and play space. The onscreen prompts are straightforward, and many are purely confirmatory (for example, to check whether you have already positioned your sensor). Several screens give you the option of selecting More Info before advancing. Steps 21–29 in "Powering On for the First Time" from Chapter 1 provide specifics.

## Playing for the First Time

Now that your Kinect is hooked up and the play space cleared, you can enjoy your new toy. *Kinect Adventures!*, described later in this chapter, or Kinect Labs, described in Chapter 11, are two great options to start with; although, you are certainly free to play any Kinect games of your choosing. Regardless of what you decide to play the first time, you need to have a basic understanding of Kinect controls.

### Kinect Controls

Kinect onscreen menus can be controlled using hand gestures or voice commands; although, availability of these options varies, depending on where you are (for example, in a game versus the dashboard).

- **Hand Gestures**—To use hand gestures to control the dashboard and the Kinect Guide (these are both discussed in Chapter 11), a video window must appear in the lower right corner of your screen. This window indicates that the sensor is active. When making selections, it is most effective to hold your hand out in front of you, with your palm facing the visual display.

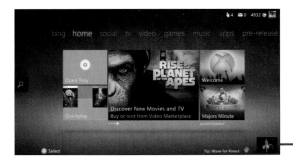

Look for this window. When you see it, Kinect is active.

- **Wave to Kinect**—When you see a Hand icon on your visual display, wave your hand, but no delicate waves like those of royalty. Move your forearm left and right, not just your wrist. Waving at the Xbox Dashboard lets you use hand gestures to move around and select menu items.

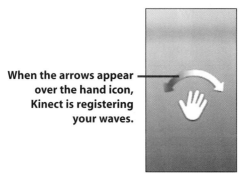

**When the arrows appear over the hand icon, Kinect is registering your waves.**

- **Hover to Select**—To select a menu option, move your hand so that the onscreen Hand icon is positioned over the item of your choosing and hold steady. A circle slowly forms around the icon, and after it comes full circle, your selection is made, and you are brought to the next screen.

**When the circle around the hand icon is completed, your selection is made.**

- **Pausing**—If you need to pause at any point while using Kinect, place both arms at your sides and move your left arm straight out at a 45-degree angle from your body.

**This icon appears when you use the pause gesture.**

- **Scrolling for More Options**—To scroll to see additional options on the left or right of the screen, hover your hand over the side you want to see, and then move your hand horizontally when the Zipper icon appears. For this control to work, your hands in the video window must appear to have a purple glow. If not, wave to Kinect.

**Move your hand in the direction of the arrowheads to slide to the next screen.**

- **Voice Controls**—The microphone icon must be present for you to use your voice to control Kinect. When you see the Microphone icon, say "Xbox," and then read one of the onscreen voice commands.

**This icon must be present for you to use voice controls.**

For more about gesture and voice navigation, turn to Chapter 11.

# Recalibrating Your Kinect

With Kinect, your body becomes the controller, making it important for Kinect to accurately track your movements. If you find that the Kinect sensor is not picking up your movements correctly, you can recalibrate the Kinect sensor. Follow these steps to recalibrate your Kinect:

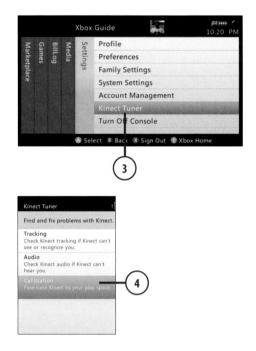

1. Get the calibration card that came with *Kinect Adventures!* or any other Kinect game you may have.

2. Press the Xbox Guide button in the middle of your controller.

3. From the Settings menu, select Kinect Tuner.

4. At the Kinect Tuner screen, select Calibration.

5. At the Kinect Calibration screen, select I Have My Card.

6. Hold up the calibration card so that Kinect can see it, and move the card around until the eyes on the card appear behind the onscreen glasses and the edges of the card match the onscreen rectangle. Kinect provides guidance on positioning.

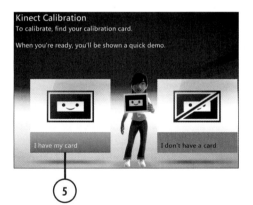

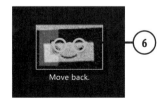

7. Hold the card's position until a green box appears around the glasses and Kinect tells you "You Got It!"

8. Repeat steps 6 and 7 until the Calibration Complete screen appears.

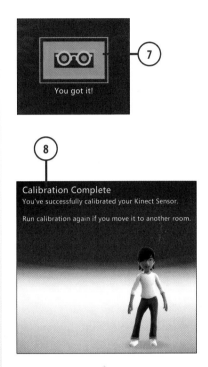

### Lost the Calibration Card?

If you lose your calibration card, you can order a replacement from Microsoft for $0.99 at www.microsoftstore.com/store/m sstore/en_US/buy/pageType.prod uct/externalRefID.B7A7A3B2, or you can search for a free down-loadable copy online and just print a copy yourself. Microsoft warns against this, but as long as you find one that prints to the same proportions as the original, it should work.

# Getting into Kinect Adventures!

*Kinect Adventures!* requires you to use full-body motion to complete a series of minigames, each of which lasts approximately 3 minutes. A total of five minigame types are available, which have four difficulty levels, providing you with 20 unique Adventures. The minigames include 20,000 Leaks, River Rush, Rallyball, Reflex Ridge, and Space Pop. Most of these provide cooperative play in two-player mode, except for Reflex Ridge, which offers competitive play. Throughout the games, your objective is to collect as many Adventure pins as possible. These pins earn you medals, whether bronze, silver, gold, or the elusive platinum, depending on the number of pins collected.

*Kinect Adventures!* supports Xbox LIVE multiplayer. Throughout the game, Kinect takes photos of you, which are shown to you at the end of the game and are stored. You can view these photos within the game, upload them to a private repository on Kinectshare.com (see "Understanding KinectShare" in Chapter 11) or share them with others on a social networking site such as Facebook. Kinect won't let anyone else see your photos unless you want them to.

>> Go Further

## DELETING PHOTOS AND TURNING OFF PHOTO CAPTURE

If your Kinect captures an unflattering photo of you playing *Kinect Adventures!*, or you decided to play au naturel and don't want anyone seeing you contorted in your birthday suit, don't fret, you can delete these unwanted photos. Select Show Off & Share from the main *Kinect Adventures!* menu (far left purple camera icon) and select Photos from the Show Off & Share screen. You now have the option to delete any photos. Simply select a photo you want to delete by hovering over it. When it finishes loading, select Delete and then confirm the deletion. The photo is now permanently deleted from your console's hard drive. Unfortunately, deleting photos is a manual process because there is no way to delete entire albums, so you may just want to turn the photo feature off.

If you don't want Kinect snapping photos of you while playing *Kinect Adventures!*, you can stop the Kinect paparazzi in its tracks. Select the Playing Options icon at the top of the main Kinect Adventures menu (far left at the top of the screen). From the Options menu, select Photos if it says "On" below it. At the Photos screen, select Off. Now you no longer need to be camera shy.

## Understanding the Game Modes

*Kinect Adventures!* has three game modes:

- **Adventure**—This is the game's story mode. You are presented with a series of preselected challenges that you progress through in a linear fashion. When you successfully complete a difficulty level, the next Adventure can be undertaken. At the end of each Adventure, you can obtain any number of awards, such as a medal, achievement, new timed play mode, new gear for your avatar, or a Living Statue, which can be uploaded to Kinectshare.com. When you earn a Living Statue, the game prompts you to celebrate this milestone by enabling you to record a few seconds of vocals and movements, which are then digitally modified to fit the character of your Living Statue.

- **Free Play**—This mode presents the same challenges as Adventure mode, but you can select the game you want to play and its difficulty level; all difficulty levels are unlocked.

- **Timed Play**—This mode is unlocked only by playing timed levels in Adventure mode. When levels are unlocked, you can start to select your own challenges, just like in Free Play. In this mode, Adventure pins are replaced by Time pins, which give you more time to finish a level. Because time is the critical gameplay element in this mode, it is game over if time runs out!

## Getting to Know the Minigames

*Kinect Adventures!* features five Adventure types, each of which demonstrate the capability of your Kinect sensor. Regardless of which Adventure you choose, it is sure to take you off your couch.

### Plugging 20,000 Leaks

In 20,000 Leaks, your avatar is in a glass-enclosed underwater observatory when suddenly leaks start to spring as various frisky marine animals begin to attack and crack the glass. You must move your hands, feet, and head to guide your avatar to plug the cracks as quickly as possible. There are three waves of attack, with each ratcheting up the difficulty level until five leaks need to be plugged simultaneously in the last wave. Successful plugging earns you Adventure pins. Each wave ends when time expires or when all leaks are plugged, with any left over time at the end of each wave added to your Adventure pin total.

**Virtual camera means Kinect is snapping some photos of you.**

## Watch Those Fish!

Paying close attention to the position of the fish and other marine life enables you to anticipate where a leak will occur. This may give you the edge needed to complete waves early, adding to your Adventure pin total.

## Riding the River Rush

River Rush has your avatar standing on a large, round raft floating down a treacherous river full of numerous obstacles and branching paths. Your goal is to collect as many Adventure pins along the way as possible. You can navigate your avatar's raft by leaning or stepping left and right. You can also get your raft airborne by jumping, which launches your vessel into the air space above the river, where additional Adventure pins are found. River Rush can be played with two players, which requires you to become in sync with the other player to ensure your raft goes the way you both want it to so that you can maximize the number of Adventure pins collected.

**Follow the arrows to get large
clusters of Adventure pins.**

## Easy Does It!

Although the game instructs you to side step to steer your avatar's raft, leaning in the direction you want to go to avoids exaggerated movements and is more likely to help you reach your targets.

## Dodging Rally Balls

Rally Ball has been described as the 3D, modern-day version of the classic arcade games *Arkanoid* and *Breakout*. The game is similar to handball, and your objective is to smash all the blocks while keeping the rallyball in play. When certain targets are hit, multiple balls come into play, and these must be handled simultaneously. There are three rounds, with each featuring a different set of blocks and targets. When all blocks and targets are destroyed or time runs out, the round ends. Any time remaining at the end of a round is added to your Adventure pin total.

**Get your whole body in on the action.**

## Use What Your Momma Gave You!

For this game, it is more effective to move around, rather than standing in one spot and just flailing your arms around. Also, you have your entire body available to block those virtual balls, so use it. When multiple balls are headed in your direction, it will be difficult to block them if you do not employ all your assets.

## Ducking for Reflex Ridge

In Reflex Ridge, your avatar rides a mine cart along a track fraught with obstacles. Your objective is to collect as many Adventure pins as possible while keeping your avatar on the mine cart. To move the mine cart, you jump, duck, or extend your limbs in ways that avoid the obstacles. You can pull on the mine cart's bars for speed. In two-player mode, you are pitted against the other player to see who can collect the most medals the fastest.

Jump for speed, but watch out for those obstacles!

### Jump Around!

Jump up, jump up, and get down! Frequent jumping gives you a speed boost, but to avoid obstacles it is best to stop jumping before you reach them.

## Jumping into Space Pop

Space Pop puts your avatar in a zero-gravity space cube. Your task is to move your avatar so it can pop as many bubbles as possible, which are generated in round holes that line the top, bottom, and sides of the room. By flapping your arms, your avatar can fly up to pop bubbles. Holding your arms out allows your avatar to hover in place, whereas dropping your arms causes the avatar to descend to the ground.

The lighted portholes signal oncoming bubbles.

## Follow the Lights!

The round holes from which the bubbles emerge light up just before the bubbles are released. Follow the lights to get in position to pop those bubbles early.

# Troubleshooting Problems

If you encounter problems while using your Kinect, you can attempt several actions to troubleshoot them before contacting Microsoft for help. What follows are some issues that could arise and solutions that may remedy the situation.

## Sensor Doesn't Work Properly

If you have tried to recalibrate your Kinect and the sensor still isn't working, try the following:

- Check that your Kinect is securely plugged into your console. If you have your Kinect hooked up to an older Xbox 360, check that the connections to the console and to the power supply are secure and that the power supply is plugged into a wall outlet. When the unit is on, the green light in front of the sensor will be on.

- Make sure the sensor is in a well-ventilated area and that its side vents are not obstructed.

- Update the sensor software. See "Installing the Sensor Software" earlier in this chapter.

## Sensor Doesn't See You

If Kinect doesn't see you, try the following:

- Check that you are in Kinect's line of sight. If you are and it still does not see you, step out of the play space, and then reenter it.

- It may be too dark for the Kinect to see you. Brighten your play space by turning on lights.

- Make sure no lights are shining directly on the sensor, such as sunlight or lamplight. Just like you can't see through glare, your Kinect can't either.

- Check that your clothing are sufficiently different from the background of your play space. Kinect can't distinguish between you and your environment if you pull a chameleon.

- Check if your sensor lens is dirty. If so, wipe it with a clean dry cloth. Microfiber cloths are best because they are nonabrasive.

- Make sure the sensor's viewing angle is not blocked by something.

- Have the Kinect Tuner assess whether Kinect can see you. To do this, activate the Xbox Guide button on your controller, go to Settings, and then select Kinect Tuner. It walks you through some tests. See "Optimizing with the Kinect Tuner" in Chapter 11 for more detailed instructions.

### Clothes Make the Man or Woman!

When you play with your Kinect, try to wear form-fitting clothes. If you wear baggy clothes, Kinect can't make out your body parts and may think you are a mutant with extra appendages.

## Sensor Motors Don't Adjust Properly

If your Kinect's motorized pivot is not moving as needed to adjust the sensor's viewing angle, never try to adjust it by hand, which risks stripping the gears and causing the motorized pivot to break. Try these actions instead:

- Check that all your Kinect's connections are secure, including to the console and to the power supply if it is hooked up to an older console.

- Ensure that nothing is blocking your Kinect's sensor from moving.

- Try making all the connections again.

## Sensor Doesn't Hear You

If your Kinect sensor stops hearing you, check the following:

- Make sure that nothing is blocking your Kinect's microphone array, which runs along the bottom of the sensor.

- Check that the sensor is not on top of something that vibrates, such as surround sound speakers, which can impede Kinect's capability to pick up sound.

- Re-run the Kinect Tuner Audio calibration to test the background noise.

Hover your hand over an item or use your voice to select it.

Control multimedia services.

Sign in using facial recognition.

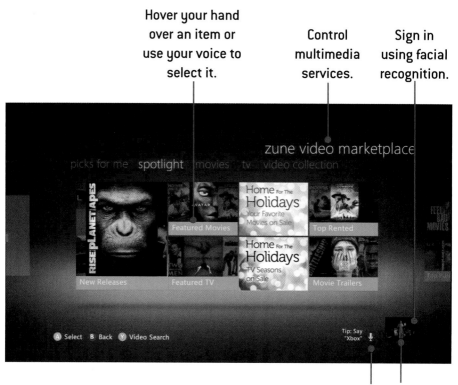

Use your voice.

Use gestures in the Kinect window.

In this chapter, you learn all about using Kinect to put yourself in complete control of the Dashboard and all of your Kinect-enabled applications.

→ Accessing and Using the Dashboard with Voice and Gestures
→ Setting Up Your Kinect ID
→ Using the Kinect Tuner to Optimize Kinect
→ Experimenting with Kinect Fun Labs
→ Video Chatting with Your Friends

# Using Kinect

Once Kinect is set up, it enables you to take control of the Dashboard and many of your apps, but rather than being tethered to your controller, you instead use gestures and voice commands to navigate the menus. Although this takes a little time to get used to, when mastered, this becomes a satisfying—and extremely cool—way to command your Xbox 360.

## Accessing Kinect on the Dashboard

After setting up the Kinect sensor, as described in Chapter 10, "Getting to Know Kinect," you can activate Kinect from the Xbox 360 Dashboard by speaking to or waving at the sensor.

---

### Who Let the Dogs Out?

Whether it's your pets, kids, or your friends and family, the one thing the Kinect does not handle well when starting up is distraction. Whether it's excessive noise or someone walking between you and the sensor, you'll have difficulty engaging Kinect with your voice or gestures if the sensor can't distinguish between you and what's going on around you.

---

## Using Your Voice

To activate Kinect by speaking, do the following:

1. At the Xbox Dashboard, say "Xbox." Speak loud and clear.

2. After the Kinect speech bar opens, say one of the commands shown.

## Using Your Body

To activate Kinect by waving, do the following:

1. Hold your right arm straight out to the side and bend your arm at the elbow. Keep your left arm relaxed at your side.

2. Wave your right hand by moving your forearm left and right. As you wave, a semicircular double-headed arrow appears above the Hand icon until Kinect registers and the icon tracks to your hand movements.

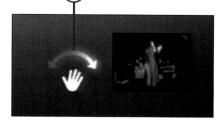

**The image in the preview window is always mirrored.**

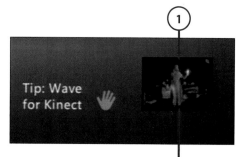

# Navigating the Dashboard with Kinect

Now that you're in control of Kinect with your voice and hand, you can use either of them to interact with the menu items on the Dashboard.

## Controlling with Your Voice

Say "Xbox" to open the speech bar. When the speech bar opens, labels appear under the items in the channels, as shown here in the Home channel.

**Say the text to launch the item.**

These labels are the commands you use to open specific items. For example, you say "Advertisement" to watch the advertisement for *Kinect Sports*. An additional set of commands is available in the speech bar. In the example shown here, there's "Bing (your search)," which runs a Bing search; "Previous," which takes you to the channel to the left; "Next," which takes you to the channel to the right; and "Cancel," which closes the speech bar.

## Controlling with Gestures

You can use a single hand to select items in the Dashboard. Once you wave to get Kinect's attention, raise your hand until you see a Hand icon on the screen.

To select an item, hover over it for a couple of seconds.

**Hover over an item to select it.**

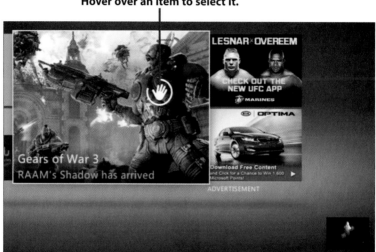

To change hands, drop both of your hands to your sides, and then raise the hand that you want to use.

Another screen of items becomes available after you move your hand over the left or right edge and move your hand in the opposite direction to slide. If you hold your hand a few seconds at the edge of the screen, guide arrows appear to indicate which direction you're sliding towards.

# Working with the Kinect Guide

Like the Xbox Guide, the Kinect Guide is a quick-and-easy way to start the most common Kinect activities. You can also view your friends, messages, and achievements and troubleshoot Kinect sensor problems from the Kinect Guide.

You can start the Kinect Guide by using motions. Follow these steps:

1. Wave to get Kinect's attention.

2. With your both arms positioned at your sides, move your left arm straight out to a 45-degree angle from your body. Hold this pose until the Kinect Guide opens. Just like with the Dashboard, the Kinect Guide is controlled with a single hand hovering over items to select them.

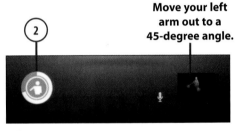

**Move your left arm out to a 45-degree angle.**

## Toggling the Mic

When using the Kinect Guide, you can turn the chat microphone on or off by hovering your hand over the Speech icon in the lower-left corner.

# Searching with Bing

While you can use motions to conduct a Bing search, doing so is an even slower and more laborious process than the already slow and tedious Xbox controller. Luckily, Kinect has an ace in the hole with its microphone, which you can use to conduct a Bing search even faster than with a keyboard. Simply say "Xbox," and once the speech bar appears, say "Bing" and a simple search term or terms.

**After the speech bar appears, you can speak your Bing search.**

For example, to search for *Gears of War 3*-related items, simply say, "Xbox," wait for the speech bar to appear, then say, "Bing Gears of War 3." After a short wait, items related to *Gears of War 3* appear.

# Setting Up Your Kinect ID

Kinect ID attempts to sign you in by recognizing your face; however, before your Kinect can do that, you need to train the sensor. Kinect can identify up to four different players at once using Kinect ID. Your Kinect ID is attached to your Gamertag.

## Creating a Kinect ID

To set up a Kinect ID, sign in with
your Xbox profile and follow these
steps:

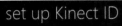

1. Select the Kinect block from the
   Settings channel.

2. Select Kinect ID Setup from the
   menu and then hover your hand
   over the Next box.

3. Hover your hand over Continue
   as [your Gamertag here].

4. You are asked to look at the sensor and then hold different poses while the sensor learns to identify you.

   Move to the green square. If you can't reach a square, wait until the square changes, and move to the next one.

5. Hover your hand over Done. After your Kinect ID is set up, you need to face the sensor for only a few seconds in the Dashboard before Kinect identifies you.

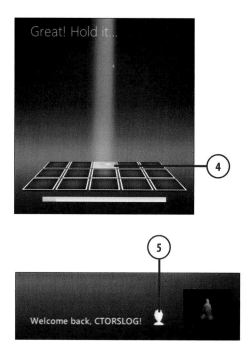

Great! Hold it...

Welcome back, CTORSLOG!

## SOMETHING ABOUT YOU LOOKS DIFFERENT...

Run Kinect ID setup under various lighting conditions to improve Kinect ID accuracy. Wear glasses sometimes? Run Kinect ID setup both with and without your glasses on. The same goes for other major changes in your appearance, like new facial hair. The bottom line is that Kinect ID remembers your previous sessions and improves recognition each time it is run, so the more looks you present to the software, the more likely it is to recognize you the next time you Kinect.

# Changing or Removing Your Kinect ID

Setting up your Kinect ID for the first time doesn't mean you're done. Kinect ID works best after it has recorded as many different views of your face under as many different conditions as possible. You do this by updating your Kinect ID with another recognition sample. You may also just want to get rid of your Kinect ID, which is provided as an option alongside updating. To change or remove your Kinect ID, sign in with your Xbox profile and do the following:

1.  Select the Kinect block from the Settings channel.

2.  Select Kinect ID Setup and then choose Update or Remove from the screen that follows to update or remove your Kinect ID. If you choose to update, you'll go through the same process from step 4 under "Creating a Kinect ID."

# Optimizing with the Kinect Tuner

There are times when you and Kinect just won't see eye to eye. Or maybe Kinect has stopped listening to you. Forget about couples counseling, you just need to use the Kinect Tuner, which helps you find and correct Kinect's body tracking and audio problems.

The Kinect Tuner can be accessed two different ways. The first way is by selecting Kinect from the Settings channel and then selecting Kinect Tuner. The second way is if you're already in a Kinect-enabled app and you select Kinect Tuner from the app's settings.

After you're in the Kinect Tuner, follow the onscreen instructions, and press the A button on your controller to continue. You're then presented with Tracking, Audio, and Calibration options, as shown here.

Tracking dot

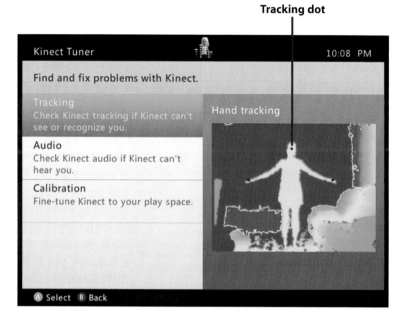

If Kinect has trouble seeing or tracking you, select Tracking using your controller, and then follow the onscreen instructions. Be sure to stand where the sensor can see your entire body. You should see an outline of your body with purple dots showing key tracking locations such as your head and hands.

If Kinect has trouble hearing or understanding you, select Audio, and then follow the onscreen instructions.

To fine-tune Kinect to your play space, select Calibration. Refer to "Recalibrating Your Kinect" in Chapter 10 for more information on the Calibration option in the Kinect Tuner.

# Using the Avatar Editor

Using the Avatar Editor with Kinect works as described in Chapter 3 under "Building an Avatar," except that you use gestures instead of a controller. After selecting Customize Avatar from your profile menu in the Social channel, wave to get Kinect's attention and then select any of the standard avatar editing categories.

When hovering over an option within a category, swipe in the direction of the moving arrows to select it, as shown in the next example.

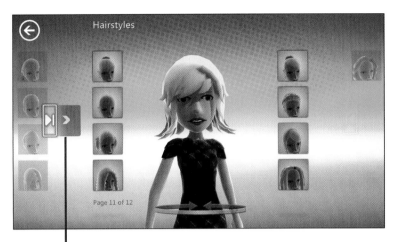

**Swipe in the direction of the
arrow to see another page.**

To rotate your avatar, hover over the circle on the rotation arrows over the avatar until you hear a click. You can now rotate your avatar left and right for a better look. Move your hand up or down to stop using the rotation control.

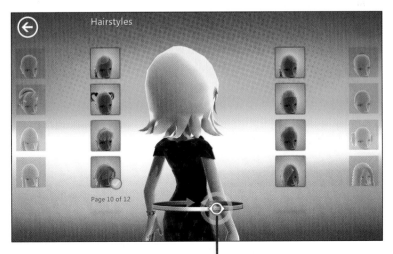

**Slide to rotate your avatar.**

# Experimenting with Kinect Fun Labs

Kinect Fun Labs is your gateway to discovering and playing with the latest advances in Kinect technology. Kinect Fun Labs enables you to download Gadgets, mini-games, and activities that make use of Kinect's bag of tricks, such as people and object scanning, background removal, and finger tracking. New Gadgets are added all the time.

## Getting Started

To start with Kinect Fun Labs, you must first download it from the Game Marketplace in the Games channel. As an alternative, use Bing to search for and find Kinect Fun Labs. To download Kinect Fun Labs, follow these steps:

1. Select Kinect Fun Labs, and then select Confirm Download when prompted to do so.

2. After the download finishes, Kinect Fun Labs is accessible under Game Hubs in Extras in the Game Marketplace in the Games channel.

## Working with Kinect Fun Labs

After you enter Kinect Fun Labs, you see all your options on a single screen. Each option can be selected using voice or gestures.

- **Last Played**—Shows the last Gadget you played. The first time you see this, it shows the first of the two default Gadgets, *Kinect Me*. After Last Played is selected, you see the standard menu options for selected Gadgets, which are described later in this chapter.

- **Last Posted**—Displays the last several items shared by your friends who use KinectShare on Kinect Fun Labs. From here you can view or play an item, flag an item as inappropriate, or flag an item as a "Like." You can also go directly to the Gadget that generated the item you are viewing and have a go at it yourself.

- **Newest Gadget**—Features one noteworthy upcoming Gadget. When selected, you can view information on the upcoming Gadget and flag the Gadget as a "Like," as shown in the following figure.

- **What's Hot**—Features a Gadget that is hot right now among the Kinect Fun Labs community.

- **My Gadgets**—Provides direct access to all your downloaded Gadgets.

- **Friends Feed**—Displays the eight most recent postings from your friends who use KinectShare.

- **New Gadgets**—Shows the eight most recently added Gadgets to the Kinect Fun Labs catalog.

- **Popular Gadgets**—Shows the four most popular Gadgets, which are determined by the amount of "Likes" each Gadget receives from the Kinect Fun Labs community.

If you experience difficulty controlling Kinect Fun Labs, press X on your controller at any time to launch the Kinect Tuner.

## Understanding KinectShare

All the Gadgets in Kinect Fun Labs make use of KinectShare, which enables you to share photos and videos of your onscreen exploits. As with other KinectShare-enabled software, by going to https://kinectshare.com/ and logging in with the Windows Live ID associated with your Xbox LIVE account, you can choose whether to print or download your content or share it on sites like Facebook and YouTube.

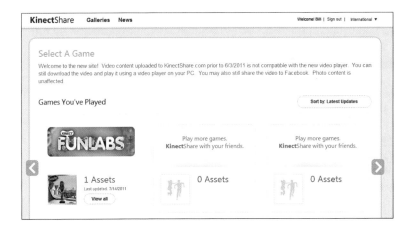

## Playing with the Gadgets

After you select a Gadget, you see a screen with several options. The main window presents a slideshow of screenshots and a brief synopsis of how the Gadget plays. The action items on the screen are as follows:

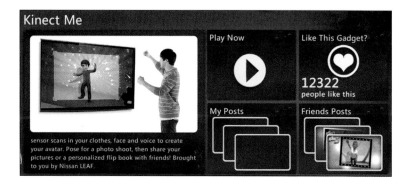

- **Play Now**—Select this option to start the Gadget.

- **Like This Gadget?**—If you like the Gadget, let the community know by selecting this option. You also see the total number of people in the community who "Like" the Gadget.

- **My Posts**—Displays all the items you've shared from this Gadget via KinectShare.

- **Friends Posts**—Displays all the items related to this Gadget that your friends have shared on KinectShare.

# Controlling the Media Services

After starting just about any of the video and music services, you have voice and gesture access to that service's Kinect-enabled features, which includes voice and gesture control of playback. Some of these Kinect-enabled features offer only a subset of options from the overall feature-set, so you still need your controller if you require access to more. To reenable controller access, press any button on your controller when in Kinect mode.

Examples of the Kinect-enabled features for some of the Xbox 360's media services are as follows:

- **ESPN**—Provides access to all functionality with gestures, though voice control is limited to major functions like navigating the Content Guide and controlling playback.

- **Zune**—Provides access to all functionality with both gestures and voice control in both the video and music marketplaces.

- **Last.fm**—Provides access to the Latest Highlights, Your Library Radio, Your Mix Radio, and Popular Stations through a special Last.fm Kinect menu. There is no access to any of the personalization features. Voice control is limited to a select number of functions.

- **Netflix**—Provides access to all functionality with both gestures and voice control.

- **Hulu Plus**—Provides  access to all functionality with both gestures and voice control.

## Using Voice

Whether within ESPN, Zune, Last.fm, Netflix, Hulu Plus, or other Kinect-enabled video and music apps, after you say the word, "Xbox," you can say any word or phrase that appears onscreen to engage that command.

Following are some of the things you can say to Kinect while watching videos or listening to music with the various services:

- **Fast forward a video**—Say "Xbox"; then say "fast forward."

- **Rewind a video**—Say "Xbox"; then say "rewind."

- **Pause music or video**—Say "Xbox"; then say "pause."

- **Play music or video**—Say "Xbox"; then say "play."

- **Skip forward**—Say "Xbox"; then say "next."

- **Skip back**—Say "Xbox"; then say "previous."

- **Exit a video**—Say "Xbox"; then say "stop."

You can't turn the console on or off with voice commands. As of this writing, voice commands are not available while watching videos from the Video Player or Windows Media Center, or while listening to music from the Music Player. Voice commands are also not available when playing movies or music from a disc.

# Using Gestures

ESPN, Zune, Last.fm, Netflix, Hulu Plus, or other Kinect-enabled video and music apps all allow for gesture control after getting Kinect's attention through the standard waving motion. The image below, which was taken from a Zune video playback, is representative of the type of control available across all the services.

**Stop**        **Seek**        **Pause**

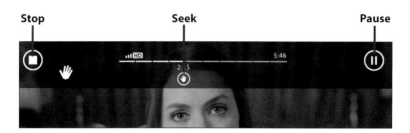

Besides the Stop and Pause icons, you can grab the Hand icon on the time-line and use it as a seek slider to rewind and fast forward the media by moving it left and right, respectively. Pulling the Hand Icon down releases the slider control.

**Move left or right to seek, or down to release the control.**

# Chatting with Video Kinect

If you have an Xbox LIVE Gold membership, you can use Video Kinect to have live video chats with your Xbox LIVE and Windows Live Messenger friends using either your Xbox LIVE Vision Camera and headset, or Kinect. Of course, as the name implies, the experience is optimized for Kinect. For instance, in addition to its built-in microphone and auto-focus capabilities, Kinect can keep you in frame using its motorized base as you walk back and forth within the room!

## Setting Up Video Kinect

To set up Video Kinect, follow these steps:

1. Select the Social Apps block from the Social channel.

2. Select Video Kinect and, when prompted to do so, select Download Now. When downloaded, you can start Video Kinect from the Social Apps block in the Social channel.

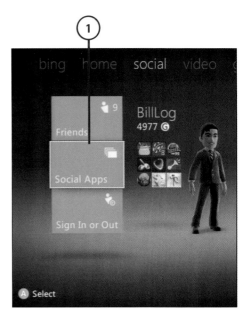

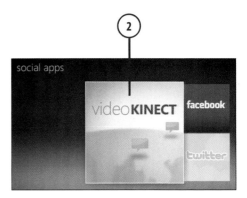

## Controlling the Chat

To control Video Kinect, you can use gestures or your controller. To initiate a chat, do the following:

1. Go to Social Apps in the Social channel and select Video Kinect.

2. The first time you start Video Kinect, you see an information screen. Hover your hand over Start or press A on your controller to continue.

3. Select a friend from the options shown, or select More Friends to access a complete listing of all friends who are presently online. You can chat only with one friend at a time.

## Accepting a Video Chat Invitation

When someone invites you to a video chat, a message appears on the bottom of your screen. To accept the invitation and talk to your friend, do the following:

**1.** Press the Guide button on your controller and select Messages.

| Xbox Guide | | 12:12 AM |
| --- | --- | --- |
| Xbox Home | | |
| Friends | 1 | |
| Party | 0 | |
| **Messages** | 1 | |
| Beacons & Activity | | |
| Chat & IM | | |
| Open Tray | | |

**2.** Select the message from your friend.

| Community | | 12:12 AM |
| --- | --- | --- |
| 0 | 1 | Messages (1 New) | 0 |
| Create New | | |
| BillLog | Wants to talk in Video Kinect | |

**3.** Select Accept Video Kinect Invite to start chatting.

| Video Kinect Invite | | 12:13 AM |
| --- | --- | --- |
| Message Received 12/22/2011 12:11 AM 1 minute ago | BillLog  Rep ★★★★★  Gamerscore 4977  Zone Family |
| Accept Video Kinect Invite | Message Text |
| Decline Video Kinect Invite | BillLog wants to video chat |
| Reply | with you. |
| View Profile | |
| Block Communications | |

4. Use your controller or gestures to control chat options.

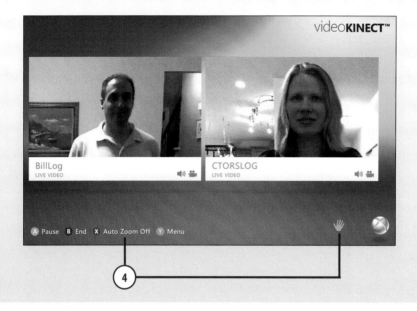

## Chatting With Windows Live Messenger Friends

To chat with your Windows Live Messenger friends, select Messenger Sign-In after you start Video Kinect. The first time you do this, you are asked for your Windows Live ID password. Avatars are used to represent your Xbox LIVE friends, and an icon of an avatar is used for your Windows Live Messenger friends.

To see the Video Kinect menu options, select the circular Menu icon, or press the Y button on your controller. The options are as follow:

- **Auto Zoom**—Tracks your movement and centers you on the screen. This is on by default.

- **Kinect Guide**—Goes to the Kinect Guide.

- **Pause**—Pauses the video chat.

- **Cancel**—Cancels the video chat.

# Finding Kinect Games

Kinect games come in the same retail, Arcade, Games on Demand, and demo configurations as regular Xbox 360 games, and they're found in all the same places (see Chapter 5, "Playing on the Games Channel"). If you are not sure which Kinect games are worth checking out, consider starting with the following five, which are all highly rated titles that make fun use of the sensor's functionality.

- ***Child of Eden* (Ubisoft, 2011)**—While perfectly playable with a regular controller, this ethereal rhythm-based shooter shines when you play it with Kinect, as it helps to seamlessly integrate *Child of Eden*'s unique sound, vision, and touch experience. The objective of the game is to save digital life form, Project Lumi, from a virus attack by shooting various onscreen objects, which produces breathtaking visual and musical effects.

- ***Dance Central 2* (Harmonix, 2011)**—The sequel to the game that was arguably most responsible for putting Kinect on the map, *Dance Central 2* is even better than its popular predecessor because it allows for simultaneous two-player gameplay in both cooperative and competitive modes, complete with drop in/drop out functionality so the party can keep moving even when your dance partner gets tired. Even if you have four left feet like a certain two authors who will go nameless, you'll find that *Dance Central 2* is an engaging, workout friendly experience that just might make you a better dancer while you have fun cutting loose to some great music.

- *Fruit Ninja Kinect* **(Halfbrick Studios, 2011)**—In the Kinect version of the popular mobile touchscreen game, you slice fruit with your hands, being careful to avoid the bombs. Though simple in premise, the responsiveness of your slicing and dicing, and simultaneous two-player mode, create an adrenaline rush that's hard to match on any other gaming platform. *Fruit Ninja Kinect* is available for purchase direct from the Xbox LIVE Arcade, and is included as a free download with *The Gunstringer*.

- *Kinectimals* **(Frontier Developments, 2010)**—In this family-friendly game, you use Kinect to feed, play with, and care for pets, which include a variety of cat and bear cubs, with the ability to purchase and download more. Activities include teaching tricks, guiding your pet around an obstacle course, and free-form play, all controlled with intuitive hand and body gestures. A new retail version was released in 2011, entitled, *Kinectimals: Now with BEARS!*, which includes the downloadable add-on, Bear Island, though it's usually a better value if you buy the original game and download the add-on separately. In addition, various licensed stuffed animals, available for offline play, come with a code to activate a new cub or toy within the game. There are even limited edition bundles that package together both the game and an exclusive stuffed animal. (You might want to keep that bit of information from the kids, though!) Finally, *Kinectimals* is also available as a Windows Phone and iOS app, enabling you to import your pets from the Kinect version and also unlock additional cubs.

- ***The Gunstringer* (Twisted Pixel Games, 2011)**—In this unique, whimsical, third-person shooter, you take control of an undead marionette sheriff betrayed by his posse. The twist is that the game is played as though it was being acted out on a theater stage, complete with an audience that responds to the quality of your performance. As one of the more complex Kinect games to control, *The Gunstringer* challenges you to use your left hand to control the marionette's movements and your right hand to aim and fire the character's gun. Certain moments of the game require you to use both hands to control two guns as the marionette moves along a set path. As a nice bonus, retail versions of *The Gunstringer* include a code for a free copy of *Fruit Ninja Kinect*. In addition, a free downloadable content add-on has also been released, entitled *The Wavy Tube Man Chronicles*, which uses live action video for its shooting gallery-style gameplay.

# Getting Help with Your Kinect and Xbox 360

Technology is a wonderful thing when it works correctly and is being used to its full potential. While we tried to cover all the bases in this book, electronics are complex and sometimes temperamental, making it impossible to account for every possibility. If you end up experiencing an issue that is not covered in this book, there are many additional resources at your disposal.

If you are experiencing technical or mechanical difficulties, your number one resource is Microsoft. Whatever you do, never attempt to open your Xbox 360 to fix what you discern to be the problem. Any sign of tampering with your

Xbox voids its warranty and may permanently damage your console's delicate insides. If you need to reach Microsoft, you can contact them at:

**Phone:** (800) 4MY-XBOX

**Web:** http://support.xbox.com/

**Twitter:** @XboxSupport

If you are trying to resolve a software hiccup or want to figure out how to accomplish a task that we do not outline, Google.com is your best friend. Type in a few keywords that describe the task or problem and you will likely find articles or posts from individuals who have been down the same road and responses from the larger gaming community with potential solutions. Of course, please use your best judgment before applying any advice.

Not getting the assistance or finding the answers that you need? We are always happy to help our readers resolve any issues they may be experiencing with their Xbox 360 or Kinect. You can contact us at bill@armchairarcade.com or christina@armchairarcade.com.

# Index

# Try Safari Books Online FREE for 15 days

## Get online access to Thousands of Books and Videos

**Safari** Books Online

**FREE 15-DAY TRIAL + 15% OFF**
informit.com/safariebooktrial

> **Feed your brain**
>
> Gain unlimited access to thousands of books and videos about technology, digital media and professional development from O'Reilly Media, Addison-Wesley, Microsoft Press, Cisco Press, McGraw Hill, Wiley, WROX, Prentice Hall, Que, Sams, Apress, Adobe Press and other top publishers.

> **See it, believe it**
>
> Watch hundreds of expert-led instructional videos on today's hottest topics.

## WAIT, THERE'S MORE!

> **Gain a competitive edge**
>
> Be first to learn about the newest technologies and subjects with Rough Cuts pre-published manuscripts and new technology overviews in Short Cuts.

> **Accelerate your project**
>
> Copy and paste code, create smart searches that let you know when new books about your favorite topics are available, and customize your library with favorites, highlights, tags, notes, mash-ups and more.

* Available to new subscribers only. Discount applies to the Safari Library and is valid for first 12 consecutive monthly billing cycles. Safari Library is not available in all countries.

Browse by Topic ▼   Browse by Format ▼   USING   More ▼

Store | Safari Books Online

# QUEPUBLISHING.COM
## Your Publisher for Home & Office Computing

**Quepublishing.com** includes all your favorite—
and some new—Que series and authors to help you
learn about computers and technology for the home,
office, and business.

Looking for tips and tricks, video tutorials, articles and
interviews, podcasts, and resources to make your life
easier?  Visit **quepublishing.com**.

- **Read the latest articles and sample chapters**
  by Que's expert authors

- **Free podcasts** provide information on the
  hottest tech topics

- **Register your Que products** and receive updates,
  supplemental content, and a coupon to be used
  on your next purchase

- **Check out promotions and special offers**
  available from Que and our retail partners

- **Join the site** and receive members-only offers
  and benefits

QUE NEWSLETTER
quepublishing.com/newsl

 twitter.com/
quepublishing

 facebook.com/
quepublishing

 youtube.com/
quepublishing

 quepublishing.com
rss

   Que Publishing is a publishing imprint of Pearson

# OWN OTHER GEEKY DEVICES? CHECK OUT THE MY...BOOK SERIES

BN 13: 9780132910736     ISBN 13: 9780132832038     ISBN 13: 9780132861366     ISBN 13: 9780132811132

## Full-Color, Step-by-Step Guides

The "My..." series is a visually rich, task-based series to help you get up and running with your new device and technology and tap into some of the hidden, or less obvious features. The organized, task-based format allows you to quickly and easily find exactly the task you want to accomplish, and then shows you how to achieve it with minimal text and plenty of visual cues.

**Visit quepublishing.com/mybooks to learn more about the My... book series from Que.**

quepublishing.com

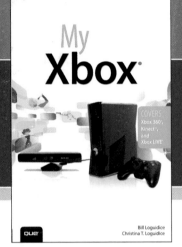

# My Xbox

FREE
## Online Edition

# Safari
Books Online

COVERS
Xbox 360®,
Kinect™,
and
Xbox LIVE®

Bill Loguidice
Christina T. Loguidice

Your purchase of **My Xbox** includes access to a free online edition for 45 days through the **Safari Books Online** subscription service. Nearly every Que book is available online through **Safari Books Online**, along with thousands of books and videos from publishers such as Addison-Wesley Professional, Cisco Press, Exam Cram, IBM Press, O'Reilly Media, Prentice Hall, Sams, and VMware Press.

**Safari Books Online** is a digital library providing searchable, on-demand access to thousands of technology, digital media, and professional development books and videos from leading publishers. With one monthly or yearly subscription price, you get unlimited access to learning tools and information on topics including mobile app and software development, tips and tricks on using your favorite gadgets, networking, project management, graphic design, and much more.

## Activate your FREE Online Edition at
## informit.com/safarifree

STEP 1: Enter the coupon code: BFDPYYG.

STEP 2: New Safari users, complete the brief registration form.
Safari subscribers, just log in.

If you have difficulty registering on Safari or accessing the online edition,
please e-mail customer-service@safaribooksonline.com

Addison Wesley    Adobe Press    ALPHA    Cisco Press    FT Press    IBM Press    Microsoft Press    New Riders    O'REILLY

Peachpit Press    PRENTICE HALL    Que    Redbooks    SAMS    SAS Publishing    vmware PRESS    WILEY    wrox